New World Choreographies

Series Editors
Rachel Fensham, School of Culture and Communication,
University of Melbourne, Parkville, Australia
Kate Elswit, The Royal Central School of Speech and Drama,
London, UK

This award-winning series presents studies of choreographic projects embedded in the intermedial and transcultural circulation of dance. Through advanced yet accessible scholarship, it introduces the artists, practices, platforms, and scholars who are rethinking what constitutes movement, and in the process, blurring boundaries between dance, theatre and performance. Engaged with the aesthetics and contexts of global production and presentation, this book series invites discussion of the multi-sensory, collaborative, and transformative potential of these new world choreographies.

More information about this series at
http://www.palgrave.com/gp/series/14729

Victoria Wynne-Jones

Choreographing Intersubjectivity in Performance Art

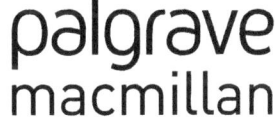
palgrave
macmillan

Victoria Wynne-Jones
School of Humanities
University of Auckland
Auckland, New Zealand

ISSN 2730-9266   ISSN 2730-9274   (electronic)
New World Choreographies
ISBN 978-3-030-40584-7   ISBN 978-3-030-40585-4   (eBook)
https://doi.org/10.1007/978-3-030-40585-4

This Palgrave Macmillan imprint is published by the registered company Springer Nature Switzerland AG
The registered company address is: Gewerbestrasse 11, 6330 Cham, Switzerland

This book is dedicated to the Elam Fine Arts Library (1950-2019)

Acknowledgements

Thank you to all of my teachers. Firstly, I would like to acknowledge the infinite generosity, patience, wisdom and expertise provided by Dr. Gregory Minissale. Secondly. I would like to thank Professor Rachel Fensham for being such an outstanding and supportive editor.

I am also deeply indebted to Dr. Caroline Vercoe, Dr. Ngarino Ellis and Professor Elizabeth Rankin from the disciplinary area of Art History at the University of Auckland, as well as Dr. Alys Longley and Dr. Carol Brown from Dance Studies. I would also like to acknowledge the support of Dr. Susan Carter and Dr. Sean Sturm from CLeaR and Professor Christopher Braddock of Auckland University of Technology (AUT).

Institutional support for this research was provided by a Doctoral Scholarship from the University of Auckland. I am thankful for a Faculty of Arts Doctoral Research Fund grant which enabled me to conduct a research trip abroad in 2015. Further development of this manuscript was enabled by a Professor Charmian O'Connor Post-Doctoral Research Award from the Kate Edger Educational Charitable Trust. Thank you to Malcolm Campbell for organising my honorary research fellowship.

Many, many thanks to Dr. Kate Bretkelly-Chalmers and Rigel Sorzano for their camaraderie, conversation and coffee.

Thank you to all of the artists who shared their practices, thoughts and resources with me, in particular: Tino Sehgal, Alicia Frankovich, Joshua Rutter, Sean Curham, val smith, Angela Tiatia, Shigeyuki Kihara, Rebecca Ann Hobbs, Mark Harvey, David Rosetsky and Juliet Carpenter. I would also like to thank curators Martijn van Nieuwenhuyzen and Hannah Mathews for sharing their reflections.

Immense moral and financial support was provided by my grandparents and parents: Jenefer, Geoffrey, Peter and Jacqueline Wynne-Jones.

Thank you to Oona.

Last, but not least, I would like to express my deepest gratitude to Daniel Strang, for his vast amounts of emotional labour, without which this book would never have been written.

PRAISE FOR CHOREOGRAPHING INTERSUBJECTIVITY IN PERFORMANCE ART

"Using the lens of theories of intersubjectivity, Victoria Wynne-Jones sheds new light on the philosophical meaning of the choreographic turn. Most importantly, she opens out the narrowly defined Euro-American discussion of this strand of contemporary practice, including important artists from the Asia Pacific region in the conversation. Her book is essential reading for global art studies."

—Susan Best, *is professor of art history and theory at Griffith University, she is the author of* Visualizing Feeling Affect and the Feminine Avant-garde *(2011)*

"This book brings together exciting choreographers and artists worldwide including the South Pacific. The transformative potential of inter-personal exchanges are wonderfully analysed through choreographed bodies, places, spectatorship, including de-colonizing choreography. A must-read for evolving understandings of dance, choreography and performance art across diverse and thought-provoking registers."

—Professor Christopher Braddock, *Auckland University of Technology (AUT), New Zealand, and author of* Performing Contagious Bodies: Ritual Participation in Contemporary Art *and editor of* Animism in Art and Performance

"As performance, participation, and choreography or 'planned move-ment' have become significant aspects of contemporary art and gallery cultures, deep questions about received art historical approaches to exhibition, reception, and art works themselves have been raised. Wynne-Jones's excellent book addresses these questions by both proposing and mapping a necessary shift in orientation from aesthetics to intersubjectivity. *Choreographing Intersubjectivity* is recommended as a project of thinking art experience agentially and ecologically, is indebted to the field of dance, and has wide relevance across visual and performing arts practices and commentary."

—Sally Gardner, *Honorary Research Fellow School of Communication and Creative Arts Deakin University*

"There's no question that major art galleries around the world are currently obsessed with choreography in the gallery—often through retrospectives of canonical performance art from the 1960s and 1970s. This book invites a critical evaluation of this trend. Rather than only looking backward, and sceptical of the museum as a European institution of subjection and control, Wynne-Jones takes a broader and more inclusive view to suggest possibilities for forms of intersubjectivity that might be yet to come."

—Theron Schmidt, *Lecturer, University of New South Wales, Sydney and author of* Agency: A Partial History of Live Art *(2019)*

CONTENTS

LIST OF FIGURES

CHAPTER 1

Introduction: Exhibitions and the Choreographic Turn

One person stands before a wall, and another approaches. They face each other. Then with arms swung backwards or held behind their back, they both tilt their upper bodies forward, lower their heads, and bury their shoulders and upper back into the chest of their counter-part. Using brute strength and the grip of their feet on the ground, each person pushes and tries to force their opponent backwards. They exert as much energy as they can, pushing and pushing, resisting the strength of the other until one person manages to shift the other's position, forcing them to step backwards. Once one has made significant gains, the other forfeits, and the contest is over. This live performance known as *Bisons* (Fig. 1.1) has been executed by Melbourne-based artist Alicia Frankovich with a range of opponents since its first iteration at a Stuttgart festival in 2010.[1] Functioning as a kind of deconstructed rugby scrum, it begins with the artist pitting herself against a known participant, someone invited beforehand to take part. From there it repeats itself; anyone can come forward, one at a time and try their luck against the artist in a "pass-the-baton" or relay-style structure.

In *Bisons* the artist/audience relationship is reconfigured into a contest of physical strength, one that is extremely raw and immediate. There is a winner and a loser. Frankovich uses her live, performing body as well as the bodies of others to re-contextualise the scrum, a convention

V. Wynne-Jones, *Choreographing Intersubjectivity in Performance Art*, New World Choreographies, https://doi.org/10.1007/978-3-030-40585-4_1

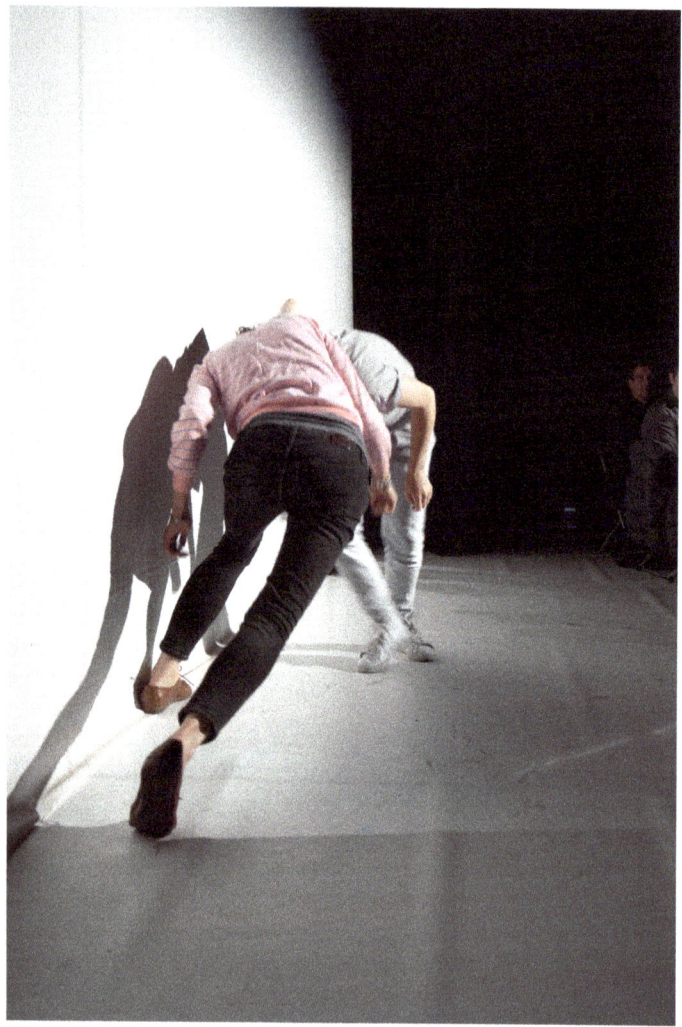

Fig. 1.1   Alicia Frankovich, *Bisons*, 2010. (Live Performance) Performed in *Floor Resistance*, 2011, HAU3, Berlin (*Photo* Conor Clarke. Courtesy of the artist)

taken from the sport of rugby football. In doing so, she also interrogates the reception of art, visitor behaviour, and museum politics—it is highly unusual for audience members to charge at an artist in the manner of a bison. When I first observed this performance at the Auckland Art Gallery Toi o Tāmaki in 2012, I was struck by how quickly the playful performance gained momentum. Once it got underway, there was no shortage of people stepping up and volunteering to engage in Frankovich's challenge. The artist reflected:

> The performance is choreographed, yet it plays out in an indeterminate way, depending on what mood I am in, and the social and physical differences of the participants. (Auckland Art Gallery Toi o Tāmaki 2012: 17–19)

The structure of *Bisons* is simple, its preconceived format allows for a rudimentary encounter between artist and participant. The performance unites the planned with the un-planned, it is repeatable, yet it is also ever-changeable, no performance will ever be the same. As Frankovich has pointed out, each time *Bisons* takes place its dynamics shift and change in accordance with the moods, attitudes, cultures, backgrounds and embodied experiences of its participants. Sometimes people teeter uncertainly on high heels, others aggressively charge and bowl the artist over. Nevertheless, the artwork always involves a shaping or orchestrating of specific relations between artist and participant and it is relations that are among the core concerns of this book. According to literary theorist Rodolphe Gasché, relations are "minimal things," though they can be small and almost elemental, they are also "the most basic and simple of all philosophical problems" (Sabisch 2011: 72). The relations realised by performance artworks are particularly complicated because their terms are neither discrete nor fixed, bodies and people are, according to human geographer Derek P. McCormack, ever-changing and "already in process" (2013: 2).

Relational Aesthetics or *Esthétique relationelle* was the title of the 1998 reflections on art by French curator Nicolas Bourriaud, ones that mark a relevant paradigm shift in contemporary art discourse. Bourriaud proposed that artworks need no longer be understood as mere products of social relations regulated by existing political and economic systems, instead artworks can "engineer intersubjectivity" and become these social relations (2002: 81). Intersubjectivity is a *relational space* that is activated when individuals meet or encounter one another, as part of a performance artwork. Performance artworks that activate interpersonal exchanges between performers and spectators blur the boundaries between art and intersubjectivity, allowing a critical examination of intersubjectivity-as-art.

It is important to note that Bourriaud has had his detractors, most notably art historian Claire Bishop (2006) who critiqued *relational aesthetics* in her 2006 *Artforum* article "The Social Turn: Collaboration and its Discontents." Bishop dismissed the aesthetic proposed by Bourriaud in favour of an emphasis on a more practical and politicised "participatory art" and socially responsible works over those producing mere sociability (2012: 2, 207). Nevertheless, Bourriaud's argument and *aesthetic* remain useful for framing intersubjectivity in relation to contemporary art practice. During the 1990s Bourriaud observed artists attempting to produce new types of relationships between people in constructed situations, rather than repeating the activation of habitual relations such as those between "supplier and client." Crucially such artworks or instances of *relational aesthetics* were presented as "time to be lived through" rather than "a space to walk through" (107). They were "process-related or behavioural" rather than "a set of objects presented" (15). As such the raw material for a work of art could be the social exchanges that took place between people within art gallery or museum spaces.

Bourriaud advocates for art that is social, relational as well as politically aspirational. One example he gives is of Thai-Argentinian artist Rirkrit Tiravanija's installation for the 1993 Venice Biennale, in which participants were presented with the means to rest and cook themselves Chinese soup. Describing art that strives to achieve "modest connections" between people, and emphasising what is relational, interactive and enjoyable, Bourriaud argues that such artists "tighten the space of relations" between people. Importantly such a work represents a social *interstice*, a space in human relations that fits into a greater overall system, yet also suggests possibilities other than those already in effect. For Bourriaud, art develops a political project when it makes relational realms an issue. Such art

> creates free areas, and time spans whose rhythm contrasts with those structuring everyday life, and it encourages an inter-human commerce that differs from the 'commodification zones' that are imposed on us. (16)

Arguing for "art as a state of encounter," relational aesthetics involves artworks that make being-together or inter-human experiences as their central theme—their very substrate is thus formed not only by social relations but by the complex of processes that expand our understanding of intersubjectivity. For Bourriaud each artwork functions as a particular invitation to "to live in a shared world," thereby activating "a bundle of relations with the world," that gives rise to other relations "and so on and so forth, ad infinitum." Tying this idea of an artwork as a bundle of relations, Bourriaud conceived of an artwork as a binomial exchange in which "someone shows something to someone who returns it as he sees fit" (24). Thus a transitive ethic that takes a direct object is utilised by an artist when she shows us something.[2] For an artist to produce an artwork is to "invent possible encounters," while to receive an artwork is to create the conditions for an exchange, just as one might return a serve in a game of tennis.

All art is relational to varying degrees and it has been argued that "transitivity is as old as the hills" (28) however what Bourriaud highlights are contemporary artistic practices focused specifically on "the sphere of inter-human relations," and the invention of models of sociability such as "meetings, encounters, events, various types of collaboration between people, games, festivals and places of conviviality."[3] These practices suggest a modification of the contracts or relations we enter into with art in the gallery or museum. Whereas paintings and sculpture exist within a gallery space, generally available to all who wish to view them, Bourriaud explains that performance art is "often marked by non-availability" it can only be encountered at specific points in time, presupposing a contract or agreement with its participants (29). The important point is that an audience is summoned by the artist, and that the work prompts meetings and invitations to appointments. Bourriaud calls such intersubjective structures the "rendez-vous" of the artistic arena that help form its relational dimension and they may include the potentially destabilising intersubjectivity of Frankovich performing *Bisons* in an Auckland gallery.

Taking Bourriaud's discussion of intersubjectivity in contemporary art as a point of departure, this book aims to develop an account of the unfolding of intersubjectivity in its multiple affective and embodied dimensions. It addresses selected performances, either live or recorded, that have involved the execution of planned movements and actions or *choreography*, as part of an encounter between various individuals occupying a gallery space. Taken from dance studies, the concept of choreography is central to this discussion because it can furnish art history with an account of the relational. Indeed, Bourriaud's thesis of *relational aesthetics* could even be seen largely as a co-option of choreographic knowledges by art theory. Choreographic theory can provide some explanation of how the social, intersubjective relations produced by performance artworks help to create specific kinds of subjecthood. They can also propose ideas as to how relations between persons and things might be challenged by their co-presence in time and space.

Worth mentioning at this stage is the proposition that just as intersubjectivity helps to produce subjecthood, in the other direction, subjects produce forms of intersubjectivity. The interpersonal structures and relational spaces we move through and live our lives within are *affective*, they shape the kinds of people we are, and through our actions, or inaction, we in turn shape them. This bi-directional phenomenon has been studied by a number of discipline-based theories. Whereas theories from the realms of philosophy, sociology and psychology might provide rigorous analysis of the subjectivity-intersubjectivity relation, choreographed artworks offer embodied, spatial, affective, kinaesthetic, somatic and experimental dimensions to this discourse. Such dimensions remind one that the interpersonal exchanges or an *intersubjectivity* temporarily produced by artworks can also be lived, personal and potentially transformative. My argument is that philosophical, sociological and psychological theories help to provide a critical framework for understanding the structure, effects and exchanges produced by performance artworks but, crucially, these works themselves have important contributions to make to the discourse on subjectivity and intersubjectivity, not least by plumbing the depths of this complex and chiasmic relationship between self and otherness. Harking back to Bourriaud, artworks do this not by representing intersubjectivity, but by producing it for the duration of the work and, arguably, in ways that can affect novel intersubjectivities long after the groups of people, choreographers, performers and audience members disperse and go their separate ways.

On another level again, this is a book about contemporary performance art, through which I argue that choreographed works like Frankovich's *Bisons* enact and produce forms of intersubjectivity, that have never existed before and which require new interdisciplinary understandings. Philosophy and art theory contribute alongside the interrelated fields of museum studies and dance studies, as I build an analytical method for the examination of these new practices of performance art in the contemporary museum and gallery setting. Through its selected case studies, this book hopes to make a contribution to readers familiar with museum studies and the politics of gallery spaces, as well as to scholars of dance and performance studies. However the concept of choreography in an expanded field of art discourse becomes critical to my understanding of the function of intersubjectivity in performance art.

Many of the performance artworks in this book were created by choreographers presenting work in the contexts of exhibitions; artists whose work utilises choreography or engages with relevant concepts developed by dance artists in twentieth-century performance art. Some of the choreographers discussed will be familiar to readers including: Tino Sehgal (Germany), Xavier Le Roy (France), Adam Linder (US/Germany), Shahryar Nashat (Germany), Dora Garcia (Spain) and Alexandra Bachzetsis (Switzerland). Others such as Mark Harvey (New Zealand), Sean Curham (New Zealand), Sandra Parker (Australia), Joshua Rutter (Germany/New Zealand), and val smith (New Zealand) may be encountered for the first time. In addition, there will be reference to many other artists who have created works that engage with important choreographic concepts, including more well-known figures such as Rikrit Tiravanija, Jordan Wolfson, Pablo Bronstein, Anne Imhof and Mark Bradford as well as others who may not be as prominent such as: Oliver Beer, Christian Falsnaes, the Bouillon Group, Oleg Kulik and Cameron Jaimie. Crucially I will also introduce artists from the South Pacific including: Louise Menzies, Kalisolaite 'Uhila, Alicia Frankovich, David Rosetsky, Juliet Carpenter and Dan Nash, Rebecca Ann Hobbs, Angela Tiatia and Shigeyuki Kihara. In terms of the methodology used for gathering information on contemporary performance artworks, the majority of the main artworks discussed were experienced in the first person. For those that I was unable to experience I have resorted to documentation and often followed this up by interviewing the artists themselves. Throughout the text it has been noted how exactly each performance was experienced.

Additionally, the history of twentieth-century performance art contains many pertinent examples, including performance practices by artists such as: Yoko Ono (b. 1933), Oskar Schlemmer (1883–1943), Allan Kaprow (1927–2006), Carolee Schneemann (1939–2019), Bruce Nauman (b. 1941), Hans Haacke (b. 1936), Gilbert and George, Paul McCarthy (b. 1945), Vito Acconci (1940–2017), Trisha Brown (b. 1936) and Gillian Wearing (b. 1963). There will also be reference to performances by

Australasian artists like Jim Allen (b. 1922), Mike Parr (b. 1945) and Stelarc (b. 1946). Such lists of artists are not meant to be an exhaustive representation of the ways in which choreographic thinking permeates performance art but rather to provide points of reference for those who see and imagine choreography in different ways and different contexts.

1.1   The Choreographic Turn: The Emergence and Flourishing of Dance Exhibitions

Since the early 2000s it has become more common for artists like Frankovich to stage sequences of movements, actions, behaviour and sometimes utterances as part of performance artworks within biennales, art galleries, and museums. This tendency can be interpreted as a *choreographic turn* in contemporary art that may incorporate both aesthetic and social factors. Bishop argues, for instance, that the prominence of dance-based works in exhibitions is linked to the rise in social media usage and the impact of smartphones on spectatorship:

> The dance exhibition emerged (and flourished) at precisely the same moment that our lives became dominated by ubiquitous portable technology: the first dance exhibitions took place in 2007, the same year as the introduction of the iPhone and the Cloud. (2018: 24)

Although the choreographic turn began earlier than 2007, there is no doubt that in the second decade of the twenty-first century it has become more prominent. Extensive survey exhibitions in large institutions such as *On Line: Drawing Through the Twentieth Century* at New York City's Museum of Modern Art in 2011 and *Danser sa vie* at the Centre Pompidou in Paris from 2011 to 2012 combined works from collections and archives that were to involve dance either literally or as a motif, together with artworks and performances by contemporary artists and choreographers. Each of these large survey exhibitions were mounted following the inclusion of performances by Berlin-based choreographer Tino Sehgal in biennales, art fairs and in a museum context from 2000 onwards. Sehgal's *Twenty Minutes for the Twentieth Century* (1999) was a work in which he danced twenty different dance styles to explore the relationship between the history of dance and the museum. The survey exhibitions were also contemporaneous with the celebration of twentieth century choreographers who had an impact on visual arts practice, and figures such as Trisha Brown, Simone Forti, Anna Halprin and Yvonne Rainer became the subject of retrospective exhibitions, performances, re-performance and new commissions. One significant exhibition that explicitly addressed the concept of choreography was *MOVE: Choreographing You* (2010–2011) mounted by the Hayward Gallery in London, before travelling to Germany.

Australasian examples include shows such as *What I think about when I think about dancing* at the Campbelltown Arts Centre, Sydney in 2009, *Framed Movements* at the Australian Centre for Contemporary Art, Melbourne in 2014 and *SCORE* at the Ian Potter Museum of Art, Melbourne in 2017. The 2016 Biennale of Sydney, under the artistic direction of Stephanie Rosenthal, with the assistance of "curatorial attachés," Adrian Heathfield and André Lepecki, featured a range of performances by choreographers and artists involved in dance. In 2017 Melbourne's MUMA hosted "Dance Remains" a yearlong programme of talks and events in conjunction with the journal Writings on Dance, and from a salon at the Biennale has evolved *Precarious Movement: Choreography and the Museum*, a research project involving scholars and curators from the University of New South Wales, the National Gallery of Victoria, Tate, Art Gallery of New South Wales and Monash University Museum of Art (MUMA).

To provide some art historical background, the artistic milieu in New York City during the 1960s provides an important touchstone for the choreographic turn in contemporary performance art. Choreographers like Anna Halprin, Simone Forti, Yvonne Rainer as well as Deborah Hay and Trisha Brown had an immense impact on artists who had been educated as painters and sculptors such as Robert Morris and Bruce Nauman. The 1960s was a time when art was becoming *transdisciplinary*, and this concept continues to have an impact on contemporary fine art practice. In 1958, artist and creator of "the Happening," Allen Kaprow concluded that.

> Young artists of today need no longer say, "I am a painter' or 'a poet' or 'a dancer'. They are simply 'artists.' All of life will be open to them. (quoted in Rosenthal 2010: 8)

Curator Catherine Wood recently gave an account of the ways in which contemporary art currently enjoys a similar trans-disciplinary environment, one in which experiments with the "choreographic" take place within museums and live bodies are often staged as works of art (2013: 113). Wood also makes the important point that this is not a teleological progression from eliminating objects or material in favour of the social. Instead, she proposes that these experiments within museums and art institutions enable one to "picture ways in which relationships constitute things, and things influence relationships" (121).

Over the past two decades there has also been substantial interest in the space of the museum and practices of exhibition-making from many dance communities. Spanish choreographer La Ribot performed her series *Piezas Distinguidas* (1993–2000) across a range of venues including art galleries such as London's Tate Modern in 2003. These included long-durational live performances as well as installations of video art. In 2009, prior to his directorship at the Rennes National Choreography Centre, Boris Charmatz published his "Manifesto for a Dancing Museum" on his website. Charmatz proposed "a living museum of dance" as part of a spirit of experimentation, evoking a desire to challenge cultural compartmentalisation, as well as a resistance to the frameworks of preconceived institutional ideas (Lista 2014: 6). Charmatz wrote of a will to transfigure the institution, arguing:

> We are at a time in history where a museum can be alive and inhabited as much as a theatre, can include a virtual space, and offer a contact with dance that can be at the same time practical, aesthetic and spectacular. (Chartmatz 2014: 236)

In 2012 Charmatz curated *Moments: A History of Performance in Ten Acts* together with Sigrid Gareis and Georg Schöllhammer at the Karlsruhe Zentrum für Kunst und Medientechnologie. This highly-scenographic exhibition brought together practitioners from dance and performance art, combining works from female artists of the 1960s–1980s as well as installations, contributions from contemporary artists, art students as well as video artist Ruti Sela. A similar "exhibition" of dance was thematised by choreographer Xavier Le Roy in his exhibition *Retrospective* at the Fundació Antoni Tapies, Barcelona in 2012. This involved a small group of performers and choreographers presenting examples of specific pieces from his oeuvre. These choreographed quotations are performed in three ways: as a still figure, an excerpt and as a narration in which the performers explain to visitors their personal relationship to Le Roy's oeuvre. Rather than following the format of a more conventional retrospective or survey exhibition in which all of an artist's works are performed or displayed, *Retrospective* exhibits a multitude of fragments that are interpreted and inflected by a range of selected people, for small groups of individuals. With *Retrospective*, Le Roy playfully inserts his work into the "physical and symbolic space" of the gallery as well as the visual art context (Lista 2013). In doing so he challenges the ways in which dance is habitually exhibited, especially the way in which this is often done in celebration of a particular individual artist or singular author. In *Retrospective* Le Roy's oeuvre becomes diffuse and complex through specific instances of reinterpretation and performance in the gallery space. In 2013 Charmatz went on to produce his work *20 Dancers for the XXth Century* at the Museum of Modern Art in New York City, a work in which performers simultaneously present interpretations of short extracts from a range of twentieth century choreographers in various rooms and corridors of the institution. The result is a highly disjunctive, partial, exuberant and idiosyncratic survey exhibition of dance.

In the second half of the second decade of the twenty-first century, exhibitions engaging with performance, dance and choreographic concerns have increased exponentially, in fact this phenomenon seems to have only just been stymied by the global pandemic of Covid-19 with its shelter-in-place orders, lockdowns and the accompanying restrictions on public gatherings. Symposia, conferences and thematic exhibitions addressing dance and choreographic concerns have been plentiful. In the past five years, Charmatz and Le Roy's work has continued to tour and solo presentations by artists like Michael Clark, Alexandra Bachzetsis, Maria Hassabi, Sharyar Neshat, Adam Linder, Trajal Harrell and Dora Garcia to name only a few, have taken place in art institutions across the globe. In April 2014, Para Site in Hong Kong organised an international conference titled "Is the Living Body the Last Thing Left Alive?: The New Performance Turn, Its Histories and Its Institutions." The conference was dedicated to the continuing relationship between dance, performance and the institutions of global contemporary art. In the accompanying publication curators Cosmin Costinas and Ana Janevski observed that this new performance turn is informed by twentieth-century performance art as well as the discourse of contemporary dance and the roles each of these play in institutional critique, postcolonial theory, and queer re-evaluations of the body and performativity (Costinas and Janevski 2017: 7). As part of the 2019 Biennale di Venezia, curator Charlotte Laubard, together with artists Pauline Boudry and Renate Lorenz, presented *Moving Backwards* at the Swiss Pavilion. The exhibition involved a film installation that explored ideas of mobilisation, resistance, postmodern choreography, urban dance, and queer club cultures, as well as letters and texts from a range of authors addressing the same concerns that were included in the accompanying catalogue (Boudry et al. 2019). In fact, the majority of scholarship in this field is currently located in exhibition catalogues.

Following the survey exhibitions and retrospectives mentioned earlier, literature addressing choreography in relation to performance art includes the publications: *Move: Choreographing You* (2010), *Sharon Lockhart | Noa Eshkol* (2012), *Show Time: Choreography in Contemporary Art* (2012), and *Framed Movements* (2014). Charmatz, together with Sigrid Gareis and Georg Schöllhammer, reflected online on their exhibition *Moments: A History of Performance in Ten Acts* (2013). Art historian Jan Verwoert has explored the relationship between choreography and contemporary visual art and performance in short essays (2010), as has Catherine Wood, senior curator of International Art (Performance) at London's Tate, Marcella Lista at the Centre Pompidou, and Hannah Mathews at MUMA in Melbourne. Even Bishop has contributed to the discourse with a series of case studies on dance in the Tate, MoMA, and Whitney Museums (2014), as well as reflections on the ascendency of exhibitions of dance and its relationship to audience attention (2018). Dance scholar Sara Wookey collaborated with Siobhan Davies Dance to produce the edited volume *WHO CARES? Dance in the Gallery & Museum* (2015) that includes a range of conversations with practitioners who have taken part in dance-related presentations within art institutions. Scholars in dance studies have built up their own literature on the exhibition of dance in contemporary art contexts, much can be found in academic journals particularly special issues such as *Dance Research Journal Special Issue Dance in the Museum* (2014).[4] Two texts from dance studies that have been particularly pertinent to this book are Petra Sabisch's *Choreographing Relations* (2011) and Bojana Cvejić's *Choreographing Problems* (2015), though both of these discuss theatrical dance rather than performance art. Sabisch's description of choreography as a "relational assemblage" focuses on the interplay of relations between bodies as well as relations to objects, music, "relations of visibility," "relations between forces," and "relations of movement and rest" (2011: 7). And Cvejić constructs a sophisticated conception of "problems" in order to craft a narrative about what drives specific instances of recent choreographic practice (2015).

However, at this point I should say that I do not wish to create a false dichotomy between authors writing about theatrical dance versus about performance art, in fact artists and theorists cross these lines all the time. Indeed, much in-depth discussion can be found in publications by performance and dance theorist André Lepecki such as *Exhausting Dance: Performance and the Politics of Movement* (2006) *DANCE* (2012) and *Singularities: Dance in the Age of Performance* (2016). It is worth noting that Lepecki's scholarship is broader than dance-related works that take place in art institutions. As part of his major publications and arguments on choreography, Lepecki focuses his attention on the concept of subjectivity and the ways in which instances of performance art might critique hegemonic social and cultural practices or values favoured by neoliberal capitalist economies. In this book, together with theories of intersubjectivity, arguments from Lepecki as well as Sabisch and Cvejić enable a more politicised and critical analysis of performance artworks than what art historical, visual analysis can offer.

1.2   DEFINING INTERSUBJECTIVITY

But what exactly *is* intersubjectivity? The term is most commonly used in the realms of social theory and psycho-therapy where it designates the "continuous and subjective interaction" between patient and therapist (Natterson 2006). Such interaction is endlessly varied, and the engagement can be largely unconscious but also multiple, inter-penetrating, and mutually transforming. I came across the concept for the first time while studying the philosophy of Emmanuel Levinas (1906–1995) and from within this context, I understand intersubjectivity to mean a sort of "coexistence," a social or dialogic relationship with another person or "Other" (Levinas 2002: 68). Levinas' conception of intersubjectivity will be explored in greater depth in Chapter 4, however, at this point, a more straightforward definition of the term can be found in social theory where intersubjectivity denotes the existence of a "between world," one that connects individual human subjectivities (Crossley 2005). It is not difficult to see why a concept of a shared, between-world with connective force might be compelling to those interested in art.

According to social theorist Nick Crossley there are two ways to approach intersubjectivity, the ego-logical and the radical or sociological. In this book I will focus more on radical or sociological approaches, however, before continuing it is worth noting how exactly ego-logical approaches to intersubjectivity function. One way of looking at a paradigm of exchange that is ego-logical is in terms of what theorist Franco Bifo Berardi has called *connection* (2012: 124–126). During exchange as connection each element remains distinct and they only interact in a functional and machinic manner. Such connection is a matter of interfacing and inter-operability. This mechanical model of intersubjectivity has been described by novelist Ursula Le Guin as a relation between transmitter and receiver, pre-coded sending and receiving, stimulus and response. A mutual, continuous interchange between two consciousnesses, a *"continuous intersubjectivity that goes both ways all the time"* (2004: 188). For Berardi this is the paradigm of exchange or intersubjectivity that is facilitated by the connective environment of electronic devices and the digital web.

In the ego-logical mode the question of whether or not other subjectivities exist is suspended to focus on the question: how it is that we come to experience and know the subjectivity of others? This was the approach of phenomenologists like Edmund Husserl (1859–1938). The philosophical tradition of phenomenology, one that focuses on embodied, first-person experience is mostly concerned with the problem of other minds in terms of social cognition or how one might attribute mental states to another person (Gallagher and Zahavi 2012; Overgaard 2012). According to phenomenology one can interpret, predict and explain another's behaviour by adopting a theoretical stance, putting oneself in their place and asking "what would I be thinking or feeling?" In tandem with research from cognitive science there is an appeal to sub-personal processes of immediate, automatic and almost reflex-like perception and understanding, so that with a knowledge of social and cultural context, as well as a perception of another's action or gestures, one can directly perceive their intentions and mental states (Gallagher in Gallagher and Zahavi 2012: 87–88). An argument from analogy posits that knowledge of one's own mind and self-acquaintance can serve as a departure point for an understanding of others. However, it is here that the problems with phenomenological approaches arise, there are many difficulties involved in any kind of self-knowledge and the analogical process itself is highly prescriptive and universalising, ignoring the diversity of others and their experiences. One example of an interactive performance artwork that cleverly choreographs a dyadic and phenomenological relation is *Three Angles* (2014) by Melbourne-based choreographer Sandra Parker (Fig. 1.2).[5] When a viewer sits down upon a chair within the darkened room of the installation, a filmed performer walks in and also sits. Motion detectors were installed within the space so that when a viewer moves, the filmed performer executes a series of pedestrian or everyday movements in response. Parker has explicitly stated her intention for the work to activate a phenomenological relationship, the aim of the piece is for participants to move and physically engage with the recorded performer in a pattern of transmission and reception, cause and effect.[6]

Phenomenological accounts of intersubjectivity are useful because they can furnish art history and performance studies with accounts of empathy, a concept that is relevant for theorising the reception and spectatorship of performers. According to phenomenology empathy is a form of intentionality directed towards others' lived experiences. Empathy is therefore an

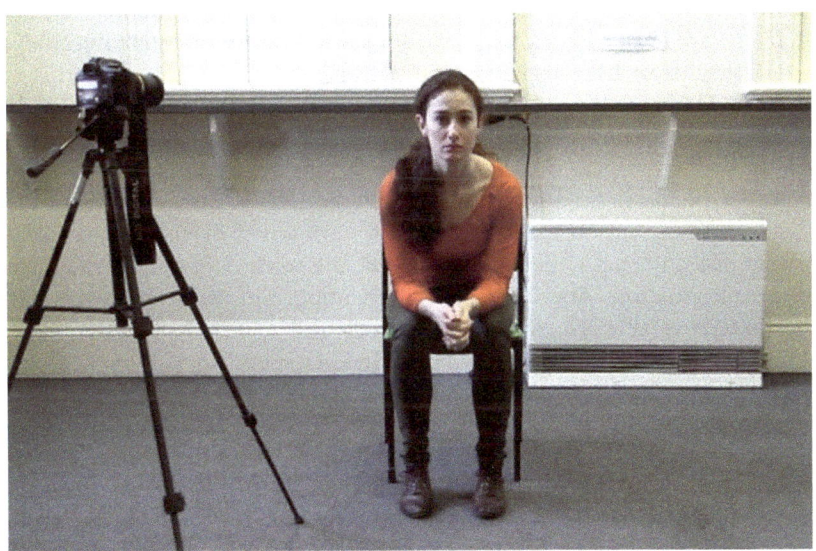

Fig. 1.2 Sandra Parker (in collaboration with Rhian Hinkley), *Three Angles*, 2014. (Single-channel interactive video installation.) Centre for Contemporary Photography, Melbourne, Australia (*Photo* Rhian Hinkley. Courtesy of the artist)

intentional act that presents another's subjectivity from a second-person perspective. It can involve perception of another's bodily presence and inference in a difficult or problematic situation. Harking back to Levinas, the emphasis is upon the face-to-face encounter, a confrontation with neither a mere body nor a hidden psyche but with a unified whole, an expressive unity. Gallagher and Zahavi state that phenomenological views emphasise "non-mentalizing, embodied perceptual approaches to questions of understanding others and the problem of intersubjectivity" (2012: 203).[7] It is important to recognise the body of the other as a lived body, one that is actively engaged in the world and radically different, so that one's perception of the other's bodily presence is unique. Rather than a mere combination of perception and inference, empathy can describe any intentional act that presents the other's subjectivity from the second-person perspective. Although empathy is based on perception of another's bodily presence as well as inference in difficult or problematic situations, a phenomenological conception of empathy involves experiencing the other directly as a person, "as an intentional being whose bodily gestures and actions are expressive of his or her experiences or states of mind" (204).

There are many issues with ego-logical accounts of intersubjectivity. Feminist scholars have argued that traditional phenomenology like that of Maurice Merleau-Ponty (1908–1961) was too focused upon description rather than sensation, the so-called body described is thin and colourless as well as urban with a certain relationship to technology. Many kinds of phenomenology failed to differentiate bodies creating a so-called abstract, "master subject" that is normative, *normate*, specifically masculinist and racist, devoid of gender and ambiguous in terms of its historical situation. Such objections are important because in the past the disciplines of performance art history and dance studies frequently appealed to phenomenological approaches. Geographer Gillian Rose has noted a suspicion of certain usages of language, stating that that there is a "queer neutrality' about the phrase 'the body' rendering it strenuously colourless" (1999: 359–361). For Rose the term "the body" creates undifferentiation, she asks "But whose, then, is the minimalist, colourless, bounded body/path that represents human agency?" Additionally, for Rose discussion of so-called "human agency" is actually masculine and constructed in the image of the master subject, therefore a very specific concept of subjecthood is involved in the various phenomenological accounts of intersubjectivity together with that of the body. Rose's concerns are echoed by Judith Butler in her specific critique of Merleau-Ponty, whose conception of the subject she finds problematic due to its abstract and anonymous status (1989: 95). Butler points out that within phenomenology it is as if the subject described were a "universal subject," one that is devoid of gender and is therefore questionable as a relevant category in any description of lived experience. The subject described "resembles a culturally constructed male subject," it consecrates masculine identity as a model for the human subject and in doing so devalues women (98).

This ties into Australian philosopher Philipa Rothfield's argument that "the subject is a false universal" and that the tendency towards universality in phenomenology represents a risk of failing to achieve any kind of generality similar to other enlightenment discourses that "covertly assume particular forms of gender, sexuality and ethnicity" (2010: 304). Returning to Rose's concerns about the term "body," Despite Merleau-Ponty's central thesis that "the world is refracted through our bodily sensibilities" and that human corporeality is the means by which the world is understood, such a relationship is articulated in overly general terms concerning "the body rather than, for example, this body" (304). Rothfield argues that phenomenological universalism brings with it:

> an ethical danger that corporeal forms of difference which occur within networks of domination will be elided; that the desire to achieve universality will blind itself to the discriminations performed in the name of sameness. (306)

Just as Gallagher and Zahavi caution that intersubjective understanding is socially and culturally embedded, Rothfield warns that there are many forms of social inequality inherent in social life and that any "universal impulse" is co-opted towards hegemonic forms of utterance and appearance, so that the universal is in fact homogenised and difference is effaced, according to dominant norms of articulation. If the world is refracted through bodily sensibilities Rothfield asks "Is there one means by which refraction occurs or are there many?" If anything can be salvaged from phenomenology Rothfield argues that it is its potential to work through difference by approaching lived bodies according to their lived situation. Hence "lived body" becomes *lived bodies*, the concept is pluralised so that it may stand as an index of differential corporeal circumstances and thereby different kinds of subjects. Rothfield asks that phenomenology relinquish the idea of universalism and recast lived bodies in pluralised terms, aiming for a "regional series of understandings" (2010: 306).

Pertinent to ego-logical accounts of intersubjectivity is Butler's point that an autonomy/dependence relation characterises human life, this dynamic is part of:

> a dialectic of the self and other which is that of master and slave: insofar as I have a body, I may be reduced to the status of an object beneath the gaze of another person, and no longer count as a person for him, or else I may become his master and, in my turn, look at him. (1989: 96)

This critique is crucial for phenomenological descriptions of inter-subjectivity as well as accounts of performance art due to the way in which they present a relation of alterity, or someone to be viewed by another. The *master/slave* is a metaphysical dynamic that posits the so-called body as always an object for others inasmuch as it is perceived.[8] Ego-logical approaches provide somewhat mechanical models of intersub-jectivity and as argued by Rose, Rothfield and Butler, situating subjects within such a relation can be problematic. The question is how to evade the undifferentiated "body" that is superimposed on false universal models of the human subject and then situated within subject/object and autonomous/dependent dynamics? One answer may be temporarily dissolving distinctions between subjects by stressing the relational and sociological or how exactly subjects involve themselves in shared relations, groups and settings. An example of a performance artwork that attempts to do this is *Composition for Mouths (Songs My Mother Taught Me) I* and *II* (2018) by British artist Oliver Beer.[9] These video works involve two performers standing upright and joining their lips in a tight seal to create a single mouth cavity, they then blend their voices to create rhythmic harmonic interactions (Biennale of Sydney 2018: 31). Beer's *Composition for Mouths* is an intersection of shared cultures of music, human voices and architecture. Two people together share an equal part in creating a single resonant cavity for music and sound that in turn resonates within the space they share, the built environment they perform within.

This enactment of inter-dependency begs a radical and sociological approach to intersubjectivity. Inspired by the theories of phenomenologist Alfred Schutz, according to this model there is no self without the other, because the very concept of self is relational and experience is depen-dent upon the other (Crossley 2005). According to this social model the group and interaction come first and a distinct individual emerges out of an interactional context. The point is, there is no "before interaction:"

> Intersubjectivity in its primary and most basic/radical form is best conceived from an interactionist and relational point of view as a fabric of social life into which individuals are born. (Crossley 2005)

We are enmeshed in interaction from the moment we are born, long before any conscious sense of self and other and it is by means of interaction that we can become aware of ourselves as well as others. As Crossley explains "I do not begin with knowledge of myself, which I then project onto others. I first interact with others and on the basis of doing so, learn to make sense of myself" (2005). The point is, subjectivity develops in and through intersubjectivity, as subjectivity develops, intersubjectivity is developed too. One example of this is language, a public, social institution one learns to use through interaction with others. From there, much of the sense of one's subjective life takes shape within language. Other examples of social institutions are art and performance. Rather than an ego-logical approach that begins with the point of view of a contemplative individual, a radical and sociological approach to intersubjectivity takes as a starting point a recognition of embodied action as the basis for subjective life and that each subject is always-already enmeshed in interactions with others.

Theories from psychology and cognitive science emphasise the unconscious processes that might take place during interpersonal interaction and although they describe general encounters, they are also useful for encounters with a performing subject. Although at first they may seem mechanical and ego-logical, in fact they are highly relational and social. From his discussion of neonate imitation or one's earliest experience of self and others, philosopher Shaun Gallagher surmises that a proprioceptive self is always already coupled with the other (2005: 82, 84). According to Gallagher the visual experience of another as well as their action and expression, is not just a matter of outward appearance. Actions and expressions communicate in a code related to oneself, such communication is organised on the basis of an innate system that does not necessarily give priority to one's own body awareness over and against perception of the other. In terms of perception of another person, visual recognition is considered very important. In particular, processes of facial recognition involve particular networks of pathways and brain areas that co-operate with other classification systems such as object and scene recognition (Minissale 2013: 64). Accordingly the process of facial recognition is perceptual and also pre-semantic. Any viewing or matching of unfamiliar faces relative to other categories of objects activates the area of the brain that is preferentially responsive to faces.

These disciplines also offer an account of more kinaesthetic acts of recognition that involve broader aspects of posture. For human brain researchers such as Riitta Hari et al. there is reliance upon unconsciously formed inferences of the other person's goals and intentions as part of direct face-to-face encounters and attempts to understand and be understood by others (2013: 105).[10] According to this argument, mutual understanding requires some similarity of perception and action to the extent that during interaction people often automatically adopt the other person's postures or movement patterns that can even lead to synchronisation. Such unconscious mirroring of other people's actions helps in the sharing of feelings, as well as goals. Psychologists Tanya Chartrand and John Bargh argue for a link between perceptions and behaviour so that perception can have an automatic, unintended and passive effect on behaviour (1999). Within an art encounter there might be a *chameleon-effect* or non-conscious mimicry of the behaviour of another person including postures, mannerisms as well as facial expressions that physically demonstrates empathy, togetherness and perhaps even interpersonal bonding. Such studies are important to my overall argument because they produce a normative account of intersubjectivity that is frequently problematised by instances of performance art.

Theses from cognitive science, particularly situated cognition which is composed of embodiment, embeddedness, and extension can also add important nuances to the social and relational aspects of cognition and phenomenology (Robbins and Aydede 2009: 3). According to the embodiment thesis cognition depends on the body, not just on the mind; the embedding thesis posits that cognitive activity often utilises structures in the social and natural environment and the extension thesis argues that the boundaries of cognition extend beyond the boundaries of individual organisms. According to each of these positions mental activity is dependent on the situation or context in which it occurs. The extension thesis in particular dictates the importance of intersubjectivity, for it argues that the boundaries of cognition extend into the social, involving other people. Philosophers Philip Robbins and Murat Aydede propose that any cognition is dependent or equivalent to a body, utilising structures in natural and social environments and extending beyond the boundaries of individual organisms. Ideas of cognitive extension are particularly relevant to theorising intersubjectivity-as-art, as cognition extends and is distributed into the socio-cultural environments of the art gallery or museum. Such interconnected accounts of cognition argue against a downwards-oriented operation of self-other, they anticipate the more fluid, dispersed and relational concepts of intersubjectivity that will be discussed throughout this book.

The paradigm of exchange is no longer one of discrete elements transmitting and receiving, it is more one of what Berardi has called conjunction and concatenation or *becoming* (2012: 122). Rather than social life as a connective modality, a functional, inter-operability of compatible linguistic units, Berardi proposes *conjunction* as "becoming-other, living and the unexpected concatenation of bodies" (123). In conjunction, singularities change when they conjoin, they become a fusion of segments and something other than what they were before their conjunction. It is this paradigm of exchange and intersubjectivity that is useful for giving an account of intersubjectivity-as-art. Berardi's conjunction resembles what Le Guin playfully describes as a model for intersubjectivity modelled on "amoebas having sex," an encounter in which organisms get together, reach out, connect and meld their pseudopodia (2004: 188–189). Intersubjectivity, as a between world between subjectivities is a generative concept, one that will be expanded upon throughout this book. For now, I will end this section with a proposition from French philosopher Louis Althusser (1918–1990), his *philosophy of the encounter*. Althusser stresses the importance of relations between a subject and an encounter that dominates with its own spontaneity, logic and operations.

> the materialism of the encounter is the materialism... of a process, a process that has no subject, yet imposes on the subjects (individuals or others) which it dominates, the order of its development, with no assignable end. (2006: 190)

Perhaps an encounter with a performance artwork as a process of *intersubjectivity-as-art* might act as what Althusser calls a clinamen or swerve, something unexpected. Althusser valorises the haphazard and aleatory as well as process, contingency, chance, displacement and freedom, a novel angle from which to approach instances of performance art. I would also argue that the concept of choreography can also be used to explain how intersubjectivity functions in performance art.

1.3   A Working Definition of Choreography

It is important to clearly distinguish between the terms "dance" and "choreography." Whereas "dance" is a general term often meaning to move rhythmically to music, following a set sequence of steps, *choreography* is the art of writing, composing or performing dances (Laermans 2008: 7). As Charmatz explains "Dance certainly includes a properly choreographic dimension, but it also happily overflows beyond this framework" (2014: 233). "*Choreography*" is a specific neologism created in 1700 at the court of French King Louis XIV, at first it referred to a form of dance notation invented by Pierre Beauchamps, dance master to the king and printed by Raoul Auger Feuillet (Foster 2010: 32). The Greek etymology of the term combines dancing and writing, choreographies were thus notated scores of dances, and choreographers were the people who could read and write the notation. Therefore, from the point at which this neologism was first used it was indelibly connected to supreme power, authority, the mechanics of bodies in space as well as reading and writing. However, over time the notion has shifted, so that since the early twentieth-century choreography has come to denote the composition of dances; it is the practice of designing or structuring which kinds of actions or sequences of steps and movements are performed. A piece of choreography constitutes a plan or score, typically a set of parameters is set up by one party in order to regulate the movement of others, for a certain period of time. What is already made evident by this short paragraph is a tension within various usages of the term. On the one hand choreography is authoritative, it prescribes movement and involves, as argued by Rosenthal, "a thought or suggestion as to a possible cause of action" (2010: 10). On the other hand choreography can function as an emancipatory project, one made up of counter-moves, it can be less prescriptive and more imaginative, a loose and casual plan involving spontaneity and freedom.

In the realm of dance, the way it usually works is that choreographers create specific, authoritative relations with the dancers who realise their works through the use of scores and instruction. Even when choreographers perform their own work, they must still follow their own previously conceived sequence of actions and are likely to follow their own training regime. Generally, in a Western theatrical dance context, the process abides by the following formula: dancers are selected by a choreographer, they then participate in a rehearsal process where they attend classes and learn the dances they will perform. And finally, they perform the given choreography as part of live or recorded performances.[11] Lepecki, together with dance historian and theorist Mark Franko, argues that a central aspect of choreographing bodies is the setting up of certain relations so that there is a subjection or "yielding" to synchronicity, instruction, and authority (2006: 9). The question of *movement* opens up the politics of mobility, how movement is actually *motivated*, requiring decisions about "*who* is able or allowed to move – and under what circumstances, and on what grounds; to decide *where* one is allowed to move to; to define who are the bodies that can *choose* full mobility and who are the bodies forced into displacement" (Allsopp and Lepecki 2008: 1).

In terms of the written component within the term choreography, Lepecki points out that any performance artwork is directly entangled with language as a force or command. Here language is a "general theory of command and obeisance, of disciplining and control, which are precisely the forces that have found, produced, and reproduced the practice and concept of choreography as a system of command." One which bodies have to subject themselves to its wills and whims (Allsopp and Lepecki). This writing of movement fulfils a corporeal need "to pedagogically and biologically (re) produce bodies capable of carrying out certain movement imperatives." The neologism of choreography was extended by Louis XIV's dance master as a way of notating ceremonial court dance in which the king's absolute authority was evoked and enacted and the movements of his dancer-subjects were heavily codified, demonstrating hierarchies and subjugation to order. Directly continuing on from this, the dancers in the French corps de ballets are still called *sujets* or subjects, submitting themselves to imperatives from dieting to gender roles, strict physical discipline as well as the precise enactment of positions, attitudes, steps and gestures. Choreography is first and foremost a structure of command that has to be reckoned with.

Choreography has been described as an "apparatus of capture," (Allsopp and Lepecki 2008: 3); it is a way of making bodies docile or subject-to, with the aid of a score or written instructions. As dance scholar Noémie Solomon explains, a choreographic score exists as a whole and as singular articulations, each is an organised system holding a conception of movement, a shaping of bodies, as well as a prompting of intersubjective relations and encounters across artistic, social and political spheres (2012: 50). A score enables a series of encounters between bodies to materialise through and as movement articulations. Thus, choreography is always already an intersubjective relation, often between a creator of a score and another as subject to the authority of the score. In terms of how relations might be structured, Lepecki's thesis is that any relationship activated by choreography is "first and foremost a structure of command that has to be reckoned with" one that "requires a series of successful surrenders to its demands" (Allsopp and Lepecki 2008: 1). Supporting this thesis, Franko cautions that choreography is a "traffic between bodies and ideologies" and the relations between dancer/performer and choreographer/artist is always a political one (2007: 19). And as Lepecki points out, what philosopher Gilles Deleuze might call *microfascisms* characterise many interrelationships and intersubjective relationships, including those between artist and performer (2013).

Those working in fine art contexts have tended to focus more on the prescriptive aspects of choreography, as was the case in the US during the 1960s when artists became interested in instructional works and scores for events. One example of an artwork that gently prescribes movement is *Grapefruit,* Yoko Ono's 1964 publication of event-scores, one example taken from the book reads: "TOUCH POEM FOR A GROUP OF PEOPLE. Touch eachother. 1963 winter" (2000: unpaginated). As made evident in Rosenthal's exhibition *MOVE: Choreographing You* (2010–2011), since the 1960s many works of art have invited visitors to exhibitions in order "to perform certain movements, effectively creating a choreography for them" (Rosenthal 2010: 10). To widen the scope further, the term *social choreography* as theorised by Andrew Hewitt refers to the more authoritarian or disciplinary aspects of choreography, as degenerated, artificial or manipulated patterns of behaviour (2005). Accordingly choreography holds a mirror up to the world, with its external powers controlling the physical, psychological and spatial aspects of our actions and reflecting back broader socio-political structures and mechanisms of manipulation. Here choreography is a structuring force similar to social organisation or the ways in which bodies are constantly managed and directed in day to day life. Lepecki argues that the "mere disposition of things in the world already choreographs, predicates or even predicts our simple and daily behaviours" (Lepecki in Rosenthal: 157). Examples of things that choreograph daily behaviour include centre-lines painted on footpaths and barriers for queues in banks or airports and even rails and stanchions in museums and art galleries. I would argue that this is why artists and curators are drawn to the thesis of choreography as a system of command—museums and art galleries are disciplinary spaces that make manifest a whole host of authoritative relations. Additionally, an interpretation of choreography as prescriptive, controlling and commanding is antagonistic and therefore can be generative for conceiving of new works of performance art. However, it is important to note that dance cannot be reduced to a field of unethical relations and un-empathetic modes of working, as reflected in everyday choreographies. The concept of *choreography as authority* is a generalisation that has been mobilised conceptually by a range of theorists and become dominant in the realm of contemporary art perhaps because it is a useful metaphor for subject-formation. There is no doubt that a very specific conception of choreography has been taken from dance studies and used to various ends, within a visual arts paradigm.

Yet there is another way of looking at choreography, one in which the concept is more expansive, making way for practices that empower artists, performers and perhaps even participants and spectators as active agents and authors of creative processes. What Lepecki calls "counter-moves," "moving otherwise" and ways of evading various forms of authority look to philosophy as an ideal model for such practices (2013). For Lepecki, the very task of choreography is "rethinking the subject in terms of the body" (2006: 5–6). It is important to note that for Lepecki, such a task is not necessarily "subservient to the imperative of the kinetic" or movement, as many of the survey exhibitions mentioned earlier have a tendency to conflate the concept of choreography with moving bodies. Corresponding with the philosophical approaches made by this book, for Lepecki, choreography is also a "task that is always already in dialogue with critical theory and philosophy."

Reinforcing the connections between performance art and choreography, theorist Bojana Cvejić argues that choreography is "characterized by experiment and by the conceptualization of working methods and of the medium of the dancing body, as well as by a proximity to performance art" (Cvejić 2015: 1). For Cvejić, choreography is one method with which to pose problems so that there might be a reinvention of "choreographic relations between the body, movement, and time in the legacy of the Western art of dance." Belgian sociologist Rudi Laermans has argued for ways in which contemporary dance is "re-choreographing" choreography (2008: 10). He posits choreography that is "total" and "open." Total in that it can include the movements of dancers as well as the presence of viewers together with sound, video, lighting, and installation. Open in that the presence of spectators or interactions of performers is not fixed. Laermans proposes what he calls *choreography in general* summarised as "*the making and modulation of assemblages*" explorative associating, coupling or bringing together of a range of elements and materials including the human and non-human (11).[12]

For Cvejić the various ways the concept of choreography has recently been inflected reflect the wider open-endedness or indeterminacy enjoyed by contemporary art in general. Hence choreography might be defined as the "the organization of movement in time and space" (2015: 8). It could involve merely the "organization of things," a "thinking about the organization of objects and subjects in time and space on stage." Another definition courtesy of Xavier Le Roy is that choreography is "artificially staged action(s) and/or situation(s)" and from choreographer Jonathan Burrows is the idea that "choreography is about making a choice, including the choice to make no choice." Choreography as doing and not doing is echoed by theorist Petra Sabisch's concern with a question that is simultaneously philosophical, political, ontological, physiological, and ethical, that of "what can a body do?" (2011: 8). More broadly, Sabisch stresses the importance of relations, or events of "qualitative transformations within the relational assemblage of choreography." Sabisch then begs the question "What can choreography do?" rather than what it is, almost tautologically she argues for: "that which choreography actually does as a can-do-determination of what choreography *is*."

From here a vital question becomes who or what does choreography do things *with*? This brings me to the importance of relations, in fact I would argue that relationality is integral to choreography. Rather than choreography as the notation or composition of dances, throughout this book the emphasis will be on the relations realised by each instance of choreography. Sabisch posits any instance of choreography as a "relational assemblage" (2011: 8) and philosopher Erin Manning concurs, conceiving of choreography "not as the organizing principle of precomposed bodies" but as an "activity of arranging relations between bodies" (Manning 2013: 76). Similarly, dance scholar Jenn Joy posits that choreographic engagement involves a positioning of oneself in relation to another, it is participation in a "scene of address that anticipates and requires a particular mode of attention, even at times against our will"

(2014: 1). Joy proposes that facing another person involves an encounter with precariousness that is the very condition of such an address:

> Yet if we engage this tenuous choreography we invent a more sensual counter-address to the legislative acts of consumption, erasure and violence. I imagine the work of the choreographic as one possibility of sensual address –a dialogic opening in which art is not only looked at but also looks back, igniting a tremulous hesitation in the ways that we experience and respond. (2014: 1)

Joy's proposition of "performance as address," her emphasis upon choreography as a positioning of oneself in relation to another, a possibility of a sensual address and a dialogic opening that involves art that "looks back," again invokes intersubjectivity, a momentary shared world or interaction connecting subjectivities.

Before continuing it is worth stressing that this disciplinary traffic is not one-way, an art historical perspective on relationality also has much to bring to choreography, especially choreography in the museum. Evidence of this is the way that Lepecki turned to the history of performance art to support his thesis of *exhausting dance* (2006). Perhaps one of the reasons that the history of art proved useful for Lepecki is that it is less concerned with customary forms of movement like ballet and since the 1960s has seen challenges to the kinds of normative bodies still generally expected in western theatrical dance. Although Cvejić perceives contemporary art in general to enjoy a wider open-endedness or indeterminacy, I would argue that what it has to offer are very specific histories and genealogies, such as that of sculpture and the material object and most importantly, the exhibition. The history of art and museum studies has many lessons and provocations to offer to choreographers who wish to step inside the museum as well as those who wish to participate in the field of the curatorial and exhibition-making.

1.4   Summary of Chapters

The point of departure for this book was the phenomenon of dance in the museum, also known as the choreographic or "new performance" turn. As observed by Wood, from at least the twenty-first century onwards, contemporary art has enjoyed a *trans-disciplinary* environment, one in which experiments with the "choreographic" take place within museums and live bodies are often staged as works of art (2013: 113). The phenomenon has its roots in New York City during the 1960s, a time when visual artists were heavily influenced by choreographers, dancers and vice versa. Similarly from at least the 2000s onwards, the traffic between dance and exhibition-making has been two-way, as makers from dance communities became more and more active in the space of the art gallery and museum. As Charmatz observed, the museum "can be alive and inhabited… can include a virtual space, and offer a contact with dance that can be at the same time practical, aesthetic and spectacular" (2014: 236). In the second half of the second decade of the twenty-first century, exhibitions engaging with performance, dance and choreographic concerns increased exponentially and were only just stymied by the global pandemic of Covid-19 with its shelter-in-place orders, lockdowns and the accompanying restrictions on public gatherings.

Responding to this phenomenon, artworks that shape or orchestrate specific relations between artist/choreographer and performer, or between performer and participants are my core concern. Selected performances, either live or recorded, involved the execution of planned movements, actions, choreography as part of an encounter between various individuals occupying a gallery space. I will argue that choreographed works like Frankovich's *Bisons* (2010-ongoing) enact novel forms of intersubjectivity. The intersubjective aspect of performance art will be unpacked, prioritising philosophy and art theory to build a case. Bringing together the interrelated fields of museum studies, dance studies and philosophy. I posit that performances have contributions to make to the discourse on the subjectivity/intersubjectivity relation. They produce subjectivity for the duration of an artwork in ways that can affect new intersubjectivities. The concept of choreography can help to explain the functions of intersubjectivity in performance art, mainly because it offers an account of the relational and ways artworks can produce or challenge subjection. The idea is that taken together, theories of intersubjectivity and choreography enable a more politicised and critical analysis of performance artworks than what art historical, visual analysis can offer.

The tensions between conformity and freedom that I have outlined in this introduction in the chorography of the contemporary art museum are well captured by Lepecki in his distinction between *choreo-policing* and *choreo-politics* (2013). In Chapter 2, I will expand on these two approaches. On the one hand is the political and kinetic practice of *choreo-policing* and taming, systems of obedience, commands, impera- tives, the controlling of movement, blocking and ensuring everyone is in a permissible place. Museums are formidable disciplinary structures, strict parameters are put in place in order to elicit managed interaction and a display of activity and engagement. The ways in which one is able to engage with art or look, walk, think and rest are manipulated within the space of the art museum by architecture, display, instruction and example as well as by parameters, scores and instruction created by either artists, choreographers or curators. Regulation, indeed self-regulation seems to be an inevitable reality of the museum, where one is choreographed by one party or another. And artists often respond self-reflexively to this unique, intersubjective environment. The antagonistic, problem-space of the gallery is immensely generative for a range of performance artists like Mark Harvey, Christian Falsnaes and Adam Linder.

On the other hand is *choreo-politics* that involve a redistribution and reinvention of bodies, affects and senses. Ways of moving politically, experimenting with movement and exercising freedom. This dichotomy runs throughout this entire book, through deliberate practices of *unset- tling spectatorship* contemporary art museums have attempted to align themselves with the choreo-political project. From the 2000s onwards, perhaps following the model of Paris' Centre Pomipdou, contempo- rary art museums were more cognisant and willing to play with a *performing museology*. As Leahy explains, the most well-known example is the Turbine Hall commissions at the Tate Modern, London from 2000. Yet even within such a space, spectators are placed within a performative framework in which one's corporeal presence is emphasised. Parameters are provided for the interaction and creative play of all its users in order to create a spectacular public space and a highly marketable image of activity and movement. Visitors are encouraged to put themselves on display, in proximity to the aura of culture provided by the museum. Occasionally they are selectively allowed to deliberately change the script and alter or disrupt the repertoire and familiar choreography of viewing. However, in doing so, as argued by Alexandra Kolb (2013) they may in fact be re- perpetuating the "experience economy" of later capitalism and as a result may not enjoy as much autonomy as previously thought.

Faced with this entanglement of conformity and freedom, a speculative project of theorising alternatives has value. Luckily there are various theo- ries of space that support the *choreo-political* project. Michel Foucault's concept of the *heterotopia* or space as a *counter-site* is important as a space of change for opening up, proliferation and the challenging of containment (Foucault and Miskowiec 1986). This ties into choreographer Carol Brown's thesis of *matrixial* space, or space as a set of relations produced by bodies, spaces and built environments as well as John Protevi's concept of *phase space* in which interaction can alter the field or situation it takes place within (2001). The idea of heterotopia sets up a space for illusion, a space that is other, different, spaces as "other places." Via Brown, space is proposed as passage, a moment for becoming, opening up and proliferation. A space in which performances and choreographies as intersubjective encounters might alter or affect the very gallery or museum in which they take place.

To expand on this within the museum space, Helen Rees Leahy has observed a *performing museology*, a shift from "the museum as a collection of objects to the museum as a site of social and corporeal practices" (2012: 2–3). In fact, as Leahy's own thesis of *museum bodies* testifies, the museum has always been a site of social and corporeal practices, using authority to create specific relations with their visitors. Like Jordan Wolfson's programmed puppet *Colored Sculpture* (2016), the practised museum spectator is always-already *subject-to*, embodied within a limited repertoire of actions that reflect and respond to: the conditions of viewing, the spaces of display and the presence of other spectators. Scripts are encoded in the rhythm of displays that regulates the direction and pace of walking. Kinaesthetic encounters with an exhibition involve a choreographing of the visitor by mechanisms of control and display chosen by the curator and exhibition designer.

In Chapter 3 I will argue that within an art historical context, choreographer Xavier Le Roy's *Self Unfinished* (1998) can be read within a broader, received narrative about US based and Western European art history, according to which cis-gendered male artists enact transformations as isolated figures within a room or enclosed space. This trope is important as it represents a certain kind of artistic subjectivity that has broader implications for modern subjectivity and the kinds of artistic subjects that may be involved in the intersubjective art encounters that take place in contemporary art settings. *Self Unfinished* demonstrates a self-reflexive awareness of how a performing body is relational, that is contingent upon the perception of others. This artwork involves experimentation with the full ontological status of subjectivity, manifesting *becoming* as well as *body without organs*, processes by which Le Roy temporarily dismantles himself, disarticulates himself, un-hooks himself from points of subjectification. In *Self Unfinished* Le Roy messes with the way in which others perceive him, he resists and problematises simple comprehension of himself as a single human body. Butler has argued that the coherence and continuity of any given person is socially or intersubjectively instituted and maintained by the norms of intelligibility. Le Roy resists this and refuses to be docile. Through a process of de-figuration, by making himself appear formless, indeterminate, not easily recognisable or identifiable he challenges and undermines his own *individuation*. Via his choreography of bodily transformation Le Roy unravels greater organisational structures and creates a temporary state of destratification. In this atmosphere of uncertainty Le Roy is no longer a definite being categorised and distinguished from other beings, he almost dissolves into a larger pool of becoming-indeterminate. In *Self Unfinished* Le Roy manifests the political potential of choreography and performance, pointing to the ways in which an emancipated subject might have implications for the units that make up intersubjectivity. An-other body is presented in *Self Unfinished*, one that undermines the constitution of a subject, temporarily evading discipline, the majority and dwelling in-between the terms at play. Le Roy, like Acconci and McCarthy before him, performs effeminisation and in doing so renders equivocal the artistic subject of the privileged, labouring, singular, unitary, male artist as genius. Accordingly, masculinity becomes an exchangeable attribute, one assigned through interpretive and intersubjective relations and one that demonstrates the fragility of the system by which its privilege is ensured.

In Chapter 4 I use political theorist Paolo Virno's concept of the multitude in order to examine intersubjectivity as a tension between the collective and the individual (2004). Such a tension is also a fruitful one for artists to explore. Theorist Félix Guattari emphasised singularity, arguing that cultivating *dissensus* is necessary for subjectivities faced with erosion (2000: 50). His concept of *ecology* can be used to challenge oppositional structures of subject/object, self/other and subjectivity/intersubjectivity. For Gilbert Simondon, subjectivity and intersubjectivity are bridged by a relational layer of affectivity, the *transindividual*, a "relation of relations," one that problematises psychic and collective individuation (Combes 2013: 25–26). Yet Guattari still wished to preserve the harshness or asperity of the other, valorising relationships between subjectivity and its exteriority, whether that be social, animal, vegetable or Cosmic. Any grouping is a work in progress, it has the potential to develop and proliferate with the aid of practices like performance art, to extend beyond previously-defined categories (40). For Guattari, the modalities of "group-being" can be implemented by experimental practices like performance art that take place on a micro-social level. As will be made evident with Frankovich's *Defending Plural Experiences* (2014), it is choreography, as a score, plan or loose series of instructions, that is instrumentalised in order to explore groups, groupings and novel forms of intersubjectivity. Instances of performance art like *Defending Plural Experiences* as well as Tino Segal's *These Associations* (2012) operate as what Guattari would call "new ecological practices," micro-political and micro-social practices that create new solidarities (2000: 50–51). Both of these performance artworks work to maintain the singularity of their performers, as well as explore ideas of group-being, multitude, mass and swarming.

An emphasis on intersubjectivity or the relational challenges ideas about spectatorship and the reception of art, as much as it probes the relationships between institutions, artists and performers. Posthumanism, as posited by Rosi Braidotti, reconceives intersubjectivity in a way that is similar to Guattari's *social ecology*, de-centring the human, especially the human as white, male, able and imperialist; opening it up to those people previously considered other, as well as objects and animals (2013). This is seen in Cameron Jaimie's *Massage the History* (2007–2009) and Anne Imhof's *Forever Rage* (2015). Choreography situates intersubjectivity in the human museum by emphasising relations that are social, animal, vegetable or cosmic. Faced with the climate emergency and ecological collapse, artists like Frankovich stress a planetary, geo-centred perspective, a *post-human becoming earth*. Intersubjectivity is thereby extended to our planet, a complex habitat in which humans are geological agents who must maintain the milieu for human and non-human alike. Such a perspective is made manifest in Frankovich's *World is Home Planet* (2016) in which performers, participants, fragrance, fruit pips, galaxies, colours and lakes are commingled within fluctuating actions, utterances and events, in illumination and darkness. Both Frankovich and Sehgal use darkness as a way to confuse unitary identity, creating groups and collectivities by making the distinctions between subjects temporarily difficult to perceive. Shared monologues, creative costuming and de-illumination are just some of the techniques used in performance art to problematise the subjectivity-intersubjectivity relation. When this book was first being conceived, I anticipated that this would be how it would end, challenging individuation by dissolving performers and beholders into a darkened mass of collectivity. However, I found that there was more to the story for two reasons: one was that the reception and production of art had been altered forever by the internet and digital technologies; and two that those decreed by the humanist museum to be *other*, those racialised and sexualised, continue to creatively undermine its structural prejudices.

In Chapter 5, I posit that Gillian Wearing's *Rehearsing for Peckham* (1994) provides an art historical precedent for recent artworks involving choreographies performed to camera, ones that are self-taught and subsequent to viewing dance content uploaded to the internet, from dancers across the globe. *Networked choreographies* like Rebecca Ann Hobbs' 2011 video works *Otara at Night* and *Mangere Mall* enact complex relations. They extend the triangulation of gallery, performance and spectator to include online video content. Access to what Harmony Bench refers to as *movement archives* has meant digital networks have become increasingly important in the creation and distribution of choreography. Such repositories have proven to be generative, for performers like those in Hobbs' works, dancing like the archive and dancing for the archive are new strategies of dance production (2017: 156). The internet and digital technologies have substantially altered subjects and intersubjectivity. Thanks to the proliferation of hand-held electronic devices, *cyborg-subjects* enjoy an intimacy of mind, body and tool (Haraway 1991). They participate within highly distributed forms of knowledge and art and have the ability to readily connect with others, confusing the polarity of public and private. Hobbs' two video works were created within a broader context of *post-internet* art practices that engage with the internet and digital technologies, as well as practices that are *post-digital*, or somewhat disenchanted with utopic conceptions of the World Wide Web.

Melissa Gronlund has posited that contemporary art explores how new technologies can both mediate and communicate the relationship between "here" and "elsewhere" in the context of the internet (2017: 120). Performers and dancers, as cyborg-subjects creating networked choreographies, can access dance content from different places and times thanks to the movement-archives. Various dance genres from very specific locales, such as dancehall in 2000s Jamaica, or vogueing in 1980s New York City, have their own stories and struggles, these can be re-visited and re-embodied in another time-place such as Auckland, New Zealand, in order to create novel choreographies. This chimes with Bruno Latour's thesis that any given interaction, or indeed any given choreography, overflows with elements from another time and place and is a "terminus point" of a great number of various different agencies and informal associations. There is always an uncertainty about the origin of action, it can often be overtaken, or "other-taken," carried out and then distributed to others (2005: 45). Cyborg-subjects enjoy unique intersubjective relations with innumerable others across the globe. Though they may be amateur dancers, they can learn from each other as well as more practised performers from the past and present. They can then test or try out various choreographies and ways of moving, permuting them and re-enacting them for their own ends.

In Chapter 6 I return to the binary logic of Tony Bennett's *exhibitionary complex* that categorises some subjects as sexualised and "other," those that deviate from dominant humanist and heteronormative systems. Choreographies that are *queer* are part of a broader counter-hegemonic, political project, using performance artworks to propose alternatives through: disobedience; actions that misbehave; other ways of moving and being. In their performance *duotones* (2014) at Auckland's Artspace gallery, val smith positioned themselves as a choreographer demanding the obedience and acquiescence of their audience members. smith's illogical and nonsensical instructions demonstrated the absurdity and arbitrariness of instruction. Demonstrating queer choreographic authority, they themselves assumed the position of choreo-police but in a way that was actually choreo-political, once again challenging the binary.

In *gutter matters* (2014) smith placed themselves and any willing participants horizontally, in the gutter, on the street as part of a "gay shame parade." In doing so, they challenged the normative vertical axis of being upright and straight up and down, reflecting Sara Ahmed's argument about *queer* involving dis-orientation and a disturbance in the usual order of things. Mapping a politics of queer pride and shame (smith 2016), the performance probed the binary opposition as one that tends to characterise and form queer identities. smith produced an affect of shame (Munt 2000) so that it could be overcome, neutralised and even used as a methodology for creating choreographies. smith reperforms the convention of the very public gay pride parade, with its relations of spectacular display and exhibitionism so that it becomes oblique as they lie horizontal on the gallery floor. In *gutter matters* they self-consciously expose themselves to alternating intersubjective relations of pride and shame, performing actions that are lowly as well as celebratory, inviting participation and complicity.

In *Meiosis* and *Homoshamanism*, both from 2016, smith used liminal, threshold spaces together with movement, action, proximity and contact to challenge the stability of identities. As Eve Kosofsky Sedgwick has argued, the *queer* operates in terms of possibilities, gaps, overlaps, dissonances, lapses and excess (1993: 8). In *Meiosis* smith engaged in a four-hour process of comprehensive transitioning to become their fellow performer, attempting to commingle or dissolve identities. Failing the brief utterly, smith evoked Halberstam's concept of *queer failure*. As a strategy for resisting received notions of mastery and success, the queer art of failure offers more creative, cooperative and surprising ways of being in the world. In *Homoshamanism* smith used a hairy, red costume as a form of drag in order to become more themselves yet also as indeterminate and illegible. With no real face, the homoshaman character undermines habitual intersubjective processes of facial recognition and identification. The costume allows for transformation to take place and the creation of a body that is defamiliarised, challenging categorisation. smith's homoshaman is an utterly post-human figure, de-familiarising but also completely entertaining, activating intersubjective relations that are light and comical.

In Chapter 7 I explore how just as writer and director Louise Tu'u reflected that her body brought into the gallery one specific instance of Pacific Island performance art, simple insertions of particular bodies within and around art institutions perform institutional critique, creating counter-hegemonic choreographies (2017: 7). This is achieved by drawing on indigenous Pacific concepts, knowledges and experiences. Through insertions of their own performing bodies, artists Angela Tiatia, Kalisolaite 'Uhila and Shigeuki Kihara activate and interrogate thresholds and colonial structures. Via instances of performance art they realise intersubjective encounters that undermine authority. As Pasifika artists they represent those previously categorised by the museum and its binary logic as sexualised and racialised others. Exceeding the disciplinary structures so omnipresent in contemporary exhibition spaces, these counter-hegemonic choreographies present their own particular permutations of relations. They evade authority, challenge subjection and enact dissensus, encouraging criticality and enabling novel or more equitable intersubjective relations.

Evoking Tu'u's "dis-ease," these three artists are disobedient, their actions promote misbehaviour, other ways of moving and being, ways that deviate. In *Walking the Wall* (2014) Tiatia challenges verticality, encouraging shifts in perspective and orientation. Her body is simultaneously defiant and sexualised, repeating movements from customary Pacific dances with difference and exposing bodily adornment in order to fight against intersubjective relations of shame and stigmatisation. Making such a body visible and exhausted draws attention to their artistic labour, as well as histories of exploitation within the museum. Sites of struggle are occupied so that choreographies might take place within them, by using the gallery for sheltering and sleeping in his *Mo'ui Tukuhausia* (2014) 'Uhila occupies the very architecture, using it to his own ends. In Kihara's *Taualuga: The Last Dance* (2006) counter-dominant ideologies are performed and presented in acts and dances that are indigenising and that manifest protest. Prior political events are recounted by presenting dances that are then reoriented towards a future that might continue to renegotiate the spaces and disciplines of colonial power.

Each of these performances, among scores of others, are part of a broader narrative about Pacific bodies performing and creating interventions in museums and contemporary art gallery spaces in Aotearoa New Zealand and beyond, as part of a response to calls to enliven the museum or Leahy's *performing museology*. Yet it is also important to remember that these occupations resist the imperialist and colonial order of things perpetuated by museums since their very inception. To those visiting the gallery from settler and colonial backgrounds, such performances are counter-hegemonic and counter-colonial. However to those artists and visitors from indigenous backgrounds they may read as *decolonising* practices that temporarily indigenise the space of the gallery: celebrating survival; intervening; revitalising; representing; gendering; negotiating and reframing (Tuhiwai Smith 1999: 142–161).

As art historian Chloe Weaver has argued, these cross-cultural encounters, in which Pasifika artists engage in museums and contemporary art contexts introduce Pacific epistemologies, ways of knowing, doing and being (2011: 53). Weaver replaces Bourriaud's *relational aesthetics* with the Pacific concept of vā, a secular, sacred, social and spiritual space of relations (Anae 2019). Weaver's thesis together with ideas from Pacific scholar and educator Melani Anae means that each of these Pasifika artists, rather than engaging in an idea imported from France in the 2000s are in fact engaging in what Anae calls *teu le va*; valuing, nurturing and caring for relational spaces.

The performance artworks that I discuss in this book are those which contribute, I would argue, to the choreographic or "new performance turn" that orchestrates specific relations between institutions, artists, performers and participants in the space of the gallery. Each of the works discussed enact, embody and use diverse choreographic approaches to activate novel forms of intersubjectivity. This is important because, as Guattari argues "if someone encounters creative autonomy in one domain, they might practice it in others," practices like performance art can act as a "catalyst for a gradual reforging and renewal of humanity's confidence in itself starting at the most miniscule level... to counter the pervasive atmosphere of dullness and passivity" (2000: 69). If so, there is the possibility that the various interactions that occur in art galleries can have broader implications for the way in which people interact with each other in the wider world. It is my hope that performance artworks that are choreo-political, post human, post-digital, queer or counter-hegemonic, can provide a way of rehearsing interactions with other people that are more sensitive, considered and ethical.

NOTES

1. *Cracker # 1 Performance Festival*, Self Service open art space, Stuttgart, Germany.
2. Here Bourriaud utilises concepts from Serge Daney. This is in contrast with what Bourriaud calls "intersubjectivity as inter-servility" as theorised by Emmanuel Levinas which will be discussed in more detail later on in Chapter 4.
3. For a critical perspective on art and interactivity, one that includes an ecological approach, see Andrew Goodman *Gathering Ecologies* (2018) Open Humanities Press.
4. It is important to note that this brief summary only addresses works published in English, it does not include the vast amount of material in other western European languages.
5. I experienced this work as it was explained by Parker in an artist presentation, as part of Helen Grogan's *SPECIFIC IN-BETWEEN (The choreographic negotiated in six parts), PART 5. Migrating frames (of space and view)* a discursive event held at ACCA, Melbourne on Wednesday 12 November 2014, as part of the exhibition *Framed Movements*.
6. Three Angles—Installation, 2014, 2016, September 29, 2016, http://san draparkerdance.com/#/past-works.
7. This emphasis on embodiment is one of the reasons why these views enjoyed such popularity with dance theorists like Maxine Sheets, author of *The Phenomenology of Dance* (1966).

8. Although Merleau-Ponty does not equate the master with the male body or the slave with the female body this master–slave dialectic returns to an argument of Simone de Beauvoir that women are culturally constructed as the Other particularly within Butler's larger critique of Merleau-Ponty's theory of sexuality.
9. Video works encountered as part of the 21st Biennale of Sydney (2018) at the Art Gallery of New South Wales, Sydney, Australia.
10. It is important to note here that psychoanalytic accounts of intersubjectivity will not be discussed in this book. According to Guattari, psychoanalytic practice is complicit with patriarchal and normative values of ordinary existence, while art and "schizoid" aesthetics suggest that one should not need to fit in to a homogenous kind of stratified subjectivity but allow non-logical, schizoid fragments to come together. For further discussion see Deleuze and Guattari's *Anti-Oedipus: Capitalism and Schizophrenia* (1983), Guattari's *Chaosmosis: An Ethico-Aesthetic Paradigm* (1995), *Molecular Revolution: Psychiatry and Politics* (1984). In many of these works Guattari is intent on dismantling the tradition of psychoanalysis established by both Sigmund Freud (1856–1939) and Jacques Lacan (1901–1981). This discussion is dense and complex and would take this project into a different direction. While there is much research to be conducted into the psychoanalytic or schizo-analytic aspects of choreographic works, I have pragmatically limited myself in this publication to discourse around the subject and intersubjectivity. Similarly, there is much literature concerning the rich sense of self pursued by art, literature and film along with its cognates, identity and individuality, for a discussion of these see Zahavi and Gallagher, and for an overview of the neurocognitive and philosophical research on the self in art (Minissale 2013: 233–251).
11. Of course there are many exceptions, since the second half of the twentieth century it has become more and more common for dancers to devise and co-create works together with choreographers and dramaturgs. For one look at this phenomenon see David Kirsh, "Creative Cognition in Choreography." *Proceedings of 2nd International Conference on Computational Creativity, 2011* (2011).
12. After art historian Thierry de Duve's proposition of *art in general* (1996 quoted in Laermans 2008: 10).

REFERENCES

Allsopp, Ric, and Lepecki, André. 2008. Editorial: On Choreography. *Performance Research* 13.1: 1–6.

Althusser, Louis. 2006. The Underground Current of the Materialism of the Encounter. In *Louis Althusser Philosophy of the Encounter: Later Writings, 1978–87*, eds. Francois Matheron and Oliver Corpet, 163–207. London; New York: Verso.

Anae, Melanie. 2019. Pacific Research Methodologies and Relational Ethics. https://doi.org/10.1093/acrefore/9780190264093.013.529.

Auckland Art Gallery Toi o Tāmaki. 2012. *The Walters Prize 2012*. Auckland: Auckland Art Gallery Toi o Tāmaki

Bench, Harmony. 2017. Dancing in Digital Archives: Circulation, Pedagogy, Performance. In *Transmission in Motion: The Technologizing of Dance*, ed. Maaike Bleeker, 155–167. New York: Routledge.

Berardi, Franco "Bifo." 2012. *The Uprising: On Poetry and Finance*. South Pasedena: Semiotexte.

Biennale of Sydney, 2018. *21st Biennale of Sydney: SUPERPOSITION: Equilibrium & Engagement Guide*. Sydney: The Biennale of Sydney Ltd.

Bishop, Claire. 2006. The Social Turn: Collaboration and Its Discontents. *Artforum* February: 178–183.

Bishop, Claire. 2012. *Artificial Hells: Participatory Art and the Politics of Spectatorship*. London; New York: Verso Books.

Bishop, Claire. 2014. The Perils and Possibilities of Dance in the Museum: Tate, MoMA, and Whitney. *Dance Research Journal* 46.3: 63–76.

Bishop, Claire. 2018. Black Box, White Cube, Gray Zone: Dance Exhibitions and Audience Attention. *TDR: The Drama Review* 62.2: 22–42.

Boudry, Pauline, Lorenz, Renate, and Laubard, Charlotte. 2019. *Pauline Boudry / Renate Lorenz: Moving Backwards*. Milan: Skira editore.

Bourriaud, Nicolas. 2002. *Relational Aesthetics*. Trans. S. Pleasance, F. Woods, and M. Copeland. Dijon: Les presses du réel.

Braidotti, Rosi. 2013. *The Posthuman*. Cambridge: Polity.

Butler, Judith. 1989. Sexual Ideology and Phenomenological Description: A Feminist Critique of Merleau-Ponty's Phenomenology of Perception. In *The Thinking Muse: Feminism and Modern French Philosophy*, eds. Jeffner Allen and Iris M. Young, 85–100. Bloomington: Indiana University Press.

Charmatz, Boris. 2014. Manifesto for a Dancing Museum. In *Danse: An Anthology*, ed. Noémie Solomon, 233–239. Dijon: Les presses du réel.

Chartrand, Tanya L., and Bargh, John A. 1999. The Chameleon Effect: The Perception-Behavior Link and Social Interaction. *Journal of Personality and Social Psychology* 76: 893–910.

Combes, Muriel. 2013. *Gilbert Simondon and the Philosophy of the Transindividual*. Trans. Thomas LaMarre. Cambridge, MA; London: The MIT Press.

Costinas, Cosmin, and Janevski, Ana. 2017. *Is the Living Body the Last Thing Left Alive?* Hong Kong; Berlin: Para Site; Sternberg Press.

Crossley, Nick. 2005. Intersubjectivity. In *Key Concepts in Critical Social Theory*, ed. Nick Crossley. Sage UK. Credo Reference. http://ezproxy.auckland.ac.nz/login?url=https://search.credoreference.com/content/entry/sageukcst/intersubjectivity/0?institutionId=181.

Cvejić, Bojana. 2015. *Choreographing Problems: Expressive Concepts in European Contemporary Dance and Performance*. Houndmills, Basingstoke, Hampshire: Palgrave Macmillan.

Foucault, Michel, and Miskowiec, Jay. 1986. Of Other Spaces. *Diacritics* 16: 22–27.

Foster, Susan Leigh. 2010. Choreographing Your Move. In *Move: Choreographing You*, ed. Stephanie Rosenthal, 32–37. London: Hayward Publishing.

Franko, Mark. 2007. Dance and the Political: States of Exception. In *Dance Discourses: Keywords in Dance Research*, eds. Susanne Franco and Marina Nordera, 11–28. London; New York: Routledge.

Gallagher, Shaun. 2005. *How the Body Shapes the Mind*. Oxford: Clarendon Press.

Gallagher, Shaun, and Zahavi, Dan. 2012. *The Phenomenological Mind*. London; New York: Routledge.

Gallagher, Shaun. 2012. On the Possibility of Naturalizing Phenomenology. In *The Oxford Handbook of Contemporary Phenomenology*, ed. Dan Zahavi, 70–93. Oxford: Oxford University Press.

Gronlund, Melissa. 2017. *Contemporary Art and Digital Culture*. London; New York: Routledge.

Guattari, Félix. 2000. *The Three Ecologies*. Trans. Ian Pindar and Paul Sutton. London; New Brunswick: The Athlone Press.

Halberstam, Judith. 2011. *The Queer Art of Failure*. Durham: Duke University Press.

Haraway, Donna J. 1991. *Simians, Cyborgs, and Women: The Reinvention of Nature*. New York: Routledge.

Hari, Riitta, Himberg, Tommi, Nummenmaa, Lauri, Hamalainen, Matti, and Parkkonen, Lauri. 2013. Synchrony of Brains and Bodies During Implicit Interpersonal Interaction. *Trends in Cognitive Sciences* 17: 105–106.

Hewitt, Andrew. 2005. *Social Choreography: Ideology as Performance in Dance and Everyday Movement*. Durham, NC: Duke University Press.

Joy, Jenn. 2014. *The Choreographic*. Cambridge, MA: The MIT Press.

Kolb, Alexandra. 2013. Current Trends in Contemporary Choreography: A Political Critique. *Dance Research Journal* 45: 31–52.

Kosofsky Sedgwick, Eve. 1993. *Tendencies*. Durham: Duke University Press.

Laermans, Rudi. 2008. 'Dance in General' or Choreographing the Public, Making Assemblages. *Performance Research* 13.1: 7–14.

Latour, Bruno. 2005. *Reassembling the Social: An Introduction to Actor Network Theory*. Oxford, New York: Oxford University Press.

Le Guin, Ursula K. 2004. *The Wave in the Mind*. Boulder: Shambhala.

Leahy, Helen Rees. 2012. *Museum Bodies: The Politics and Practices of Visiting and Viewing*. Farnham, Surrey; Burlington, VT: Ashgate.

Lepecki, André. 2006. *Exhausting Dance: Performance and the Politics of Movement*. New York: Routledge.

Lepecki, André. 2012. *DANCE*. London; Cambridge: Whitechapel Gallery; The MIT Press.

Lepecki, André. 2013. Choreopolice and Choreopolitics: or, the Task of the Dancer. *TDR: The Dance Review* 57.4: 13–27.

Lepecki, André. 2016. *Singularities: Dance in the Age of Performance*. London; New York: Routledge.

Levinas, Emmanuel. 2002. *Totality and Infinity: An Essay on Exteriority*. Trans. Alphonso Lingis. Pittsburgh: Duquesne University Press.

Lista, Marcella. 2013. Xavier Le Roy: A Discipline of the Unknown. *Afterall* 33: 27–37.

Lista, Marcella. 2014. Play Dead: Dance, Museums, and the "Time-Based Arts." *Dance Research Journal*. 46.3: 6–23.

Manning, Erin. 2013. *Always More Than One: Individuation's Dance*. Durham: Duke University Press.

McCormack, Derek P. 2013. *Refrains for Moving Bodies*. Durham; London: Duke University Press.

Minissale, Gregory. 2013. *The Psychology of Contemporary Art*. Cambridge: Cambridge University Press.

Munt, Sally R. 2000. Shame/Pride Dichotomies in Queer as Folk. *Textual Practice* 14.3: 531–546.

Natterson, J. (2006). Intersubjectivity. In *The Edinburgh International Encyclopedia of Psychoanalysis*, ed. R. Skelton. Edinburgh University Press. Credo Reference. http://ezproxy.auckland.ac.nz/login?url=https://search.credoreference.com/content/entry/edinburghpsychoa/intersubjectivity/0?institutionId=181.

Ono, Yoko. 2000. *Grapefruit: A Book of Instruction and Drawings by Yoko Ono*. New York: Simon & Schuster.

Overgaard, Soren. 2012. Other People. In *The Oxford Handbook of Contemporary Phenomenology*, ed. Dan Zahavi, 460–482. Oxford: Oxford University Press.

Protevi, John. 2001. The Geophilosophies of Deleuze and Guattari. Delivered at the November 2001 meeting of SEDAAG (Southeastern Division of the Association of American Geographers). http://www.protevi.com/john/SEDAAG.pdf. Accessed 16 June 2016.

Robbins, Philip, and Aydede, Murat. 2009. A Short Primer on Situated Cognition. In *The Cambridge Handbook of Situated Cognition*, eds. Philip Robbins and Murat Aydede, 3–10. Cambridge: Cambridge University Press.

Rose, Gillian. 1999. Women and Everyday Spaces. In *Feminist Theory and the Body: A Reader*, eds. Janet Price and Margrit Shildrick, 359–370. Edinburgh: Edinburgh University Press.

Rosenthal, Stephanie. 2010. *MOVE: Choreographing You*. London: Hayward Publishing.

Rothfield, Philipa. 2010. Differentiating Phenomenology and Dance. In *The Routledge Dance Studies Reader*, eds. Alexandra Carter and Janet O'Shea, 303–318. Abingdon; New York: Routledge.

Sabisch, Petra. 2011. *Choreographing Relations: Practical Philosophy and Contemporary Choreography: In the Works of Antonia Baehr, Gilles Deleuze, Juan Dominguez, Félix Guattari, Xavier Le Roy and Eszter Salamon*. München: epodium.

smith, val. 2016. Mapping a Politics of Queer Pride and Shame. valvalvalsmithsmithsmith. https://valvalvalsmithsmithsmith.blogspot.com/2016/07/mapping-politics-of-queer-pride-and.html. Accessed 11 October 2016.

Solomon, Noémie. 2012. Across the Score: Eshkol, Lockhart, and the Choreography of Encounters. In *Sharon Lockhart | Noa Eshkol*, eds. Eva Wilson and Daniela Zyman, 50–53. Berlin: Sternberg Press.

Tuhiwai Smith, Linda. 1999. *Decolonizing Methodologies: Research and Indigenous Peoples*. London, New York, Dunedin: Zed Books Ltd, University of Otago Press.

Tu'u, Louise. 2017. *Performing the Margins: An Anthem of Hope*. Christchurch: The Physics Room, We Should Practice.

Verwoert, Jan. 2010. *Tell Me What You Want, What You Really, Really Want*. Ed. Vanessa Ohlraun. Rotterdam; Berlin; New York: Piet Zwart Institute; Willem de Kooning Academy; Sternberg Press.

Virno, Paolo. 2004. *A Grammar of the Multitude: For an Analysis of Contemporary Forms of Life*. Trans. Isabella Bertoletti, James Cascaito, and Andrea Casson. Los Angeles, New York: Semiotexte.

Weaver, Chloe. 2011. *Art As Experience: Collaborative and Participatory Practice in Contemporary Pacific Art*. Thesis MA Art History, The University of Auckland, New Zealand.

Wood, Catherine. 2013. People and Things in the Museum. In *Choreographing Exhibitions*, ed. Mathieu Copeland, 113–122. Dijon: Les presses du réel.

CHAPTER 2

Museum Bodies: Choreo-Policing and Choreo-Politics

A metallic marionette of an oversized boy is suspended from heavy chains, attached to a large gantry that fills the entire space of the gallery. At the back of the room can be seen the machinery of a movement generator. The boy resembles depictions of the fictional character Huckleberry Finn, with bright red hair, freckles, rosy cheeks and a forced gap-toothed smile. He is not wearing any shoes, his blue trousers appear frayed at the bottom and seem to be held up by a piece of rope. In the course of this work, Jordan Wolfson's *Colored sculpture* (2016, Fig. 2.1), described as a "robotic performance" by critic Karen Goldberg, the boy is violently and repeatedly dragged, spun, jerked, hoisted and dropped from a height onto the concrete floor, the heavy slack of chains falling around and sometimes on top of him, making a deafening sound (2016: 222).[1] Though he was highly-finished and polished to begin with, over the course of the exhibition his paint began to wear away, revealing patches of the metal below, as if grey like bruised skin. Suspended from three chains, one at the top of his head, one on his left wrist and one his left leg, the puppet often hangs, gliding across the space before the audience. Sometimes he is still. At intervals an easy-listening ballad from the 1960s is played at high volume and then abruptly cut off.[2] Goldberg described the programmed series of movements as a "punishing cycle," a "brutal loop" as part of "a very precise choreography."

V. Wynne-Jones, *Choreographing Intersubjectivity in Performance Art*, New World Choreographies, https://doi.org/10.1007/978-3-030-40585-4_2

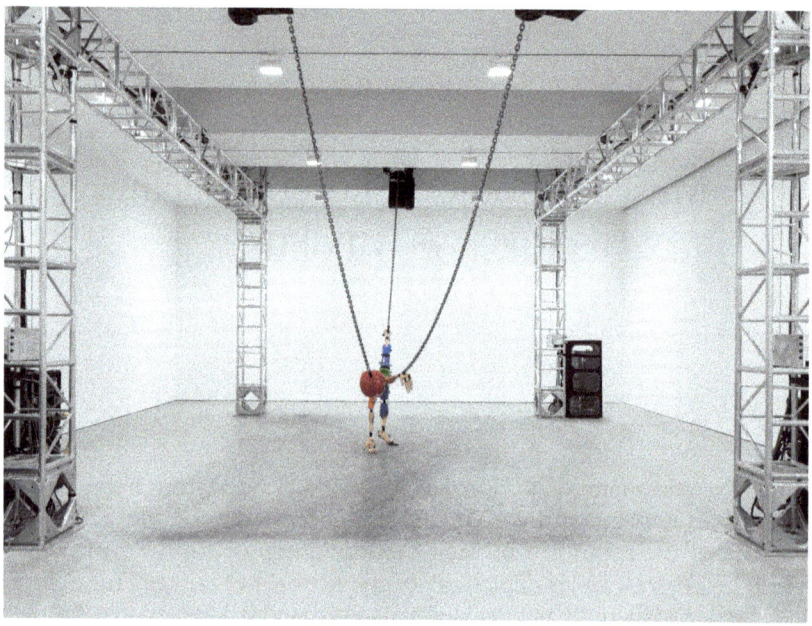

Fig. 2.1 Jordan Wolfson *Colored sculpture*, 2016. Installation view. *Jordan Wolfson*, David Zwirner, New York, 2016 (© Jordan Wolfson. Courtesy the artist, David Zwirner and Sadie Coles HQ, London)

Wolfson's sculpture involves the presentation of a boyish figure whose programmed actions are mechanically controlled, they are in fact, as Goldberg argues, mere "side effects of violent, larger forces," all decided by the artist as master puppeteer. The obsession with a device that could imitate human capacities and sometimes even exceed them has been an art historical trope with origins in antiquity, but is perhaps best known in European thought in Heinrich von Kleist's frequently-quoted 1810 essay "On the Puppet Theatre" (Von Kleist 1976). One reason for the ubiquity of the device is the way in which it so perfectly illustrates tensions between the autonomy one may or may not enjoy over one's own movements, how control might be exercised by external forces or mechanisms of manipulation and the ways in which such controlling intersubjective relations might impact upon subjecthood. As an emblem of subjection and submission, Wolfson's puppet can be interpreted as an illustration of the way in which one might be controlled by external forces, whether they be another person, an artist or an institution.

This chapter follows this image of the manipulated subject, in order to examine the tension between conformity and freedom, it begins with the history and politics of the relations created between art museums and visitors, from early nineteenth-century examples before moving on to the modernist "white cube" and its more hybrid twenty-first century permutations. Michel Foucault's historicised accounts of power and discipline have enabled scholars to perceive that the ways in which visitors to museums can look, walk and behave have always been manipulated by a combination of architectural devices, regulations, textual and graphic prompts, guidance and example. Examining these phenomena is in fact a study of subjection, the various ways bodies can be managed and made docile.

Dance theorist André Lepecki has observed that "behaviour, or conduct, oscillates between habitus and conformity, rebellion and freedom" (2013: 18). This tension between the political and kinetic projects of *choreo-policing* and *choreo-politics* is central to this chapter and indeed to this entire book. According to Lepecki's definition, *choreo-policing* involves: systems of obedience; the issuing of commands; imperatives and their implementation; controlling movement; ensuring everyone is in a permissible place; diminishment; blocking and above all conformity. Yet thankfully, there is another side to the story, with the aid of French philosopher Jacques Rancière, Lepecki counters *choreo-policing* with the proposition of *choreo-politics* which:

> requires a redistribution and reinvention of bodies, affects, and senses through which one may learn how to move politically, how to invent, activate, seek, or experiment with a movement whose only sense… is the experimental exercise of freedom. (Lepecki 2013: 20)

I will analyse artworks that manifest various kinds of manipulative relations between choreographers, the dancers who perform their works in museums or galleries and the visitors who participate in the works. Performances by artists like Louise Menzies, Adam Linder, the Bouillon Group, Sharyar Neshat and Dora Garcia all manifest individuals like Wolfson's puppet. They are entangled within complex relations, with various authorities, that dictate their movements, whether they be religious, salutary, professional, psychoanalytic or choreographic. Regulation, indeed self-regulation seems to be an inevitable reality of the museum, where one is choreographed by one party or another. Thus my focus is upon how subjection and submission to control, makes bodies docile and how intersubjective encounters and spaces might make them more resistant to manipulation by the gallery or museum.

Lepecki has posited that choreography "as a peculiar invention of early modernity" is similar to the museum in that it was initially formed in order to function as a "technology that creates a body disciplined to move according to the commands of writing" (2006: 6). Curator Stephanie Rosenthal concurs with this conception of choreography as a commanding and disciplining force, referring to it as a "manipulative strategy" (2010: 18). By problematising institutional spaces of subjection, certain performance artworks undermine the operations of choreo-policing and explore how performers as artistic subjects or gallery visitors might deviate from such forms of structure and control. In doing so, the very spatiality of the museum of contemporary art is transformed and this is where Foucault's concept of heterotopia or space as a counter-site is important (Foucault and Miskowiec 1986). For Lepecki, negotiating the oppositional forces of choreo-policing and choreo-politics is the task of the contemporary dancer, however I believe that the exploration of this tension is also the task of any artist creating works of performance art within the contemporary art museum. It should also be a concern for curators facilitating said works, as well as art historians responding to them. I propose that given the right circumstances, performance artworks can enable the museum to become a site of what Lepecki calls "choreographic imagination" (2013: 20) one in which highly mobile, political subjects can appear away from "preassigned modes and spaces of circulation" and perhaps even enact, even if only temporarily, forms of intersubjectivity that are also political, or ones that might make manifest experimental exercises of freedom.

2.1   MUSEUM BODIES: SELF-REGULATION

The art gallery I attended as a child was the National Gallery of Victoria in Naarm, Melbourne. This immense building of monumental scale stretches along a significant portion of St. Kilda Road, still dwarfing those who approach it. As a small child its bluestone façade, waterwall entrance and towering Great Hall filled me with awe. According to Manchester-based museologist Helen Rees Leahy, art museums enjoy a very specific form of cultural authority: even before entering the building, there are certain expectations about what one should do and feel when one visits. Museums themselves take for granted the "corporeal techniques, skills and methods" that visitors bring with them (2012: 14). Leahy surmises that a "repertoire of bodily practices or 'bodily habits' has become totally incorporated within the museum audience." *Museum bodies* are both real and discursive, actual bodies moving through galleries, as well as bodies that are socially inscribed in space and practice. The museum has its material and physical dimensions, yet it is also a site of institutional, social and corporeal practices, it is in fact enacted by its visitors. In this case, subjects contribute to the production of specific intersubjective relations. Leahy investigates how exactly "museums and exhibitions have inculcated and accommodated different modalities of looking, walking, hearing, sitting and talking (but less frequently, touching, tasting or smelling)" since their emergence in the eighteenth century (3). According to Leahy the visual, ambulatory and performative practices of art spectatorship have been produced by the explicit regulations of institutions, the guidance offered by museum managers and curators- and, most interestingly, "by the exemplary conduct of more sophisticated and practised visitors."

Leahy points out that visiting an exhibition or museum always involves intersubjectivity, as every visit is populated by "a series of transient encounters with other visitors: strangers in public with whom we share the private experience of looking at art" (99). Vienna-based architectural theorist Christian Teckert reflects on the subjectivity of the spectator in relation to their encounters with the architecture and ideologies of exhibition spaces (2014). Teckert's description of spectators at nineteenth-century exhibitions is important because it draws on Tony Bennett's argument that institutions of exhibition, such as museums as well as temporary expositions, formed an *exhibitionary complex* of disciplinary power relations (1995: 59).[3]

For Teckert, mechanisms of overview, surveillance, observation, discipline and visual control were inscribed into the spatial structures of classical museum architectures of the nineteenth century (2014: 115–117). The vision of the spectator was organised in relation to the *panopticon* or rendering of everything as visible to a surveying eye, as well as that of the *panorama* or spectacular view. Such a "technology of vision" regulated a crowd "by rendering it visible to itself, by making the crowd itself the ultimate spectacle." Examples of this phenomenon come from the panoramic vantage points provided by temporary exhibitions such as London's Crystal Palace in the Great Exhibition of 1851, or the Eiffel Tower in the 1889 Paris Exposition. Such architectural features provided viewing positions from which one could "see and be seen, to survey and yet always be under surveillance, the object of an unknown but controlling look." Teckert adds that panopticism was encouraged by other features such as an extensive use of reflective glass in vitrines, light-filled rooms without internal supports and exhibition zones with paths to create a regulated flow of motion (114–115). Each device contributed to a sense of being on display, increasing awareness of one's visibility and the possibility of being observed, both subject and object of a controlling gaze. Hence the exercise of attending an exhibition became a "form of coercion" as part of "schemata of restraint" (Bennett 1995: 63–64). A self-monitoring system of looks made up a regime of self-control and it was by these means that "the many headed mob" could be made to conform and be transformed into an "ordered crowd" (72).

This self-monitoring ties into Lepecki's proposition of *choreo-policing* as "taming" (2016: 92).[4] Lepecki describes an iterative process by which humans learn to hold themselves and break themselves in like animals. By extension, one can break-in another person by forcing them to conform and repeat a certain act, gesture or movement again and again. For Lepecki, there is a link between the "normative self-taming of humans and choreographic acts of repetition," where, in the end something becomes natural "when it conforms perfectly and without apparent effort to accepted models." In terms of actions that are performed for self-improvement and to demonstrate certain beliefs, we might consider what Greenfield (2013) would call the filmdance *Peloha* (2009) by Auckland-based artist Louise Menzies. In this 16 mm film, projected in a darkened room, a naked figure can be seen executing a series of movements upon the porch of an old colonial homestead.[5] According to Menzies, the routine of stretches and bends was choreographed in reference to an exercise manual from the School of Radiant Living, founded during the 1930s by English psychologist Herbert Sutcliffe in Havelock North, New Zealand (2013: 14). The school, known for its public exercise demonstrations, disseminated written material and recorded lectures designed to promote physical, mental and spiritual alignment. A cheerfully-delivered, predominantly Christian outlook combined self-help with exercise and dietary advice. One of the exercises reads: "Turn smartly to the left, shoot out arms side-ways on a level with the shoulders, clenching fists (sniff once); relax fists and bring arms back to shoulders…. Repeat the whole exercise several times, and remember to smile!!" In this performance there is a play between the authoritative relations of religion or a belief-system whose exercises promote self-care, and certain choreographed actions that must be performed for the sake of self-amelioration.

A connection can be made between the conformity of action demanded by such belief systems and that of the museum, they are both systems that demand obedience. In the museum, similar models of decorum or good conduct are promoted; self-taming and subjection is produced with the help of architectural devices such as look-outs, reflective glass, light-filled rooms and clearly designated paths. The kinds of movements and behaviours expected of museum visitors were anticipated by architecture as well as the arrangement of objects, in order to reflect very specific nationalist ideologies.

For Bennett, institutions such as the British Museum used their authority in terms of the nation-state to create specific relations with visitors by positioning them within configurations of imperialist power. Bennett argues that exhibitions located their preferred audiences at the very pinnacle of the exhibitionary order of things they constructed.[6] Within a museum, the whole world was metonymically present as an assemblage of commodities, all of which were subordinate to the dominating gaze of a white, bourgeois, metropolitan and male eye (1995: 84). The order of things, within a taxonomy and developmental framework that ran from past to present, raw to manufactured to fine, and primitive to civilised, organised its implied public, "the white citizenries of the imperialist powers… conceived as the realization, and therefore just beneficiaries, of the process of evolution and identified as a unity in opposition to the primitive otherness of conquered peoples" (89). This point about the imperialist authority of the museum will be revisited in Chapter 7 as part of a discussion on decolonising choreographies (Fig. 2.2).

Just as Teckert argued that the ideology and architecture of any exhibition space has ramifications for the subjectivities and processes of subjectivation of its spectators, Judith Butler (b. 1956), after Foucault, argued that *subjects* are produced and constituted by political systems or certain fields of power. Such systems "set out in advance the criterion by which subjects themselves are formed, with the result that representation is extended only to what can be acknowledged as a subject" (1990: 1–2). Any subjects regulated by such structures are therefore "by virtue of being subjected to them, formed, defined, and reproduced in

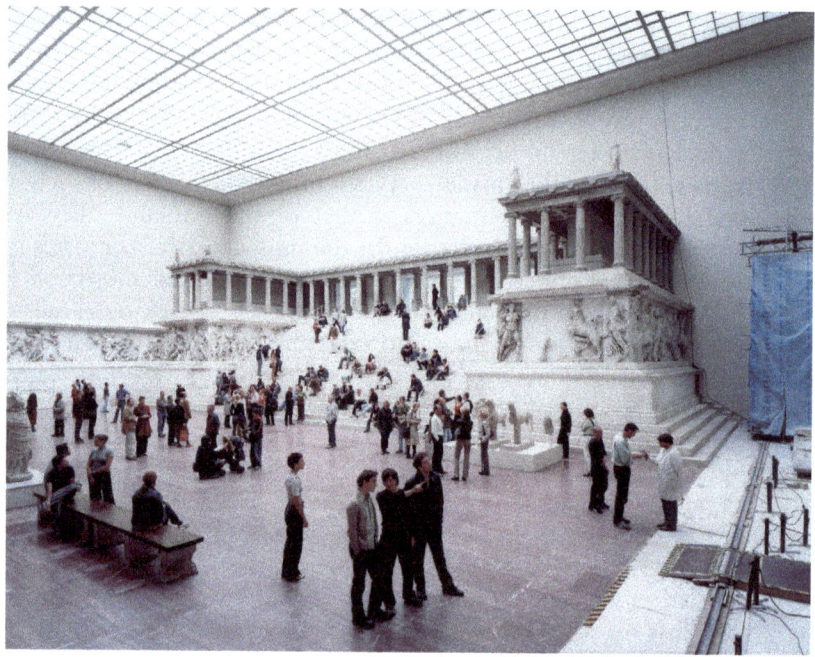

Fig. 2.2 Thomas Struth, *Pergamon Museum 1, Berlin 2001* (Chromogenic print, 197.4 × 248.5 cm) (© Thomas Struth)

accordance with the requirements of those structures." The etymology of the term is *sub-jectus*, designating one who is placed under or beneath, someone who submits or is subordinate (Tomès 2005: 7–9). Butler adds that such subjects are "produced [and legitimised] through certain exclusionary practices that do not 'show' once the juridical structure of politics has been established." Even the best of intentions may go awry as art institutions and art history could be considered what Butler refers to as "domains of exclusion" with "coercive and regulatory consequences of that [subject] construction, even when the construction has been elaborated for emancipatory purposes" (1990: 4).

Butler ties into arguments about museum bodies, the exhibitionary complex and choreographic taming with her assertion that the body is "a passive medium on which cultural meanings are inscribed;" it is a "mere *instrument* or *medium* for which a set of cultural meanings are only externally related" (8). Such processes of inscription recall the ways in which early choreographer Raoul Auger Feuillet worked to capture a basic vocabulary of positions and steps that could function as a rubric that could be translated and inscribed onto the printed page (Foster 2005: 87). For Butler, the body is a "construction" and "myriad bodies" come into being in and through assigned attributes such as the marks of gender or designations such as "visitor," "artist" or "dancer." Like the paper scores of the early choreographers, the very boundaries and surfaces of bodies are thereby politically constructed, signified and maintained. This emphasis upon the practical and physical dimensions of subject construction is crucial to the ways visitors are physically manipulated by the art gallery apparatus. It is also relevant to performance art that often involves practices, or individuals physically performing acts that might challenge dominant systems of ideas.

For Lepecki the act of *choreo-policing* par excellence is to determine the subject who performs interpellations as a Subject "with a capital S," an authority who interpellates ordinary subjects (Althusser 1971: 167).[7] Foucault argued subjects are part of a process of subjection, one that makes bodies docile that is, "subjected to, used, transformed and improved" (1977: 136).[8] Here disciplines, analogous with Lepecki's *choreo-policing*, involve "meticulous control of the operations of the body, that ensures the constant subjection of its forces and imposed upon them a relation of docility-utility" (137). Foucault posits that subject constitution is a material process that takes place "through a multiplicity of organisms, forces, energies, materials, desires, thoughts, etc." (Foucault 1980: 97). And the effects of power or relations of force are *concentrated upon* the body. Tying into the panopticon and panorama of the museum, individuals might be carefully fabricated according to "a whole technique of forces and bodies" (1977: 217) with the aid of instruments and techniques. The operations of disciplinary power used by institutions include enclosure or physical division, organisation, temporal regulation, as well as bodily articulation or manoeuvres.

What can be taken from Foucault is that so-called subjects are produced and constituted by apparatuses, institutions and fields of power in museology and art history. There are requirements and sets of criteria by which one can be acknowledged, produced, legitimised and designated an artist, museum visitor or even an artefact. Examples of personalised requirements for museum visitors include: paying an entrance fee, purchasing a ticket, queuing one behind another, reciting one's postal code for data collection purposes, remaining on the right side of barriers and keeping one's voice lowered. Designation of an artistic-subject by an ideology and its apparatuses is what Foucault describes as processes of subjection in which, via the meticulous control of operations of bodies, disciplines make them subject-to, that is docile, of use, tamed, transformed and improved. Finally, for Foucault a discipline or discourse, such as art history, sets up "given" places such as the white cube exhibition space described in the next section—in which such subjects can be formed.[9]

2.2   THE TWENTIETH-CENTURY EXHIBITION SPACE: THE WHITE CUBE AS A MECHANISM FOR VIEWING

The modernist exhibition space, as described by art historian Walter Grasskamp, is a mode of display that developed in Western Europe at the end of the nineteenth century. Its central components were the hanging of paintings at approximately eye level before a monochrome, neutral background (Grasskamp quoted in Teckert 2014: 116). The aim was for this "white cube" to create a neutral container which might provide immersion into the aura of art and an avoidance of political or economic contexts. Artist and art-writer Brian O'Doherty has written at length on the ideology of such a gallery space and contemplated the significance of performers inserting themselves into such a space. According to O'Doherty, the white cube is "an evenly lighted 'cell," a "space of isolation" that works by removing "all cues that interfere with the fact that it [an entity] is 'art" (1986: 14). This white cube becomes a "sacramental space," one in which entities may become art because that is "where powerful ideas about art focus on them;" a certain type of gaze might be employed, so that there is a "transposition of perception from life to formal values." O'Doherty describes such spaces as "Unshadowed, white, clean, artificial – the space is devoted to the technology of esthetics" (15).

According to O'Doherty's narrative about art history, it was a collage attached to the surface of a wall, Pablo Picasso's 1911 synthetic cubist work *Still Life with Chair Caning* that opened up the "impure space" in front of it, the secular world of the spectator's space, so that "pockets of voids" or gallery spaces could become "generative forces." Space then became an "undifferentiated potency" in which things could make space happen and the space between the walls became "a unit of discourse" (39). When walls as well as more minor architectural features like light switches, power-points and cables are all the same colour white, the gallery space becomes an almost undifferentiated *environment* and spectators become surrounded. O'Doherty argues that the gallery becomes a "transforming force," or a "chamber of transformation," once objects or entities are placed within such a context they can be transformed, "the gallery will make it art anyway" (16). Importantly, O'Doherty describes the way in which the performance of certain gestures or actions within a gallery space, as a chamber of transformation, might create interruptions or breaks in "conventions of ordinary life." Precise gestures can be quickly interpreted when collaged into a set situation or environment "from which they derive energy" (47). According to O'Doherty, the indeterminacy of a gallery context is "favourable ground for the growth of new conventions," it creates what art historian Lucy Lippard called "an art context, framework or awareness" as it "quotes" whatever is placed within it, de-familiarising content and making it art (49).[10]

By the 1960s artists began to create situations that might draw attention to the space surrounding them in art galleries, making evident the white cube's mode of construction. One way of evading timelessness and injecting temporality was through an insertion of performing bodies. Allan Kaprow's meticulously scored *18 Happenings in 6 Parts* took place at the opening of the Reuben Gallery in New York City in October 1959. It included performers and spectators as well as "movement, live and recorded sounds, spoken word, smells, electric lights, films, action painting and sculpture" (Solomon 2010: 41). Similarly in *Up to and Including her Limits* (1973–1976) Carolee Schneemann inserted her own body into a white cube like space. Naked and suspended from a harness, she would swing back and forth in order to draw directly onto the walls around her, activating them by rendering them actual supports upon which to create art, rather than mere surroundings. Importantly, such interaction with the white cube encourages a certain kind of spectator as well as "the subjective perception of individual artworks" (Teckert 2014: 117).

An idealised viewer, on the other hand, is too often framed and perhaps invisibly controlled by a gaze that seems to emanate from the white walls of the gallery space. Historical and local context is occluded and the ideological equipment of the institution is made invisible. Such an apparatus recalls my earlier discussion of space in relation to discipline and historical processes of rendering bodies docile. Foucault explains that discipline "proceeds from the distribution of individuals in space" (1977: 141). This could involve *enclosure*, a "protected place of disciplinary monotony," a place heterogeneous to all others and closed in on itself. Enclosure functions on a principle of basic location or *partitioning* so that "each individual has his own place. And each place its individual" (143). The aim of disciplinary spaces is "to establish presences and absences, to know how and where to locate individuals, to set up useful communications, to interrupt others, to be able at each moment to supervise the conduct of each individual, to assess it, to judge it, to calculate its qualities or merits." Discipline organises an analytical space, harking back to O'Doherty, for Foucault "disciplinary space is always, basically, cellular." This proposition of a highly regulated and discursively determined space may seem bleak, but it is also somewhat necessary for the kinds of art that have emerged since Marcel Duchamp's conceptual artworks in the 1910s. As argued by art theorist Arthur C. Danto, following on from Lippard, the bracketed space that is removed from that of everyday life is required for everyday objects and actions to be aesthetically contemplated and judged as such (1981).

Such a space was certainly invoked historically by Oskar Schlemmer (1883–1943) in his stage workshop at the Bauhaus art school in Dessau, Germany, if only to utilise it more fully as a structured environment. In typical Bauhaus fashion Schlemmer approached performance from a very "basic and elementary standpoint," initially addressing fundamentals (Schlemmer 1996: 81). In examining the most basic elements he began with *space*, the art of the stage was therefore a *spatial art*. For Schlemmer, performance occurs within an "architectonic-spatial organism" in which "all things happening to it and within it exist within a spatially-conditioned relationship" (85). What is relevant to the white cube is the notion of "space as space" signifying nothing more than itself. This evokes a concept of space theorised by English physicist Issac Newton (1642–1727) as an "absolute" or "void space," one that exists purely as a frame for motion (Falkenstein 1997). Schlemmer would go on to write that space is "primarily a thing of dimensions and proportion" that determines "the laws for everything that happens within its limits" as well as the gestures of figures within that space (Schlemmer 1978: 118). Schlemmer breaks form down, so that it "is manifest in extensions of height, breadth, and depth; as line, as plane and as solid or volume" (1996: 21). According to Schlemmer, the human figure contrasts with the cubical abstracts of space, he advocates a deference of the human to geometry, in this situation a human figure is affected by abstract space and is thereby "recast to fit its mould" (23). For Schlemmer, cubic space is made up of an invisible, linear network of planimetric and stereometric relationships and this rubric corresponds to the inherent mathematics of the human body, the "measure of all things." The value to the white cube of such a geometric-choreographic method is that it enables one to think beyond the pictorial space of painting and the placement of the so-called plastic arts, as argued by O'Doherty it can be more of an environment for different kinds of objects, entities, bodies and activities.

As a disciplinary space, therefore, the white cube presupposes what art historian Miwon Kwon has called a "universal viewing subject" who is in possession of a "corporeal body" as espoused in the model of phenomenology or first person experience (Kwon 2005: 33). Such a subject, as part of a normative model, views artworks and performances that are coherent and legible, harking back to a cybernetic model of art in which a message is transmitted from emitter to receiver. I have already pointed out how problematic the conception of such a subject is in Chapter 1, but various theorists have further ruminated upon the gallery as a space, arena or a kind of stage. Such a space can isolate a single figure, it can be intersubjective, enabling one person to observe another or others (Brook 1968) and it can be undifferentiated, involving both performers and spectators. The exhibition room as a stage-like, empty space may be open and undifferentiated, "a scene of action" that is "a single, undivided locale without partitions of any kind" as theorised by French dramatist Antonin Artaud (1896–1948), but it can also be one shared by performers and spectators simultaneously.

> Direct contact will be established between the audience and the show, between actors and audience... the auditorium will be enclosed within four walls stripped of any ornaments... In effect the lack of a stage in the normal sense of the word will permit the action to extend itself to the four corners of the auditorium. (1999: 74–75)

As Belgian sociologist Rudi Laermans observed, without the so-called fourth wall to separate the real bodies of audience members and the "represented or enacted bodily realness" a performance becomes more and more like a live installation (2008: 9).

According to art historian Rosalind Krauss, during the 1960s US-based artists used a variety of techniques including performances or "Happenings" in an attempt to undermine habitual kinaesthetic responses and the axiomatic understandings of space and perspective (Krauss 1981: 218–239). Harking back to O'Doherty, artists 'theatricalised' the sculptural space of the white cube to the extent that spectators could become more aware of how their very presence, movement and participation within the white cube completes an artwork. Devices that artists used to make such theatricality explicit included: assaulting the various senses of audience members and treating performers as inanimate props or depersonalised instruments in an impersonal or "supra-personal" way (232–233).

Using the idea of the score or instruction, Los Angeles and Berlin-based artist Adam Linder created a series of choreographic service works from 2013–2016. *Some Cleaning* is a transaction in which a client may contract a subject, based on an hourly rate, to choreographically clean a given location (Howe 2015: 81). Linder explicitly uses action to maintain the cleanliness of the exhibition space. Such cleaning utilises a variety of movements that might symbolically and experientially address a particular place. Each of Linder's four service works involve conditions of engagement with an institution or client, and services of a slightly absurd nature such as cleaning through movement, transforming art criticism into actions, physically riding the cadence of a written text or "performing hair-care." There is an interweaving of: the institution in which the work is performed; choreography; labour; profession; expertise; recuperation and the cultural capital of public programming. In this example, the exceptional space of the white cube gallery becomes a context or place for striking out against conventional assumptions about how experience is generally formed in daily life and in the outside world. Linder's *Some Cleaning* series moves away from choreo-policing and towards choreo-politics as he uses his rigorously trained body to perform absurd and mundane tasks, rather than the refined and artistic movements and dances usually demanded of him.

2.3   Twenty-First Century Contemporary Art Museums and the Experience Economy

Returning to the twenty-first century, contemporary art museums, especially in the age of block-buster international shows, are still affected by the conventions of nineteenth- and twentieth-century exhibitions. What remains includes galleries as places of *choreo-policing*, where one is aware of being seen as well as seeing, and the way in which the white cube creates a context-less zone; encouraging, directing and sometimes disrupting visual perception. Leahy points out that, more than a mere "eye that roams demurely," the practised museum spectator is embodied within a limited repertoire of actions to reflect on and respond to: the conditions of viewing, the spaces of display and the presence of other spectators (2012: 5–6). Gestures, attitudes and postures make up *somatic embodiments* of the viewing position and signify one's competence and successful performance of spectatorship.

> The empirical *performances* of individual visitors may conform to, ignore or resist the prescriptive institutional *performative*. Each of these incorporated responses reveal a degree of 'habit acquisition' – in this context, familiarity with the operation of the museum – that provides the visitor with a repertoire of potential appropriate and situated actions. (100)

For Leahy, the bodily techniques of the museum spectator are normative, acquired and required, harking back to Lepecki's taming. All museums have a part to play in structuring particular aspects of propriocepsis or "how the body knows its own boundaries and orientation in space." According to Leahy, visitors' performance is a process that occurs "at the intersection of their embodied subjectivity and the materiality of the museum."[11] One example is the acquired habit of conjoined walking and looking, a walking that "choreographs visuality within the museum" (75). In terms of corporeal interaction, there are a range of performances, both scripted and improvised that visitors are allowed to enact inside the museum.[12]

Dance scholar Franziska Bork Petersen and museum professional Minnie Scott have also examined the parameters of exhibition spectatorship, specifically the degree to which it involves authoritarian choreography (in Butte et al. 2014). Placing an emphasis upon the "kinaesthetic encounter with an exhibition," Bork Petersen and Scott draw attention to the way in which an exhibition visitor's walk is characterised or determined by pace, order/arrangement/selection/repetition, perspective, conscious embodiment and the way in which each exhibition, with its own aesthetic and didactic ambitions, proposes an approved mode of engagement and a correct way of behaving in relation to these factors. This draws on the social codes of the host venue, which in turn call upon what Leahy has described as the internalised conventions of the regular museum- or gallery-goer, in relation to such spaces. Forces or modes of control shape or constrain one's path, range of movement and line of vision. Power is imposed through an exhibition's control mechanisms. Bork Petersen and Scott describe a choreo-policing toolbox of spatial techniques that is used in curatorial practice to indicate and enforce the choice of route, proximity to artworks and how to pace oneself. Such spatial techniques include: angled walls, attraction techniques, unicursal routes, wall colour, arrows, clustering and sharing or withholding the exhibition's scale. These are the mechanisms used by curators and exhibition designers to install and connect works in an attempt to support their overall objectives and to create a stable display with the requisite degree of control over the visitor's movement.

Tying into the importance of a preconceived plan or score for choreography, or the logics of moving through its spaces, there are correct and incorrect readings of the institutional script. Rules about behaviour are often posted by the entranceway or explained by those selling tickets. Scripts can be encoded in the rhythm of displays that regulates the direction and pace of walking, and in the organisation of pictures on the gallery wall that engenders a specific modality of looking (Leahy 2012: 100). The London-based artist Pablo Bronstein has made explicit the way in which museums control or physically choreograph their visitors in his 2010 installation *Interim Performance* at the Chisenhale Gallery in London (Fig. 2.3). The work involved a maze-like configuration of municipal stacking chairs that snake their way around, forming lines of chairs often facing towards each other. The chairs were then animated by the crowd of visitors responding to the choreographic and "aggressive" prompts. Some people sat in rows facing each other, others were frustrated, pacing back and forth when they found they could not get to where they wanted to go. According to the artist "Architecture is able to choreograph in an obvious and direct way – you can walk through here, but you can't walk through there" (Wood 2011: 69). Bronstein self-reflexively takes the convention of museums providing chairs as a respite for fatigued bodies and twists it, so that it becomes another mechanism for choreo-policing or conformity, guiding bodies through certain paths, allowing or preventing the flow of motion.

The way in which the architecture of art museums physically corrals its visitors either through the directions of staff members or maze-like barriers is therefore mirrored in *Interim Performance* as a form of institutional critique. This artwork involves an authoring of kinaesthetic encounters, that performance studies scholar Barbara Kirshenblatt-Gimblett describes as the shift from an informing to a *performing* museology. Such

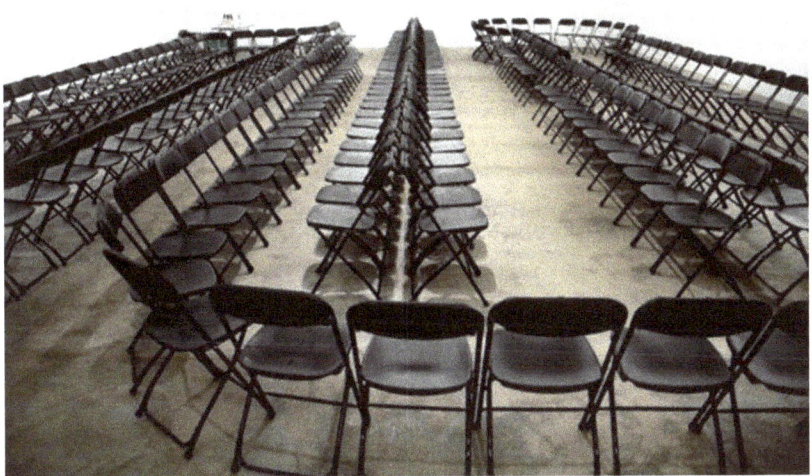

Fig. 2.3 Pablo Bronstein, *Interim Performance*, 2010. (Live performance) Chisenhale Gallery, 2010. Produced and Commissioned by Chisenhale Gallery, London

a reorientation of museum theory and practice was a response to the contested formation of collections and a re-examination of assumptions about the transmission of knowledge and cultural value (Kirshenblatt-Gimblett quoted in Leahy 2012: 2–3). Leahy summarises a crucial "shift in attention from the museum as a collection of objects to the museum as a site of social and corporeal practices." A *performing museology* enables an institution to adopt a more reflexive position in relation to its own operations, functions and processes. The museum as a technology, a set of skills, techniques and methods can thereby have the possibility of being visible or explicit to its visitors. However, Teckert points out that even today most contemporary architectural approaches to museum architecture still follow the conventional path of delivering standardised, white cube exhibition spaces, albeit sometimes within a larger envelope of either minimalist boxes or sculptural designs that re-appropriate organic forms (2014: 124).[13]

With a focus on the late twentieth century exhibition space of the Centre Pompidou in Paris, France, Teckert argues that the new architecture of museums and exhibitions has been utilised to reproduce an image of an all-inclusive public sphere. The panopticon is thereby "democratized" and the spectator conceived as a "performatively framed subject whose corporeal presence becomes central" (122–124). The art institution in the twenty-first century has therefore become, for Teckert, "a point around which a lifestyle crystallises" with its promise of intellectualism and cultural distinction. No matter how close one can be to its processes and status, the degree to which one can be engrossed or immersed in the rooms of the art institution becomes a critical feature (Leahy 2012: 106). For Teckert, the spatial conception of the museum is highly theatrical; each subject must respond with "constant efforts to improve her own performance and adjust her pose" (2014: 122).

Lepecki follows up a point made by art historian Claire Bishop, that the disciplinary space of the museum is now more of what philosopher Gilles Deleuze has described as a "control-based system" (Lepecki 2013: 15). Whereas in the disciplinary space of the museum the mechanisms of confinement and sources of imposition or choreo-policing are easily locatable, for example with guards, the control-based system of the museum of contemporary art operates by "continuous control and instant communication." Nothing and no-one is left alone for long and an apparent freedom of movement is under strict control, thanks to constant surveillance. We might return here to Wolfson's *Colored Sculpture* (2016) which has facial recognition software built in to its design so that the figure can track and return the gaze of his beholders. Choreo-policing becomes self-policing, as Teckert explains, the imperative for the spectator is to put oneself permanently on display either physically or through images of oneself in the museum posted on social media: "The beholder, who was allowed to enter this stage set, is now an actor in his own right and, in a neoliberal logic of the public, a performer of his own more or less creative biography" (2014: 123). The theatricality and self-imaging encouraged by such a milieu ties into Bishop's observation that dance exhibitions coincided with the invention of the smart phone (2018). It is this very device that enables visitors to broadcast their engagement with and proximity to art in the museum.

Many artists, on the other hand, have contributed to an *unsettling of spectatorship* with artworks that disrupt visitors' habits and their expectations of museum comportment, by distorting or interrupting their experience of gallery spaces. One example is the annual commission that has been given by the Tate Modern in its Turbine Hall since 2000, some of which are discussed in this book. Commissions such as the three huge slides in Carsten Höller's *Test Site* (2006) often interrogate or restage the triangular relationship between body, artwork and space. Monumental in scale, the Turbine Hall works "dramatize visitors' corporeal interaction" by extending and challenging their repertoires of cultural consumption. For Leahy, participating in such works involves an "interplay of mutual self-regard, reflexive panopticism and self-display." Such commissions, in my view, act as machines that provoke and manage individual and group encounters, often licensing a more relaxed and playful occupation so that, with the blessing of the institution, visitors might temporarily abandon the decorum of the white cube. One way of looking at the Turbine Hall Commissions, after some arguments made by theorist Kai van Eikels, is that visitors may think that if the contemporary art gallery allows such "refreshingly unconventional performances" and instances of disruption to take place, then they cannot be too bad (2008: 89). The question then becomes, when a museum "deliberately changes the script and disrupts the repertoire," altering the familiar choreography of viewing, what exactly happens? (Leahy 2012: 100).

Auckland-based artist Mark Harvey's performance *Political Climate Wrestle* (2013) self-reflexively realises relations and enacts forms of intersubjectivity affected by neoliberalism. Performed as part of a collateral event at the 55th Biennale di Venezia the work began with Harvey, dressed in a business shirt, trousers and dress shoes, openly soliciting passers-by, asking them whether they would like to participate in a performance. Individuals were asked whether they would like to discuss the issue of climate change with the artist and also whether they would like to wrestle with him. If they accepted they were required to fill out a legal waiver. Harvey then engaged each participant in discussion and eventually wrestled them.[14] The intersubjective relations set up by this performance were legal and contractual, as well as argumentative and physically adversarial. An intimate politics of mobility is activated where the choreographer/performer invites and coerces a participant to perform certain movements. Acts of solicitation, hand-shaking, polite discussion and conversation were followed by an unexpected shift in which participants were forced to engage more athletic relations, physically wrestling with the artist. Such an engagement meant that participants found themselves physically coming to terms with the brute matter of another body. Harvey's performance is dyadic and direct, as the choreographer/performer manipulated his participants one-on-one.

While visitors to art museums, such as those of the Tate's Turbine Hall commissions or the Venice Biennale, are selectively allowed to change the script and alter or disrupt the repertoire and familiar choreography of viewing, in doing so they may be re-perpetuating the "experience economy" of late capitalism and be subject-to even more insidious forms of authority and control. In staging such works, museums may be using their authority to engender certain relations with visitors that are not as progressive as they may seem. Sometimes it is difficult to discern between performances that are choreo-policing from ones that instantiate choreo-politics. The tension within the term choreography between the authoritative and the emancipatory is enacted once again. Concentrating upon *econo-political* implications, dance theorist Alexandra Kolb theorises that the trend for performances in the 2000s for turning spectators into active participants, requiring them to move rather than remain seated and to physically interact with performers, was part of an overall desire to provide immersive experiences that actively engage participants. Those who take part in participatory or immersive performances are units to be organised, they are required to temporarily suspend their own agency and follow the script or choreography in order to realise the artists' intentions. Often it is the case that in such relational works, the power only moves one way, from the top-down. Kolb also notes that there seems to be little questioning of whether audience members desire or need to interfere actively with a performance, or the requirement of a spectator to eschew her alleged passive role as a mere viewer.

Kolb argues that contemporary performances have direct parallels with the *experience economy* as described in 1999 by businessmen and academics Joseph Pine and James Gilmore. The outputs of the experience economy are distinguished by direct engagement with *guests* and the provision of differentiated experiences that stimulate multiple senses and in which they may actively immerse themselves. The kinds of experience in this new economy may be manifold however the "most exciting and unusual experiences are said to be those that permit immersion, meaning that the guest 'goes into' the experience and becomes an active part of it" (37). If social interaction, participation, collaboration, cooperation and human contact are central to present-day working practices, as well as contemporary choreography, according to Kolb it begs the question of whether such instances of intersubjectivity-as-art reflect rather than oppose the recent shift towards new forms of producer and consumer culture. The experience economy integrates the relationship between production and consumption, so that *the consumer intervenes in an active way in the composition of the product*. Thus audience participation could be seen as buying into and proliferating the ideas of activation and formation of creative subjects that are so central to post-industrial conceptions of labour.

Instruction, control, orders, organisation and forced interaction directed by an artist, in tandem with the cultural authority of the art museum, were explicitly presented in Danish artist Christian Falsnaes' work *Moving Images* (2015).[15] The installation involved a darkened room with large, immersive video projections filling two opposing walls. The footage projected alternated between fast and chaotic montages of images taken from online image libraries or Google searches, and performance videos made by the artist filmed in the same room in which the installation takes place. The artist induced exhibition visitors to become participants in an interactively conceived performance by placing within the installation a live performer who forcefully engages visitors in performative actions. She repeats the instructions and questions that are heard in the voice-over of the film. Visitors are gathered, commanded, asked to look at the screens, asked individually to explain how they feel and why. At one point one visitor is singled out and asked to dance for the others. One of the commands heard in the film, spoken by an electronically-generated male voice says: "I want you to explain how you feel to the other people in the room." During my own encounter with this work, a domineering performer firmly demanded that all those present in the room gather in the centre and answer this question, one by one. The voice-over was played back at a deafening volume, the tone of voice was harsh and domineering and the questions although simple were not necessarily the things one feels like sharing with a group of strangers. However, to participate in this performance meant relinquishing control, "playing along" by submitting to the artist and performer's authoritative demands. Sometimes very physical commands were issued, at other times participants were asked to perform certain actions, such as forming a line, gathering in a circle or pointing out a certain feature in the filmed performances.

Kolb points out that issues of respect, agency, and the need for boundaries in audience participation are vital ones that often arise in this context. Immersive works raise questions about how much pressure is being placed on members of the public to participate, pressure that has the potential to be intrusive or embarrassing. There may be a denial of choice and agency that manifests what Kolb calls a "low-level fascism" in treatment of "the 'up for it' audience" (45–47). As I have suggested in my analysis of Falnaes' *Moving Images*, this work produces uncomfortable and awkward intersubjective relations, because it explores what it means to be a subject or subject-to. Participatory performances like *Moving Images*, that adopt performance parameters and terminology therefore run the risk of furthering values that coincide with the wishes of current governments and powerful economic interests rather than liberating audiences or offering alternative visions of society. Recalling the value of qualities of reflection and deliberation as well as practices of contemplation and concentration, these need not be automatically side-lined in favour of activities that seem to engage people in more immediate ways. Untangling the liaison between intersubjectivity and subjectivity, spectatorship is not always already passive, it might also involve active translation and interpretation of the material presented. Artists like Bronstein, Harvey and Falnaes choreograph gallery situations that deal self-reflexively with the choreo-policing of contemporary exhibition spaces. However, in doing so they may in fact be re-perpetuating the "experience economy" of later capitalism and as a result may not enjoy as much autonomy as previously thought.

2.4   Choreographed Bodies: Institutions, Instruction and Choreo-Politics

Whereas the previous section looked at performances that self-reflexively engage with the choreo-policing functions of art institutions, before moving onto the emancipatory project of *choreo-politics* I would like to briefly mention selected performance artworks in which a submission to authoritative choreographies or dictates is creatively performed. As mentioned in Chapter 1, according to a definition of choreography as a *choreo-policing* function, choreographers create specific, authoritative relations with the dancers who realise their works through the use of scores and instruction. An initial process of selection decides who is able or allowed to move, often based on what kinds of bodies are desired. A subsequent training regime or rehearsal process is a further way to control or discipline those who move. The intersubjective and choreo-policing relations are between choreographer and dancer, one who has created a score and those who follow it and are subject-to. This can also be extended to an artist and the participants within a participatory or immersive performance. Choreography is a traffic between bodies and ideologies, a way of making bodies docile subjects who yield to authority, instruction and often synchronicity. The circumstances of movement are prescribed and what is executed or performed is a given choreography, a previously decided sequence of actions. A plan, set of parameters or score is set up by one party, in order to regulate the movement of others, for a period of time. Choreography, as I have suggested, can be regarded as a structure of command, an authoritative relationship that requires a successful surrender to its demands. Such authoritative structures involve the suggestion of or instruction for the performance of particular movements by one party, and as demonstrated by the performances discussed, can be perpetuated by religious, pseudo-spiritual, fiduciary, psychoanalytic as well as aesthetic parties.

Recalling Althusser's description of how belief is reinforced by physical practices, the way in which religion dictates the repetition of certain gestures and actions as part of worship is subverted in *Religious aerobics* (2010–2013) by the Georgian Bouillon Group. This instructional work, performed both live and installed in a gallery as a video was created by a group from the Caucasus, a place where West Asia meets Eastern Europe that has a complex mix of cultures, histories and faiths (Nagesh 2015: 126). This video work involves a male instructor with a "class" or small group of people behind him. He addresses the camera, beginning with the words "Attention. Hello, let's start to exercise. If you want to achieve the desired result try to repeat all movements." The instructor and the class behind him proceed to go through a sequence of actions in three parts, all performed for eight counts twice and accompanied by walking on the spot.[16]

The actions to be learnt and performed are taken from acts of worship from Christian and Islamic faiths; they include: raising hands and touching thumbs to fingers, making a sign of the cross with fists together, cupping the ears with the hands, covering the face, touching lips with hands and then gesturing away, putting the left palm in the right one and bending forward, bowing with hands resting on thighs, placing the right palm on chest and with the left hand touching the ground, walking in a circle, to the right and to the left, kneeling on one knee then the other, turning to one side, kneeling and then placing one's head and hands on the ground and crossing and uncrossing the feet. At the very end of the piece all of the gestures are performed with an up-beat tempo;

the pace is relentless, the actions are difficult to remember and follow. There is a cycle of instruction, demonstration and execution accompanied by encouragement, approval and the reminder to smile and breathe. *Religious aerobics* is a choreographed work that produces relations that explore what it means to be a subject practising worship, involving a selection of isolated actions taken from many different faiths. These are combined and repeated until they involve a significant amount of exertion and mental concentration. The movements demonstrated and displayed refer to religious practices, as well as the mass parades of socialist states and the late capitalist idea of exercise for self-improvement.

Another work *Parade* (2014) highlights the extent to which acts of choreo-policing function to determine corporeal complicity with instructions. *Parade* is a videodance with dancers, including Adam Linder referred to earlier, performing to the dictates of the choreographer and artist, Shahryar Nashat.[17] The work is a series performed by three dancers in a theatrical stage set dominated by grey, faux-marble panels and a green-coloured opening. Explicit about the concept of capture, each of the three performers wears a cage-like element of costuming, constructed of cane basketry. Linder wears a skeletal frame of cane shaped like men's underwear and the cages worn by the two female performers resemble vestiges of corsetry. Throughout the duration an authoritative voice-over barks commands "Again! Again!" and announces his judgement and approbation "Right, right! Good, good, good." In the "Acrobat" section Linder appears to rehearse, repeating the same steps over and over as the authoritative voice demands, "Again!" Linder shakes his head, exhales and rubs his back expressing his fatigue and frustration. The voice of the choreographer recites comments, suggestions or platitudes that are meant to encourage the dancer, but are in fact so ambiguous as to be meaningless "Yeah, it's definitely a trade-off. Right, right. Stability will come in ebbs and flows, okay, but keep focused on the incentives." *Parade* presents aspects of polished performance, as well as moments of what appears to be a rehearsal process, as a dancer practices the same movements over and over again before a choreographer until he expresses his satisfaction.

The Sinthome Score (2013) by Barcelona-based artist Dora Garcia, combines the language of psychoanalysis with pedestrian forms of dance from the 1960s. A live act for two characters, a *reader* and a *mover* dance for each other, not paying any attention to the audience. The idea is that the performance is a kind of play, their rhythms of reading aloud and moving adjust gradually, until they go together in harmony, synchronised (Farmer and Garcia: 2016).[18] The provocation for the work was a sentence Garcia read while part of a psychoanalytic reading group: "The Unconscious is the body pierced by language." Taken from a seminar by psychoanalyst Jacques Lacan "Joyce Le Sinthome Seminar XXIII Jacques Lacan," Garcia described the seminar as "beautiful enough to be read aloud and arcane enough to create a secret community." Another sentence from the same text includes the term *condansation*, describing something surprising that serves more than the body. In terms of movement, Garcia looked towards a type of contemporary dance that anyone can do, in particular the supposedly non-virtuosic work of choreographers like Yvonne Rainer during the 1960s and more recent works by Jonathan Burrows.[19] Garcia made drawings of various positions that would form a book or score. The idea was that anyone could pick up the book/score and read, move or play, there was no need for training and all renditions would be equally good. A small circle of chairs was formed in the performance space, creating a physical limit, a part of the room. In Garcia's *Sinthome Score*, performers move according to the dictates of a psychoanalytic text as well as graphic representations of positions taken from recent dance history.

The Sinthome Score expresses something specific about this history of subjectification and its relationship to psychoanalytic techniques and approaches. Harking back to Foucault, subjectivity or individuation depends on certain psychic operations to take place that are enabled in and through language. In psycho-analysis language can be constructive and helpful rather than merely coercive. Personally, I found this performance to be delightful and capricious, Lacan's text is simultaneously cryptic and compelling. There is something pleasing about the mover copying the scored movements, testing them out and approximating them with her own body, it seems like a fun game to participate in. There is also an element of chance, when watching and listening there are sometimes enjoyable congruencies or oppositions in the movements being made and the words being uttered. Although in some sense it is prescriptive, I felt the work was more choreo-political than choreo-policing. The capriciousness and randomness of Garcia's *Sinthome Score* means that neither the reader nor the mover resemble Wolfson's puppet, each opens the text or score at random and proceeds to engage with them on their own terms.

In terms of Wolfson's performing puppet, the intersubjective relationship between choreographer and dancer is often described as manipulative and compared to that of puppeteer and marionette. As theorist Bruno Latour explains, the word for "hand" is still hidden within the Latin etymology of the word "manipulate" alluding to the way in which a puppet is subject-to or controlled by the puppeteer (2005: 59–60). Conceptions of choreography as manipulation, analogous to the puppeteer relation, correspond with Leahy's thesis of museum bodies in which visitors bring within them very particular habits that are then encouraged by architecture, signage, guidance and display. However, Garcia's *Sinthome Score* is a reminder that there are positive aspects to being designated a subject, by either a discipline like psychology or by museum institution, it facilitates subject formation. As argued by Latour, it is in such instances and spaces that one might:

> be able to observe empirically how an anonymous and generic body is made to be a person: the more intense the shower of offers of subjectivities, the more interiority you get. (2005: 208)

Psychoanalysis, like the museum can function as providing some people with many offers of subjectivities. As explained in Althusser's example of a police officer hailing 'Hey, you there!' subjects can be recruited by acts of interpellation. By responding to the command one becomes a subject, recognising that it is really her who is being addressed and hailed (Althusser 1971: 167). Yet the importance of choreography as command cannot be overstated, it is endemic to contemporary societies, or what Deleuze has called "societies of control" (Deleuze 1995: 174–175). For some artists such a concept of choreography is fruitful, as it provides something to push back against, but for others a more positive, autonomous and emancipatory concept is more generative for making and this is where the project dubbed *choreo-politics* comes in (Lepecki 2013).

Before moving on to explore choreo-politics further in the next section, it is worth noting that Latour recounted that domination cannot be simply transported through strings to the puppet without translation, sometimes marionettes suggest that the puppeteers do things they would never have thought possible by themselves. Puppets cannot control their handlers, but they might encourage an uncertainty about action. A good puppeteer will multiply the amount of strings and accept surprises about acting, handling and manipulating. Even though marionettes are bound to the puppeteer, emancipation is not just about cutting all the strings: "The only way to liberate the puppets is for the puppeteer to be a *good* puppeteer" (Latour 2005: 215). Dance critic Laurent Goumarre extends this identification of the dancer with the marionette, adding that the character of Pinocchio is a puppet who is disobedient, one who opens the door and dashes out into the street before he is even finished (2014: 275–277).

2.5 THE CHOREO-POLITICAL PROJECT

Such an shift in thinking about the potential for autonomous action, as well as handling and manipulating the boundaries of the museum is proposed by choreographer William Forsythe for whom choreography could be instead an "enabling practice," one that instead might "promote the dancer's autonomy" (quoted in Franko 2007: 16). The question remains, as Lepecki asks, of how, within a larger choreo-political formation one might "move otherwise" (2006: 18)? Indeed this question is central to this book as a whole, and it will be returned to again and again.

Keeping in mind Forsythe's proposition about a dancer's autonomy; Latour's narrative about marionettes somehow suggesting movement to their puppeteers and Goumarre's provocation of Pinocchio as a disobedient puppet who runs into the street; there exists the prospect of problematising and undermining the operations of choreography and institutional spaces of subjection, such as the museum of contemporary art. Therefore the final part of this chapter begins to explore how performers as artistic subjects or gallery visitors might deviate from such forms of structure, control and subjection, as part of a broader *choreo-political* project. As mentioned, a core provocation is that choreographed works might enact intersubjectivity in ingenious ways that can affect new intersubjectivities.

As posited by Lepecki, although choreography has a "deep relation to obedience and command," it also has a "political unconscious" that might be considered an emancipatory project (2013: 23–24). A non-authoritarian choreography, one that might also be non-authorial is, for Lepecki, "the occasioning for a *political thing* to come into the world as *movement* and circulate through subjects" (22). For Lepecki, it is "danced techniques of freedom" that might suggest choreography as a "technology for moving freedom." The choreo-political might involve collective plans that take place at the intersection of creativity and a persistent "iteration of the desire to live away from policed conformity" (23). Experimentation, or "experimenting art" is key, as it is this which allows for the political to be re-discovered and re-produced. Crucially,

Lepecki's notion of the choreo-political is highly intersubjective, social and relational:

> The political is a social and personal force that must be built with others, must be set into relation, and must be danced, collectively, into existence. Once in existence, it has to be learned, sustained and experimented with. Again and again, lest it disappear from the world. (22)

His calls for experimentation and the relationality of choreography will be revisited throughout, particularly in Chapters 4–7, but here I would like to provide some principles that will underpin my argument about the choreo-political.

This chapter began with a narrative about the ways in which the site of the museum acts as a choreo-policing force, so the question is, what kind of site can allow for the choreo-political to occur? How might this be theorised? To begin with, the idea of collectively moving away from policed conformity, moving otherwise and physical deviation recalls Foucault's concept of space as a "counter-site" or *heterotopia*, that opposes the kinds of spaces made into a places via partitioning, in which individuals are distributed, enclosed and managed (Foucault and Miskowiec 1986: 22–24). A heterotopia as a "space of change," one that allows for opening up and proliferation anticipates arguments made by Melbourne-based choreographer and educator Carol Brown regarding space that is *matrixial*, a set of relations produced by bodies, spaces and built environments that I want to explore further below (2010). Equally useful to my argument about museums is a concept of *phase space* in which interaction can alter the very field or situation in which it takes place (Protevi 2001).

Whereas Artaud and Schlemmer described a space that is somewhat elemental, Carol Brown's thesis starts with the premise that "space has a history." Central to the way in which performance or dance takes place is "being present within the space and time of a shared experience" (2010: 62). And harking back to O'Doherty, such a performance is in some ways determined by the historical conception of the space within which it takes place. According to the UK choreographer Siobhan Davies, cited by Brown, the white cube of the gallery space brings with it "received conventions and habits of viewing" (65). There is an emphasis upon the visual, rather than the kinaesthetic or proprioceptive senses and the gallery brings with it modernist ideas about oppositions between absence and presence as well as space as something that is bare, empty, universal and homogenous. I have considered how this space has shaped certain uses by spectators and artists in the first half of this chapter.

Brown elucidates that in the early to mid-twentieth century, modern dancers, particularly in Central Europe, rediscovered space as *raum* or the material of choreography, so that it became tangible, "a dynamic field of forces acting on and through the body" (58). Space was conceived as a pre-requisite for movement and yet movement was also a visible aspect of space. In sympathy with developments in architecture, *Raumempfindung* or "felt" volume in space was conceived. Echoing Schlemmer, such space was a "pliable, abstract volume" that could be measured and divided with the aid of academic rules.[20] Brown goes on to argue that in the twenty-first century "space is fractured," for the kinds of world embodied by performers and dancers is "an effect of the ways in which we understand the spaces and times in which we live." According to Brown the ubiquity of the digital, surveillance, armed conflict and relativity have meant that "the limits of the kinesphere are radically reconfigured" (61).

Rather than a "three-dimensional container, a passive receptacle or void, whose form is given by its content" space is proposed as "a moment of becoming, of opening up and proliferation, a passage from one space to another, a space of change, which changes with time" (Grosz quoted in Brown 2010: 61). A performer is thereby "a conduit between spaces," so that space is transformed according to a dancer's relations with it. According to Brown's proposition of *matrixial spaces*, choreography takes place:

> As an emergent matrix of relationships shaped by states of flux between the body and the built, performers and audience, corporeality and virtuality, ephemerality and the seemingly permanent. (58)

Brown argues that once bodies are untethered from anthropocentric points of view, the biases of Euclidean geometry and modernist conceptions of space, what can then be explored is a continuum through enfolding inside and outside, interior and exterior, so that performers might "embody, incorporate and extrude spaces," assimilating places as given, via somatic awareness and going on to generate a sense of place by manipulating space (59). In articulating or disarticulating space, making it affective vectors or fields, a set of *matrixial* relationships between bodies, spaces and the architectural can be produced. According to Brown, space is an agent within any performance "a discontinuous, plurality of spaces containing multiple dimensions." Thus space is not prior to an act, it can in fact be constituted by acts, such *matrixial fields* could be a "transgressive threshold of co-emergence for the dancing subject and the unfolding spaces within choreography as encounter."

Yet space, as Foucault reminds us, is also heterotopic, a counter-site, in some ways it presents or represents other kinds of relations and places. Foucault conceives of *heterotopia* as a way of transcending categories of space, problematising containment, placing or what he refers to as *emplacement*. Instead he points out the importance and predominance of "simultaneity," the dispersed, a "network that connects points and intersects with its own skein." They can take on varied forms, they are "different spaces," or "other places." One type of heterotopia described by Foucault are heterotopias of deviation, "those in which individuals whose behaviour is deviant in relation to the required mean or norm are placed." In many ways this is fitting for a description of art galleries in which artists perform, as they often exhibit forms of behaviour that could be perceived as deviant to societal norms.

The gallery space of performance is *different* or *other*, it deviates in relation to norms, several spaces might be presented within one; fleeting, transitory, precarious temporal spaces or *heterochronies* might be activated. Such a space might also be conceived as a *matrixial field*, a series of relationships between bodies, interiors, exteriors, architecture and audience. The prior, so-called "objective," Newtonian conception of space is transformed into a subjective space of possibilities, a topological space where space is consciously stylised and performed, it is made qualitative rather than quantitative. Such a space contests the male, abstract space of the temple, the natural quantitative space that just *is*. If there is a mutually reinforcing relationship between a figure and ground, or performer and the white cube, what happens when the coherence of such a performer is questioned? Perhaps then such a masculine, Newtonian space can be complexified and begin to challenge prior categories, a previously cis-gendered space might be challenged, opened up and become heterotopic.

The theorist John Protevi has another way of expanding our ideas about the museum when he argues "the activities of a system change the very nature of the space itself" and "the interactions of actual agents serve to change the virtual field" (2001). What he calls *phase space* becomes something that is affective, rather than something that is extended or quantitative, something into which bodies are inserted. Instead each space is something unique created when bodies come together in a particular way, for a specific purpose, perhaps inflected in a certain way by a performance or choreography.

The project of this book is to consider how the gallery and museum has been, and might be, subjectivised or more importantly inter-subjectivised as a meeting of subjectivities. Such a heterotopia, matrixial or phase space will make for qualitative and intensive choreographies that have the possibility to be creative, open-ended and un-predictable. Perhaps such a space could be considered to be more of a topological site. Such a site might be activated by the presentation of a relational body, one that can manifest the political potential of choreography and performance. This chapter therefore ends with the prospect of choreographies that might work against normative phenomenology by deconstructing, recoding, and making a-signifying recognisable movements from ordinary experience. With the museum space becoming a vector of movement, sensory experience and embodiment, it will be charged by what takes place within it. Following on from Lepecki's proposition of the choreo-political I will argue that such processes can be initiated by specific instances of performance art, ones in which the political emerges from "planned, dissensual, and nonpoliced disposition of motions and bodies" (2013: 22). The following chapter will examine how strangely syntactical movement perceptions of subjectivity are activated by Xavier Le Roy's *Self Unfinished* (1998) and other examples of performance art.

NOTES

1. Exhibited in *JORDAN WOLFSON* May 5–June 25, 2016, David Zwirner, 525 West 19th Street, New York.
2. Rhythm and blues singer Percy Sledge's "When a Man Loves a Woman" (1966). Read in the context of the Black Lives Matter protest movement, the title of Wolfson's "coloured" sculpture seems to hint at the historic lynching of African Americans.
3. As Bennett argued, historically, museums played a pivotal role in the formation of the modern state, whose endorsement gives them the ability and authority to be perceived as "a set of educative and civilizing agencies." According to Bennett, it was during this period that the general public became witnesses whose presence was essential to a display of imperial power "precisely in continually displaying its ability to command, order, and control objects and bodies, living and dead" (1995: 66–67).

4. Taken from French philosopher Henri Lefebvre (1901–1991).
5. As seen exhibited in *Freedom Farmers: New Zealand artists growing ideas* at Auckland Art Gallery Toi o Tāmaki, 26 October 2013 to 23 February 2014.
6. Museums also installed visitors at the threshold of greater things to come. It could be argued that biennales and contemporary art gallery still position their viewers at this threshold, and at that of contemporaneity.
7. Althusser also notes that "God thus defines himself as the Subject par excellence."
8. Foucault supports Butler's conception of subject formation as affected by fields of power, emphasising a need to question "how things work at the level of on-going subjugation.... We should try to discover how it is that subjects are gradually, progressively, really and materially constituted through a multiplicity of organisms, forces, energies, materials, desires, thoughts etc. We should try to grasp subjection in its material instance as a constitution of subjects" (Foucault 1980: 97).
9. This argument about the way in which observers of art are historically constructed was brought to fruition in Jonathan Crary. *Techniques of the Observer: on vision and modernity in the nineteenth century* (1990).
10. O'Doherty writes that "occupancy" of a gallery space as an environment is a large subject, "the effect on the spectator who joins them is one of trespass."
11. The term subjectivity here is opposed to "objectivity." The suffix creates an abstract noun from the term subject.
12. The varied deportment of museum visitors has been extensively explored by Thomas Struth's series of museum photographs (Fig. 2.2).
13. For the minimalist box see the New Museum by Kazuyo Sejima and Ryue Nishizawa or SANAA in Brooklyn, New York City, for the sculptural envelope see Frank Gehry's Guggenheim, Bilbao, Spain.
14. I witnessed this performance as part of the exhibition *The Maldives Exodus Caravan Show* (2014) at Te Tuhi in Auckland, New Zealand.
15. Christian Falsnaes' *Moving Images* (2015) was included in the Preis der Nationalgalerie 2015 where I saw it at the Hamburger Bahnhof—Museum für Gegenwart in Berlin.
16. I viewed this video work as part of the *8th Asia Pacific Triennial of Contemporary Art* (2015) at the Queensland Gallery of Modern Art in Brisbane, Australia.
17. *Parade* (1917) had a scenario by Jean Cocteau. It was performed by Serge Diaghilev's Ballets Russes with set and costumes by Pablo Picasso, music by Erik Satie and choreography by Léonide Massine. Ironically Linder himself actually choreographed this contemporary version of the ballet (Heiser 2014: 214). I viewed this work as part of the 20th Biennale of

Sydney (2016) at the Museum of Contemporary Art (MCA) in Sydney, Australia.

18. I encountered this performance at the Arsenale in Okwui Enwezor's exhibition *All The World's Futures* as part of the 56th Venice Biennale in 2015.

19. For more on Burrows see Daniela Perazzo, *Jonathan Burrows: Towards a Minor Dance* (2019).

20. In terms of art history this recalls the Minimalist sculpture of artists like Donald Judd, for example his brass floor work *Untitled*, 1968.

REFERENCES

Althusser, Louis. 1971. Ideology and Ideological State Apparatuses (Notes Towards an Investigation). In *Lenin and Philosophy and Other Essays*. Trans. Ben Brewster, 123–173. London: New Left Books.

Artaud, Antonin. 1999. The Theatre of Cruelty—First Manifesto. In *The Theatre and Its Double: Essays by Antonin Artaud*. Trans. Victor Corti, 68–78. London: Calder Publications Limited.

Bennett, Tony. 1995. *The Birth of the Museum: History, Theory, Politics*. London; New York: Routledge.

Bishop, Claire. 2018. Black Box, White Cube, Gray Zone: Dance Exhibitions and Audience Attention. *TDR: The Drama Review* 62.2: 22–42.

Bork Petersen, Franziska, and Scott, Minnie. 2014. The Unruly Spectator: Exhibition Analysis on Foot. In *Assign and Arrange: Methodologies of Presentation in Art and Dance*, eds. Maren Butte, Kirsten Maar, Fiona McGovern, Marie-France Rafael, and Jörn Schafaff, 131–150. Berlin: Sternberg Press.

Brook, Peter. 1968. *The Empty Space*. London: Penguin Books.

Brown, Carol. 2010. Making Space, Speaking Spaces. In *The Routledge Dance Studies Reader Second Edition*, eds. Alexandra Carter and Janet O'Shea, 58–72. Abingdon, Oxon: Routledge.

Butler, Judith. 1990. *Gender Trouble: Feminism and the Subversion of Identity*. New York; London: Routledge.

Crary, Jonathan. 1990. *Techniques of the Observer: On Vision and Modernity in the Nineteenth Century*. Cambridge, MA: MIT Press.

Danto, Arthur C. 1981. *The Transfiguration of the Commonplace: A Philosophy of Art*. Cambridge, MA: Harvard University Press 1981.

Deleuze, Gilles. 1995. *Negotiations, 1972–1990*. Trans. Martin Joughlin. New York: Columbia University Press.

Falkenstein, Lorne. 1997. Space. In *Encyclopedia of Empiricism*, eds. Don Garrett and Edward Barbanell. London: Routledge. Credo Reference. http://ezp roxy.auckland.ac.nz/login?url=https://search.credoreference.com/content/entry/routemp/space/0?institutionId=181. Accessed 18 May 2016.

Farmer, Geoffrey, and Garcia, Dora. 2016. Nobody Is Sleeping in the Sky. *Mousse* 54: 250–259.

Foster, Susan Leigh. 2005. Choreographing Empathy. *Topoi* 24.1: 81–91.

Foucault, Michel. 1977. *Discipline and Punish: The Birth of the Prison*. Trans. Alan Sheridan. London: Penguin Books.

Foucault, Michel. 1980. Two Lectures. Lecture One: 7 January 1976. In *Power/Knowledge: Selected Interviews and Other Writings 1972–1977*, ed. Colin Gordon, 78–109. New York: Pantheon Books.

Foucault, Michel, and Miskowiec, Jay. 1986. Of Other Spaces. *Diacritics* 16: 22–27.

Franko, Mark. 2007. Dance and the Political: States of Exception. In *Dance Discourses: Keywords in Dance Research*, eds. Susanne Franco and Marina Nordera, 11–28. London; New York: Routledge.

Goldberg, Keren. 2016. Agenda: Jordan Wolfson. *Mousse* 54: 222.

Goumarre, Laurent. 2014. Disobedience and DIY. In *Danse: An Anthology*, ed. Noémie Solomon, 275–282. Dijon: Les presses du réel.

Greenfield, Amy. 2013. Filmdance: Space, Time, and Energy. In *Choreographing Exhibitions*, ed. Mathieu Copeland, 192–199. Dijon: Les presses du réel.

Heiser, Jörg. 2014. Perfect Pretence. *Frieze 166*. October: 212–215.

Howe, David Everitt. 2015. Dance in the Ruins: Trajal Harrell, Adam Linder and Alexandra Bachzetsis on Their Work, Its Institutionalization, and the Art World. *Mousse* 50(October): 76–89.

Kolb, Alexandra. 2013. Current Trends in Contemporary Choreography: A Political Critique. *Dance Research Journal* 45: 31-52.

Krauss, Rosalind. 1981. *Passages in Modern Sculpture*. Cambridge, MA: MIT Press.

Kwon, Miwon. 2005. One Place After Another: Notes on Site Specificity. In *Theory in Contemporary Art Since 1985*, eds. Zoya Kocur and Simon Leung, 32–54. Malden: Blackwell Publishing.

Laermans, Rudi. 2008. 'Dance in General' or Choreographing the Public, Making Assemblages. *Performance Research*. 13.1: 7–14.

Latour, Bruno. 2005. *Reassembling the Social: An Introduction to Actor Network Theory*. Oxford; New York: Oxford University Press.

Leahy, Helen Rees. 2012. *Museum Bodies: The Politics and Practices of Visiting and Viewing*. Farnham, Surrey; Burlington, VT: Ashgate.

Lepecki, André. 2006. *Exhausting Dance: Performance and the Politics of Movement*. New York: Routledge.

Lepecki, André. 2013. Choreopolice and Choreopolitics: Or, the Task of the Dancer. *TDR: The Dance Review* 57.4: 13–27.

Lepecki, André. 2016. *Singularities: Dance in the Age of Performance*. New York: Routledge.

Linder, Adam. 2016. Adam Linder. http://www.adam-linder.net. Accessed 28 September 2016.

Menzies, Louise. 2013. Louise Menzies: Peloha. In *Freedom Farmers: New Zealand Artists Growing Ideas*, ed. Natasha Conland, 14.

Nagesh, Tarun. 2015. The Social Medium. In *The 8th Asia Pacific Triennial of Contemporary Art*, 118–161. Brisbane: Queensland Art Gallery | Gallery of Modern Art.

O'Doherty, Brian. 1986. *Inside the White Cube: The Ideology of the Gallery Space*. San Francisco: The Lapis Press.

Protevi, John. 2001. The Geophilosophies of Deleuze and Guattari. Delivered at the November 2001 meeting of SEDAAG (Southeastern Division of the Association of American Geographers). http://www.protevi.com/john/SED AAG.pdf. Accessed 16 June 2016.

Rosenthal, Stephanie. 2010. Choreographing You: Choreographies in the Visual Arts. In *Move: Choreographing You*, ed. Stephanie Rosenthal, 8–21. London: Hayward Publishing.

Schlemmer, Oskar. 1996. Theatre. In *The Theatre of the Bauhaus: Oskar Schlemmer, Laszlo Moholy-Nagy, Farkas Molnar*, 82–105. Baltimore: John Hopkins University Press.

Schlemmer, Oskar. 1978. The Mathematics of Dance. In Hans Maria Wingler. *The Bauhaus, Weimar, Dessau, Berlin, Chicago*. Trans. Wolfgang Jabs and Basil Gilbert. Ed. Joseph Stein, 118–119. Cambridge, MA: MIT Press.

Solomon, Noémie. 2010. Allan Kaprow: 18 Happenings in 6 Parts (1959) Reinvented in 2010 by Rosemary Butcher. In *Move: Choreographing You*, ed. Stephanie Rosenthal, 40–43. London: Hayward Publishing.

Teckert, Christian. 2014. The Mobilized Spectator: Some Speculations on the Architectural History of Museum Scripting and Staging. In *Assign and Arrange: Methodologies of Presentation in Art and Dance*, eds. Butte et al., 113–127. Berlin: Sternberg Press.

Tomès, Arnaud. 2005. *Le Sujet*. Paris: Ellipses.

Van Eikels, Kai. 2008. This Side of the Gathering The Movement of Acting Collectively: Ligna's Radioballett. *Performance Research* 13.1: 85–98.

Von Kleist, Heinrich. 1976. Puppet Theatre. *Salmagundi* 33/34: 83–88.

Wood, Catherine. 2011. Pablo Bronstein: Sprezzatura. *Flash Art International* 276: 68–71.

CHAPTER 3

Xavier Le Roy and the Male Subject as Performance Artist

Xavier Le Roy positions himself in an empty room, seated in front of a desk. Throughout his performance, *Self Unfinished* (1998) he returns to his desk again and again, it becomes a location where he ends one sequence and begins another.[1] This repeated action signals the constitution of the solo, male performer and choreographer as theorised by art historian Amelia Jones with her thesis of the "Pollockian Performative" and by dance theorist André Lepecki in his description of a solipsistic, masculine choreographer. Le Roy's act of sitting at a desk signals an enactment of subject constitution, indeed solo performances as chamber pieces involving men in rooms, performing certain actions or labouring, are endemic to late twentieth-century performance art. What makes Le Roy different from other male performance artists such as Paul McCarthy or Stelarc, is the way in which he self-consciously alternates between a singular, authoritative, unitary subjectivity and something that is less straightforward to comprehend. There are moments in *Self Unfinished* when Le Roy seems unreadable or un-recognisable, thereby disrupting intersubjective processes of recognition. By scrambling his recognisability with the aid of various choreographic and technical devices, Le Roy implicates viewers and audience members in the very constitution of his artistic subjectivity.

V. Wynne-Jones, *Choreographing Intersubjectivity in Performance Art*, New World Choreographies, https://doi.org/10.1007/978-3-030-40585-4_3

79

Le Roy's placement of himself at a desk could signify an intention to conduct bureaucratic labour before his audience. Artist and art-writer Brian O'Doherty has described the labour of a solo, performing artist as often futile, marked by *pathos*, failure and inadequacy:

> There is something infinitely pathetic about the single figure in the gallery, testing limits, ritualizing its assaults on its body, gathering scanty information on the flesh it cannot shake off. In these extreme cases art becomes the life of the body. (1986: 64)

Le Roy's presentation of himself as a labouring, solo, male performer could also be read as a riff, response, interrogation, extension and exaggeration of the idea or myth of a singular, unitary, male artist as genius (see Jones 1998: 86; Schneider 2005: 35). Although Jones has written extensively on subjectivity in relation to self-imaging technologies and performance art, it is her early discussion on male performance artists and their relationship to the figure of US painter Jackson Pollock (1912–1956) that is most relevant here.[2]

Her point of departure is a selection of photographs and film footage taken around 1950 by Hans Namuth (1915–1990) of Pollock "standing above or within his huge canvases, overtly and theatrically *performing* the act of painting" (1998: 53). For Jones, the images enabled an artistic subject to be conceived and perceived as self-consciously enacting or performing his role, so that the relationship between himself and his work would be forever altered by the presence of others as photographer, viewer or audience member. Jones describes how Harold Rosenberg, whilst writing on Pollock, proposed painting as a mythic event, a physical "*act*" of performance that took place within the *arena* of the canvas" that had everything to do with the angst-ridden and expressive body of the artist. In the previous chapter I have emphasised the concepts of act and arena as they refer to Artaud's ideas about performance as action and it is in these writings in art history that the painter becomes also understood as an embodied performer.

For Jones, artistic subjectivity is itself indebted to intersubjective relations, any act of performance is "contingent on the act of reception" (57) therefore Pollock's performative persona was open to and even *dependent upon* "intersubjective engagement" (83). Pollock has been discursively shaped and defined by art history as postmodern, given the milieu in which he functions, although paradoxically, Pollock self-consciously performs himself as a quintessentially modernist subject. In his repeatedly performing, Pollock adheres to or is obedient to a previously conceived role, script or score, that of the labouring, heroic, mystical, male action-painter. For Jones, a performative, artistic subject is generally assumed to be masculine, and "implicitly aligned in Western culture with whiteness, heterosexuality, and an ambivalent antibourgeois positionality." Jones sees this "Pollockian model of artistic genius" as dominant throughout art history and such normative masculinity became a legacy to be grappled with, mimicked, parodied and assaulted (94). Jones' art historical narrative involves performances that interrogate the aggressive *masculinism* of Pollock with the whiteness, heterosexuality and class implications attached to his privileged subject position. In the 1970s, performance artists like Vito Acconci and Paul McCarthy explicitly reacted to the persona of Pollock and many other male solo performers identified with that thesis.

Before continuing it is worth explaining that although this chapter is situated within art history and critical museum studies, there has already been a significant amount of discourse in dance studies on Le Roy by dance scholars such as Gerald Siegmund (2006) Susanne Foellmer (2009) and Laurence Louppe (2007).[3] There are effectively two readerships of Le Roy's work, those within dance studies and those within the field of art or museum studies. The fact of the matter is, Le Roy is somewhat endemic as a case study and his work is often framed around discussions of subjectivity. This has also occurred in writing by André Lepecki and Petra Sabisch whose work I will draw on. This particular reading of Le Roy's *Self Unfinished* has much to offer art history and performance studies but perhaps less to offer dance studies itself, as this is where many of its insights have been sourced from. Nevertheless, dance scholars may be interested to see what happens when Le Roy's choreographic practice is interpreted by art historians as we come to terms with the impact of works like *Self Unfinished* once they have entered into contemporary fine art contexts. In this chapter I will make the case that within art history, questions of artistic subjectivity have a different lineage via male performance artists in the last quarter of the twentieth century.

I would argue that Le Roy's *Self Unfinished* therefore can be read as a presentation of a non-normative, artistic body operating in a mode of hyperbolic, exaggerated masculinity and masquerade. Le Roy presents once again an expressive body within an arena, someone self-consciously and overtly enacting or performing the role of the artist as unique genius, as a labouring existentialist hero and one who is contingent upon acts of reception. I argue that by performing his own choreographed solo, Le Roy blatantly signals his individual creativity, referencing Jones' trope of self-conscious and particularised self that might dismantle the universality of the privileged body of Pollock.

Lepecki also takes up this idea of a less than coherent self when he uses the term *idiotic* to describe Le Roy's positioning of himself alone and in front of a desk, appealing to the etymological sense from the Greek *idiotes* meaning an "isolated, self-contained *one*" a private, separate individual removed from social responsibility (2006: 33). "[T]he solitary male dancer" is also a solipsistic figure that lingers or "haunts" the site of dance, and Lepecki describes such performers as:

> men moving alone in explicitly enclosed and empty spaces – empty chambers, empty studios, empty rooms, sombre voids where haunted solitude, concentration of will and precision in execution all fuse to create what can only be described as solipsistic excess. (19)

The trope of the solitary, masculine figure in "studious privacy," extends therefore not only to their absorption but also to their movements within the physical space of the "chamber," whether it be the studio or an exhibition space. Striving to undergo some sort of transformation, testing limits or gathering scant information, according to performance theorist Rebecca Schneider, the twentieth century was "uniquely hospitable to, and enamoured of, solo performance" and "the single body increasingly performed in a piece authored and/or choreographed and/or staged and/or deigned by that single body" (2005: 27, 32). From the 1960s onwards, US body art practices, as well as European and Australasian reactions to such practices, all yield examples of such "chamber pieces" involving men in rooms performing certain actions or labouring, to their own ends.

Examples include the experimental activities Bruce Nauman conducted and documented in his sublet studio in Mill Valley in the winter of 1967–1968 such as *Walking in an Exaggerated Manner around the Perimeter of a Square* and *Dance or Exercise on the Perimeter of a Square* (van Bruggen 2012: 81). Both works involve the artist walking or stepping upon and around a masking-tape square on the floor of his studio with a metronome used to provide regulation of his movements. Applicable to Le Roy, is Lepecki's reading of Nauman's performances, as examples of the artist locking himself in the "cranial space" of his empty studio.

The studio as a "space of thought moving" for a series of "self-contained, cloistered, choreographic solipsistic explorations – under the excuse of philosophy" (2006: 30).

Later examples that also involve artists pacing, walking, mapping or measuring the available space of a room include those by New Zealanders from the 1970s onwards. Jim Allen paced and read poetry amongst running chainsaws in *Poetry for Chainsaws* at the Experimental Art Foundation, Adelaide in 1976. Bruce Barber negotiated an obstacle course in Kerikeri Memorial Hall under conditions of sensory deprivation in *Bucket Action* (1973). Peter Roche executed extreme vocalisations whilst pacing in his performance *Get the Fuck Out Got to Get Out* at Elam Art School, Auckland in 1979. Similarly Australian artist Mike Parr frequently isolates himself alone in a room for prolonged periods of time in works such as *Aussie, Aussie, Aussie, Oi, Oi, Oi, [UnAustralian]* (2003).

For Lepecki, artists like Nauman evoke the *choreographic* in their works as a "vigorous, methodical, monomaniacal execution of a set of previously established steps" (2006: 23). Nauman as well as Allen, Barber and Roche, performed various acts of pacing within a room or chamber. Nauman himself reflected that when working in his studio he in fact spent most of his time pacing around and drinking coffee, coming to the conclusion that he may as well film himself doing just that (Coosje van Bruggen quoted in Lepecki, 29). According to Lepecki, the way in which Nauman's pacing is controlled, mapped out, measured or "chronometric" and repeated means that it is "formalised," making it in fact a "choreographic exercise" (29, 31). From its mapping of space and marking of time, the choreographic chamber becomes, according to Lepecki, "an accumulator of subjectivity," however in my view, this consideration of the male artists in a room begs the question of what kind of subjectivity it accumulates (30).

3.1   THRESHOLD SPACES AND MACHINIC VOICES

Lepecki's argument about the function of the choreographic chamber means that it is difficult to disentangle an artistic subject from the institutional and intersubjective space he performs in. Additionally, performance artworks that take place in art galleries confuse the distinction between the prior activities of the studio as a space of preparation and the artwork as an event. The gallery itself becomes a processual space where things unfold and the unexpected may occur. By entering into the gallery space as an apparatus of visual arts, from the stage of performing arts, Le Roy's *Self Unfinished* experienced a significant change to its aesthetic dispositif or set-up. The performance has shifted or crossed from one space to another, in the physical sense as well as the disciplinary one. Many contemporary works have explicitly activated these physical, cultural frameworks and thresholds. One example is Ukrainian artist Oleg Kulik's 1994 performance *The Mad Dog or Last Taboo Guarded by a Lone Cerberus*. Kulik, together with the poet Alexander Brener guarded the entrance to the M. Guelman Gallery on Jakimanka Street, Moscow, 23 November 1994. In this performance Kulik, naked, stood on all fours wearing a leash. An account follows:

> Naked in the frost, losing his bearings, Kulik barked, rushed on a chain, pushed spectators off their feet and bit them. His throat hoarse with barking, unaware of cold and danger, Kulik rushed into the thick of the traffic and managed to stop it. (Watkins and Kermode 2001: 72)

Kulik explicitly makes the gallery entranceway a space of risk and danger. The so-called neutrality, transparency or "innocence" of the space of the white cube, with its accompanying presumption of a universal viewing subject, as espoused in the phenomenological model, had been deflated and challenged earlier by US-based conceptual artists like Michael Asher. In the early 1970s Asher highlighted the institutional frame and its machinations by removing gallery walls, revealing the offices and storage facilities normally hidden behind them (Kwon 2005: 35).

The artists' studio space also has its traditions, it has been valued as a mysterious and masculine space of production, a liminal site that has been set apart for philosophical exploration, a social place for gathering and manufacture as well as a monastic space that strives towards absolutes and elimination. Within such a space there may be openness and indeterminacy, creative energies, an anxious and antagonistic masculinity as well as obsession, virility and kinaesthetic thinking.[4]

The art gallery as a white cube that was discussed at length in Chapter 2 is a very specific unit of discourse, constructed in art history over time. It is also an intersubjective environment, one that is occupied by performers as well as spectators creating interruptions or breaks in everyday life. It may be a space of isolation that enables observation, one that is undifferentiated, involving performer and spectators simultaneously. In some sense this space is a cell, a chamber of aesthetics or transformation, it involves the space of spectators, with an undifferentiated potency, one that consists of pockets of voids or even generative forces. Such a space as an apparatus or *dispositif*, as constructed by disciplines of art history, curatorial practice and museology is unique, it encloses those within it and partitions them within rooms. Most importantly, via a process of spatio-subjectivisation, the white cube sets up criteria for the formation of very specific kinds of viewing and artistic subjects.

Using the choreographic as a template, there are ways to measure and regulate the structures of the gallery space, like the eight-hour working days British artists Gilbert and George's spent performing *Singing Sculpture* (1969) (Dutt 2004). According to art historian Helen Molesworth, the early twenty-first century has been marked by radical transformations of the global labour force, "As commodities are now almost exclusively produced in developing and non-Western nations, the labour of developed nations has increasingly become the management of information and the production of experience" (2003: 18–19). This last point harks back to Pine and Gilmore's experience economy discussed in the previous chapter, but the kind of service labour that Le Roy prepares himself to perform for his audience involves more extensive human contact and interaction.

After Le Roy has sat still at the desk for a spell he starts to move in slow isolated movements, making a "vvvvvr" sound with his mouth in varying pitches corresponding to the movements of various body parts, as if his body were a robotic machine. He continues to match his movements with sound effects that are produced in a ventriloquist manner so that one cannot even see his mouth move. It creates the impression that his body is a hydraulic machine. In this part of his performance Le Roy performs a very different kind of pacing around a room. Le Roy's moving and walking in a robotic fashion could be read as performing a body that is passive, managed, regulated, made docile and machine-like, one that adheres to rules, codes or prior instructions, one that is very similar to Jordan Wolfson's metallic puppet. After walking like a robot Le Roy goes from an animate mechanical being to an inanimate object. Le Roy moves gradually backwards until he reaches the back wall of the performance space. He crouches, then lies down, his face towards the wall, his arms and body extended along it so that his toes touch the wall. Fifteen minutes into his performance, he remains completely still.

As defined by Michael Hardt and Antonio Negri, labour that is immaterial is often *affective*, "focused on the creation and manipulation of affect" (2000: 292). This concept of labour that is affective, corporeal yet still immaterial, produces experiences for others, intangible products such as "a feeling of ease, well-being, satisfaction, excitement, or passion" (293). Such affective labour recalls the pathetic, futile testing of the single figure in the gallery, exemplified by Le Roy, as well as Artaud's proposition within his essay "An Affective Athleticism" of performer as a *heart athlete* or "crude empiricist," someone who is in possession of an "affective organism" or "musculature" (1999: 88–89). It is equivocal as to whether this optimistic conception of affective labour is achieved by performance artists such as Le Roy, however, what matters is that the labour he is preparing himself to perform, before an audience, in an art institution involves the prior assignation of a task that is in this case a choreography, as well as labour that might be affective but is also probably futile.

Le Roy's positioning of himself resting on the side of his body, stretched along and facing the wall highlights the object-ness of his body and there are many instances of performance artists throughout the twentieth century presenting their bodies as mass, a physical solid or object. Australian artist Stelarc considered his body as a weight that is ordinarily prey to the forces of gravity in his suspension performances that took place over 25 years, in particular his *Rock Suspension* (1980) where his naked body, suspended from hooks embedded in his flesh was suspended in the midst of hanging rocks within a white cube gallery setting. Stelarc rendered his own body sculpture, still as the rocks, or slightly swaying so that audience members could wander around him like a statue. *Rock Suspension* also manifests a sort of puppetry of the artist that subverts or problematizes spatio-subjectivisation by making space a problem, making the white cube explicit as a visible support rather than covert, gaining strength and power from the way in which it is generally invisible and so-called neutral.

As indicated in Jones' argument about the Pollockian Performative, the relationship between artistic subjectivity and intersubjectivity is complex. Throughout the twentieth-century artists performing within white cubes were expected to be avant-garde, exhibitionist, productive, and efficient. Artists such as Acconci and McCarthy explored and actively disrupted these prior models. In pacing or motivating themselves within enclosed spaces, artists like Nauman, Allen, Barber and Roche explored the ways

in which certain spaces might accumulate certain forms of artistic subjectivity. The very thresholds of such spaces were made explicit in works by
Asher, Kulik and others.

Choreographic strategies employed by Le Roy, Gilbert and George and
Stelarc, who make movement schematic and machine-like, contribute to
an interrogation of the expectations for performers, in particular their
propensity for successful or efficient actions. Paradoxically, performances
that position the performer as object-like begin to evade fixity and chart
a line of flight from subjection or the always-already subject, to what
Sabisch refers to as a "proliferation of a different dynamics of change."
According to Lepecki, within his performance Le Roy "drops the notion
of the subject" as well as the potential to be fixed within the categories of "masculinity and femininity, human and animal, object and
subject, passive and active, mechanical and organic, absence and presence" (Lepecki 2006: 40). In *Self Unfinished,* according to Lepecki, Le
Roy replaces categories and binary oppositions with "a series of pure
becomings."

3.2   BODYMADES: METAMORPHOSIS
AND TRANSFORMATION

The remainder of this chapter will examine in more detail how exactly
male artists use their bodies to undermine the mutually reinforcing relationship between figure and ground, or subject and the white cube.
O'Doherty's white cube as a chamber for transformation is a place in
which the performance of certain gestures might create interruptions or
breaks in the conventions of ordinary life. Additionally, various aspects
of the studio might be co-opted so that the white cube gallery becomes
a space for performance. One such aspect might be what drama theorist Phillip Zarilli has described as a metaphysical studio, a place of
propositions and possibilities, one in which to practice philosophy in the
flesh.

Echoing this concern with practical philosophy, I posit the transformation of a body in relation to a larger ontological argument about how the
always-already subject is part of a greater system of organisation and how
this may be evaded via: acts of transformation, the creation of bodymades,
executing choreographed movements, still-acts that are unreadable or a
body stripped of meaning. French philosophers Gilles Deleuze and Félix
Guattari state that it is inevitable that one is "nailed down" as a subject,

but that it is possible to dismantle the self, to "disarticulate," to "unhook ourselves from the points of subjectification," ceasing to be an "organism" (2008: 177–179). The subject is thus replaced by the *body without organs* (BwO), flows of intensity, fluids, fibres, continuums and "conjunctions of affects." Similar to becoming, this involves:

> Opening the body to connections that presuppose an entire assemblage, circuits, conjunctions, levels and thresholds, passages and distributions of intensity, and territories and deterritorializations measured with the craft of the surveyor. (179)

Here the BwO is a kind of call to arms, a re-imagining, an appeal to radically re-conceptualise concepts of the body. Above all, BwO is a "practice, or 'set of practices' that involves 'biological' and 'political' experimentation" (166). Deleuze and Guattari explain that the BwO swings between the surfaces that stratify it or submit it to judgement and the plane of consistency that sets it free, unfurling and opening itself to experimentation.

> This is how it should be done: Lodge yourself on a stratum, experiment with the opportunities it offers, find an advantageous place on it, find potential movements of deterritorialisation, possible lines of flight, experience them, produce flow conjunctions here and there, try out continuums of intensities segment by segment, have a small plot of new land at all times.... (176, 178)

Lepecki, for instance, posits that Le Roy's *Self Unfinished* is an example of such experimentation, and it is this that makes him within his performance "ontologically unfinishable" (2006: 40).[5] The dismantling of the universal body is however part of a larger argument about bodies as sites of resistance, or as places with the power of *ex-scription*. Philosopher Boyan Manchev et al. argues that dance is one form of experimental practice that might express the transformability of both body and subject (2014: 117). Manchev stresses that a performing body might rebel against preconceived ideas about its functionality, by showing a dysfunctional and disorganised body. Manchev posits that suspension of a body's organic functionality might erase all of the "systems of identification and aesthetics, social, political and biological codes" attributed to it (121–122).[6]

Returning to the hierarchical structures and discourses of performance and art history, Le Roy enjoys a certain amount of authority as an artist, performer and choreographer within the white cube, an art historical field of power that makes up the plane of organisation. Yet there is the possibility that from within this plane of organisation, enjoying its very privileges and authority, he has been able to create movement-percepts both in his own body and with others. Via a choreography of bodily transformation that undermines or unravels the organisational structure to create a destratification, Le Roy creates a disruptive encounter with the labour of seeing and being seen, by manipulating representations of his body and its outward expression. It is important to note that this trans-formation is dependent on the audience's sightlines, a theatrical device usually afforded by the proscenium space when audience members are seated on one side and view the performer from one orientation.

The molecular parts of Le Roy's *Self Unfinished* could be understood as movement-percepts or fragments that are recognisably masculine or feminine learned actions, or ones that are inhuman. However much a body is fixed in actuality, it can assume other forms of life and attempt to perform what is not its own. In this work, Le Roy uses costume as a tool or prosthetic for transformation. A simple tube of black fabric allows him to mask certain parts of his body, making them invisible to the audience whilst highlighting other parts (Fig. 3.1). Le Roy's use of fabric to alter the appearance of his body, as well as dilate and augment his movement recalls a similar use of fabric in earlier works by US-based choreogra-phers such as Martha Graham's *Lamentation* (1930) and Katherine Litz' *The Glyph* (1977). The remaining visible body parts, in Le Roy's case, feet, hands, trousers and encased upper body are then utilised as parts or particles, ones that can enact relations of movement and stillness as well as speed and slowness.

Manchev has described Le Roy's apparently headless figure as "a morphologically primitive form, with undifferentiated organs, a torso or trunk and tentacles waving as if dying" (125). What is emphasised is a process of metamorphosis, so that Le Roy presents research into "the conditions of life that exist *in* the metamorphosis, the passage of the forces, the *traffic* of intensities, forces and rhythms: it's the body as the open and not as figure, even if the figure is that of a monster" (Manchev, 125–126) (Fig. 3.2). This fabric-masking technique also points to the influence of Le Roy's collaborator, French video artist Laurent Goldring and his technique of producing what he calls *bodymades* via performers

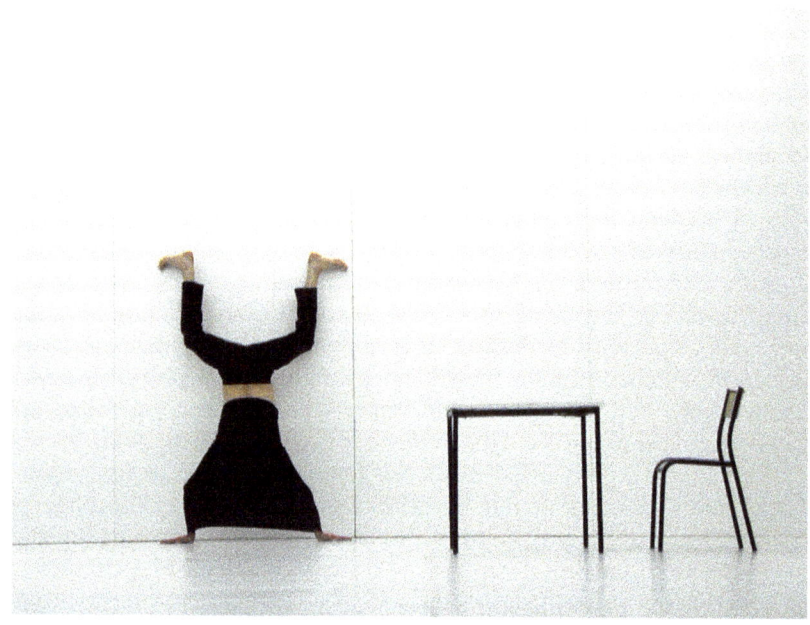

Fig. 3.1   Xavier Le Roy, *Self Unfinished*, 1998 (*Photo* Katrin Schoof)

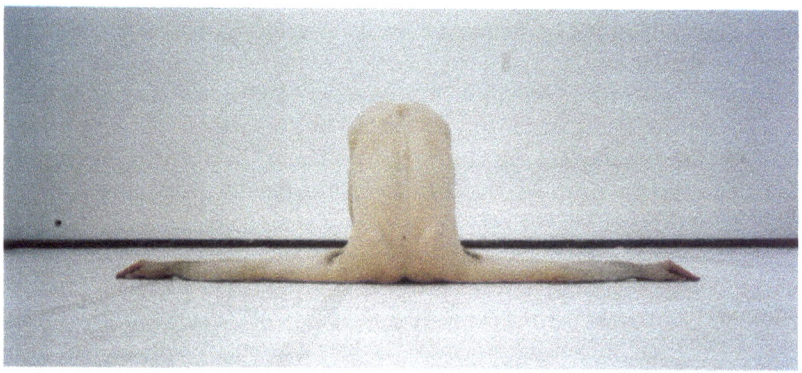

Fig. 3.2   Xavier Le Roy, *Self Unfinished*, 1998

and video monitors. *Bodymades* are images of bodies freed from picto-rial and functional reduction, each pushed "to a zero degree point where it becomes an effective critique of representation" (Sabisch 2011: 168–169).[7] Goldring has described his process as one that is "asignifying," the aim is to make a body "unreadable" via images that seize upon moments of transmission, or the ways in which a body might communicate certain signs. Goldring presents the body as "a certain number of organs:"

> There remains the skin, members, debris that move around on both the inside and the outside, that migrate and rearrange themselves, or in other words, that assume different shapes. (quoted in Sabisch 2011: 169)

For Goldring, attempts to produce a body "shorn of connotation" and meaning is to rid it of all signs and themes until what remains is a body, or "portrait of a body."

One way that LeRoy attempts to dismantle the body image is by momentarily showing a female body or body image, moving to a different dynamic in relation to Deleuze and Guattari's concept of *becoming-woman*. Becoming involves an appeal to a plane of proliferation, a level of strata that exists prior to organisational structures such as sexual differ-ence. Beginning with the form, subject and function he might be said to fulfil, Le Roy starts as a male choreographer, dancer, performer. It is from here that he must extract particles between which he establishes the relations of movement and rest, speed and slowness that are closest to what he is becoming. If becoming is an *involving* that forms a block or runs its own line between the terms in play (masculine/feminine) and beneath assignable relations, Le Roy enters into a particular zone of prox-imity with the recognisably female as performance artists McCarthy and Acconci have done before him.

Le Roy's presentation of himself clothed in the dress-like tube of black fabric enables him to present a body image that can be read as female, evoking Deleuze and Guattari's thesis on *becoming-woman*. Accordingly "all becoming is a becoming-minoritarian," where minoritarian involves that which is in a subordinate relation to a majority as a state or stan-dard of white-man and adult-male (2008: 320–321). It takes a minority to serve as "the active medium of becoming," hence "women, children, but also animals, plants, and molecules are minoritarian." Relevant to Le Roy here is his donning of a dress as "it is perhaps the special situation of women in relation to the man-standard that accounts for the fact that becomings, being minoritarian, always pass through a becoming-woman." Although Deleuze and Guattari advocate for all becoming-minoritarian passing through the alterity that is becoming-woman, in this case Le Roy steers away from a hierarchy or linear timeline of becomings, with his becoming-woman occurring part way through his performance. The very concept of such experimentation means allowing oneself to become, moving into or entering into becoming, gestures, rhythms and sensations that are non-habitual, unexpected and perhaps even astonishing when witnessed.

There are many other precedents of cis-gendered male artists trans-forming themselves or becoming woman, whilst isolated within a room or chamber. From the 1980s onwards Parr made a series of "Bride" performances dressed in a white gown. In his 1975 performance *Sailor's Meat*, Paul McCarthy wore women's lingerie and a silvery blond wig, his face heavily made up with blue eyeshadow, eyeliner, lipstick and tinted foundation (Dziewior 2003: 100). Throughout the performance, orig-inally seen only by audience members via a monitor linked to a video camera, McCarthy executes a series of actions upon a bed in an aban-doned hotel room (McCarthy 2015). *Sailor's Meat* had no script, instead McCarthy used objects as triggers to perform certain actions, in this case the scantily-clad artist performs a series of sexual manoeuvres, sounds and acts upon himself in conjunction with meat, ketchup, dressings and bandages, mayonnaise and a hollow, dildo-like appendage. McCarthy's actions range from slow rocking and auto-erotic caresses to suggestively, repeatedly and violently thrusting a mayonnaise-covered sausage into his own mouth. In the case of *Sailor's Meat* McCarthy used make up, costume and props to become-woman as well as perpetuate upon himself the violent sexual acts so often perpetuated by men in reality, pornography and Hollywood cinema.

Acconci also used the medium of film and video in the early 1970s to perform feminising acts upon himself, particularly in the works *Conver-sions* (1970) and *Openings* (1970). These works often involved body hair removal as well as hiding his penis between and behind his thighs. *Conver-sions* included photographs of the artist "Putting a match to my breasts; burning off the hair. Pulling at my breasts (trying to develop female breasts). Extending the sex-change (removing my penis, hiding it between my legs)" (Acconci et al. 2006: 210–211). In his notes Acconci seems to evoke becoming, he writes "Pulling –performance as shifting a boundary (going from one region into another)." In his fifteen minute, Super 8 film *Openings*, Acconci pulls hairs out from his stomach, as it becomes smooth and hairless it can be read as more feminine. Again Acconci's notes seem to discuss becoming: "I've deprived my body of hair –my deprived body can be used as a new body... my drive against my body results in a drift into another form." Acconci speaks of his removal of body hair as a "cleansing, opening up new ground: a way to get through to some hidden region." Acconci, like McCarthy, Parr and Le Roy, all use performance to enact instances of becoming-woman that momentarily undermine the constitution of a subject that is the privileged, labouring, singular, unitary, male artist as genius. What is presented is another body, a series of body images that exist between the terms at play, in this case masculine and feminine. Each artist performs an effeminisation in order to assume a subordinate relation to a male majority using the minoritarian feminine as an active medium of becoming. There is a break, if only for a moment from a major identity, a withdrawal from the majority, a deviation triggered by a little detail. To evade discipline and the majority for even a moment is significant, Foucault notes that each little moment of discipline is meaningful, in "a political anatomy of detail... every detail is important since, in the sight of God, no immensity is greater than a detail" so that there is the "great tradition of the eminence of detail" (1977: 139).

I would argue that in enacting instances of becoming-woman via performance, to incorporate an otherness that is femininity, artists Le Roy, Acconci and McCarthy probe the very limits of subjectivity, in so far as it can be defined by the male artist. Such artistic subjectivity is paradoxical, bounded by the fragility of masculine privilege, the legitimising function of male bodies (even when it comes to performing incoherence) as well as an ability to incorporate otherness, in order to reinforce status and privilege. These are the constraints that can be resisted, challenged or reconfigured in performance art that is performed and presented in the gallery. Becoming-woman might be one process as a performance of *effeminisation* that can temporarily render a subject equivocal (Jones 1998: 108).

Becoming-woman, as performed by Le Roy as well as Parr, McCarthy and Acconci before him, implies a withdrawal of the artist from his majority together with a rising up to prominence of minority that is femininity, momentarily creating an alliance between the two. However, these processes also activate paradoxes at the core of subjectivity, that were previously posited by Jones in relation to Acconci's performances.

The argument is that such artists perform the "dynamic of the failure of normative masculinity to exclude otherness from itself." This failed coherence depends on otherness in order to "sustain its mythical claim of coherent plenitude and empowerment" (1998: 143, 116–117). The two main aspects of the thesis are: masculinity as a corporeal style and the always-already legitimising function of the male performing body.

It takes a certain amount of privilege, opportunity and visibility to publicly ironicise the normative, coherent, male artistic subject. Self-exposure is always-already self-confirmation, even though performances of *pathetic masculinity* might deliberately fail to attain Pollock-like greatness, they also flirt with such coherence and by reiterating such a so-called norm, ensure it maintains its legitimising aspects (104, 106). Masculinity is a *corporeal style* that has the ability to "craft a body" which goes on to enjoy the status of majority and the cultural privilege of genius. Yet there is also a fragility to masculinity, it is an "exchangeable attribute" that is assigned "through the interpretive" and I would argue intersubjective "relation" (107). Such fragility extends to the plane of organisation or system by which masculinity ensures its privilege.

Any performance that incorporates otherness, for example, the alterity of the feminine can in fact make a male performance artist appear to be more coherent (149). Le Roy enjoys a certain amount of authority as an artist within the white cube and he operates from a position of privilege and authority. Although an ambivalence towards masculinity might seem "radical and de-stabilising," simultaneously it reaffirms its privileges (138). In its struggle for legitimacy, a male body is in fact always-already legitimate. Sexual difference is precarious, so that it must be continually restaged in performance, yet it is also always-already a "failed staging of plenitude" (144–145).

3.3   Becoming-Animal

Aside from attempts to incorporate the alterity of femininity, another strategy for attempting to disrupt the coherence of male subjectivity, via performance art performed and presented in the gallery is that of *becoming-animal*. This process was notably attempted by Ukrainian artist Oleg Kulik, as part of his *Zoophrenia programme*, Kulik attempted to transform himself into a whole host of animals, though his first "dog performance," *The Mad Dog or Last Taboo Guarded by Alone Cerberus*

(1994) remains the most interesting. Kulik was to repeat his "dog performances" many times in a host of different venues, including galleries and
museums. He has also performed with cows, a goat named Charles, a
caged orangutan as well as attempting to: fly like a bird, swim with live
carps for half an hour and fight with a fighting cock. He has covered
himself with reflective plates like an armadillo, spent time with pigeons
and even performed with a black dog. Kulik's experimental performances
of becoming-animal ally the artist with a whole host of different creatures,
so that the artist became, if only for the duration of the performance, in
close proximity to them.

There are precedents in dance studies for becoming-animal via performance, particularly in *butoh*, a form of dance theatre born in Japan out
of the turmoil of the post-World War II era, a response to the bomb-
ings of Hiroshima and Nagasaki and to encroaching Western materialism
(Fraleigh 2010: 11). Butoh remains a relevant lens through which to
read becoming-animal in performance art as it is a kind of dance knowledge that functions as a technology for becoming. What is pertinent
about butoh is its emphasis on shape-shifting or metamorphosis, recalling
Manchev's discussion of transformability. Butoh emphasises *a body that
becomes* and it involves cultivation of the in-between and passage. The
dancing of animal essences is quite common in Butoh and metamorphosis
takes place within a watery, subtle body that is ready to dissolve and go
under. As a discipline critical of Western materialism in general and the
mind/body dualism in particular, transformations according to Butoh
require an elastic body/mind that is willing to risk and learn. A transformation such as *becoming-animal* requires the study of various forms
and images, in order to physically transform one must let go of one's
material sense of self in order to take upon the psychological shapes, physical forms, affect and appearance of something else. Within Butoh, any
becoming or transformation involves a performer's ability to cross over
from image to image, shifting shapes and bodily forms whilst remaining
conscious and open to the elements, places and people that surround her.
When one is *being becoming*, one performs changing states in relation to
others and the outside world, the very horizons of being are transitive and
nothing is settled or fixed. Crucially, within butoh the body is relational
rather than representational, metamorphosis or embodying otherness is
the very core of such practice (Fraleigh 2010: 48).

The Butoh scholar and phenomenologist Sondra Fraleigh writes of an
experiential somaticity, that is a body sensibility and capacity widely cast

to incorporate varied materials and images. Any metamorphosis requires a butoh dancer to have a capacity for an embodiment that is relational, empathic and somatic or experienced by the self in relation to others and the environment. Animal becomings involve a rapid dissolving into serial forms, such forms can be shared and exchanged by many, so that the jumble of parts of subjectivities can be delayed by rhythms of intersubjective exchange.

It is my suggestion that the animal becomings of Butoh provide one way that artists can use their bodies to undermine the mutually reinforcing relationship between figure and ground, or subject and white cube. As I have argued earlier, other relevant phenomena are the ways in which performances in art galleries provide both temporal and spatial interruptions or breaks in ordinary life. Artists enact or activate the space of the metaphysical studio, foregrounding their labour, so that they might practice philosophy in the flesh before their audiences. Through their actions and still-acts performance artists realise physical experiments, in the hope that these might also function as part of biological and political experimentation as part of broader project that is the body without organs or ways of undermining greater systems of organisation and categorisation that were described in Chapter 2, via acts of transformation.

There is however an important difference between Le Roy's instances of becoming-animal and that of Kulik. Le Roy creates the *illusion* of transformation, whereas Kulik appears to be shamanistic in his transformations, particularly in relation to becoming-dog. A similar distinction could be made between Acconci's instances of becoming woman and those of McCarthy. This begs the question of what the difference is between appearing to transform oneself and believing one actually does transform. Do instances of becoming-animal within performance artworks that are less illusive and more radical enable more of a reconfiguration of the limits of subjectivity? Or is it enough, as in the case with Le Roy that they appear to be so to their beholders and audience?

In *Self Unfinished* Le Roy deliberately and playfully uses theatrical conventions, or the theatrical *dispositif* in order to draw attention to the ways such apparatus function. This tension between theatricality and transformation, or creating the illusion of transformation, versus earnest attempts to realise transformation in instances of performance art is another way of analysing and interpreting its history. In relation to dance history it is worth noting that Yvonne Rainer rejected the use of the theatrical within dance, in her 1965 "No manifesto," she wrote

"No to spectacle no to virtuosity no to transformations and magic" (quoted in Sabisch 159). Le Roy's embrace of theatricality anticipates choreographer Mette Ingvartsen's 2004 *Yes Manifesto* in which she posits "we live in the times of 'everything is possible,' so why not spectacle, virtuosity, glamour, style, involvement" (Cvejić, 171). There is even an interesting link between wilful theatricality and *becoming-woman*. Rainer's denunciation is contemporaneous to art critic Michael Fried's dismissal of theatricality as an "infectious," "corrupting" and "perverting" force that "served to negate and degenerate art." Jones has connected such thoughts to a quotation from Nietzsche for whom theatricality is not only antipathetic to art, it is also associated with femininity: "In the theatre, one becomes people, herd, female, Pharisee, voting cattle, patron, idiot" (1998: 108). This masculinist determination of theatricality argues that theatre is merely "a feminine mode of presentation" aligned with "inauthenticity," and a "debasement of the virility of 'pure' modernism." Why is it that theatricality gets denunciated and then celebrated in turn, by both artists and critics? Perhaps it is because it offers very real challenges to unitary identities and because in being theatrical a performer is more explicitly dependent upon the presence of beholders and an audience, it is always-already intersubjective.

In an affirmative sense then, I have argued that Le Roy's *Self Unfinished* demonstrates many of the hallmarks of the kinds of transformations enacted in butoh: performing changing states in relation to others and the outside world, evading the settled and fixed, presenting a relational body and attempting to embody otherness in processes of metamorphosis.[8] It allows both approaches, the theatrical and the transformational to unfold in turn, the performance is a knotted and contradictory one. Although Le Roy ends his performance as a man in trousers, fully dressed, he does so only after enacting a series of transformations. He attempts to create new relations with himself in the hope of achieving, if only momentarily, to display himself as "unfinished," radically incomplete, open, processual—a work in progress. Yet as Jones has argued, whenever male performers incorporated alterity, they are in fact making themselves more coherent. Via choreography, Le Roy uses the practical means of his body in order to evoke the possibility of evading the assignation of subjectivity, a probing of his dependence upon the disciplinary structures of dance and art as well as an attempt at independence.

Although Le Roy enjoys the privileges and authority of a white, cisgendered male, solo performer he literally bends subjectivity, that is, his corporeal self, backwards in an attempt to challenge, undermine and subvert this power. The inversion or transgression may be only temporary but there is an eminence of detail. A small detail, according to Foucault, is still a deviation. Any withdrawal from the majority and evasion of discipline is still meaningful.

NOTES

1. Created in collaboration with Laurent Golding. This account is of the 2003 version performed in Ponderwil, Berlin. MCB-DV-1154, Mediathek für Tanz und Theater, Mime Centrum, Berlin. *Self Unfinished* was originally created for an event about performance and theory, it has since been reiterated on multiple occasions in various art galleries and fine art contexts, for example at the Centre Pompidou in Paris in 2000 and 2014 and at the Museum of Modern Art, New York City in 2011, though it is important to note that such instances occurred as timed performances within quite theatrical settings. In the iteration described by André Lepecki, performed at the Kitchen, New York in 2003 Le Roy sat at his desk greeting audience members as they entered the performance space (Lepecki 2006: 41).

2. I have chosen to utilise Jones' earlier conception of masculinity rather that her recent arguments about: the ways in which identity and identification might affect the interpretation and valorisation of visual culture as seen in *Seeing Differently: A history and theory of identification and the visual arts* (Jones 2012); or her examination of the ways in which technologies of visual representation are utilised in an attempt to capture or confirm the so-called self *Self image: technology, representation and the contemporary subject* (Jones 2006).

3. Siegmund (2006) has argued there was a deliberate return of dancers and choreographers to the stage in the 1990s for example Meg Stuart's *No Longer Readymade* (1993). In order to distance themselves from site specific performances and works in galleries, dancers decided to "go back" and challenge the very conditions and apparatus of the dance theatre, and this is a perspective from which to view Le Roy's work both in the proscenium and in the gallery.

4. See Mary Bergstein, "The Artist in His Studio: Photography, Art and the Masculine Mystique." *Oxford Art Journal* 18.2 (1995): 45. And Brian O'Doherty, Phillip Zarilli and Daniel Buren in Hoffmann, Jens, ed. *The Studio*. London; Cambridge, MA: Whitechapel Gallery; The MIT Press, 2012.

5. This argument has previously been heavily debated and rebutted in Siegmund (2006) and Laurence Louppe (2007).

6. Importantly, Le Roy himself reflects that "on the one hand, there is the impossibility of fixation, and, on the other, the fact that without fixation we can neither understand or move forward." Xavier Le Roy, quoted in Boyan Manchev, Xavier Le Roy, Franz Anton Cramer "Dance, the Metamorphosis of the Body" (Solomon 2014: 126). Indeed Deleuze and Guattari stress that the creation of BwO is delicate and must be approached with caution "It is easy to botch it, it can be terrifying and dangerous, even fatal" (Deleuze and Guattari 2008: 169). Foucault questions how far the line of the body can be unfolded "without falling into a breathless void, into death." How can it be unfolded "without losing touch with it, to produce an inside co-present with the outside, corresponding to the outside." He adds it is a matter of "practices" or make existing into a "way" or "art." Perhaps this "endurable zone" that is utilised as a place to pause, breathe, confront things and reflect might be the space of the art gallery. Deleuze and Guattari also note that one needs to know when and how to keep "enough of the organism" there is also "a necessity for a minimum of strata, a minimum of forms and functions, a *minimal subject*" (Deleuze and Guattari 2008: 298, 178).

7. The term "zero degree point" is taken from semiotician Roland Bathes' (1915–1980) publication *Writing Degree Zero* (1953). The hallmarks of such a degree zero, theorised by Barthes in relation to writing are: absence, a negative momentum and an inability to be maintained within the flow of history (Barthes 1967: 11).

8. Le Roy himself undertook informal, amateur research into the butoh dance form, as recounted in his lecture-performance *Product of Other Circumstances* (2009) see (Le Roy 2001). In this case his research took place some time after the initial conception of *Self Unfinished* (1998).

References

Acconci, Vito, et al. 2006. *Vito Acconci: Diary of a Body, 1969–1973*. Milan; New York City: Charta.

Artaud, Antonin. 1999. An Affective Athleticism. In *The Theatre and Its Double: Essays by Antonin Artaud*. Trans. Victor Corti, 68–78. London: Calder Publications Limited.

Barthes, Roland. 1967. *Writing Degree Zero*. Trans. Annette Lavers and Colin Smith. London: Cape Editions.

Bergstein, Mary. 1995. The Artist in His Studio: Photography, Art and the Masculine Mystique. *Oxford Art Journal* 18.2: 45–58.

Deleuze, Gilles, and Guattari, Félix. 2008. *A Thousand Plateaus*. Trans. B. Massumi. London: Continuum.

Dutt, Robin. 2004. *Gilbert & George: Obsessions & Compulsions*. London: Philip Wilson Publishers.

Dziewior, Yilmaz. 2003. *Paul McCarthy, Videos 1970-1997*. Hamburg, Koln: Kunstverein in Hamburg, Verlag der Buchhandlung Walther König.

Foellmer, Susanne. 2009. Am Rand der Körper: Inventuren des Unabgeschlossenen im zeitgenössischen Tanz. Bielefeld: Transcript Verlag.

Foucault, Michel. 1977. *Discipline and Punish: The Birth of the Prison*. Trans. A. Sheridan. London: Penguin Books.

Fraleigh, Sondra. 2010. *Butoh: Metamorphic Dance and Global Alchemy*. Urbana, Springfield: University of Illinois Press.

Hardt, Michael, and Negri, Antonio. 2000. *Empire*. Cambridge, MA; London, England: Harvard University Press.

Hoffmann, Jens. 2012. *The Studio*. London; Cambridge, Massachusetts: Whitechapel Gallery; The MIT Press.

Jones, Amelia. 1998. *Body Art: Performing the Subject*. Minneapolis: University of Minnesota Press.

Jones, Amelia. 2006. *Self Image: Technology, Representation and the Contemporary Subject*. New York: Routledge.

Jones, Amelia. 2012. *Seeing Differently: A History and Theory of Identification and the Visual Arts*. London; New York: Routledge.

Kwon, Miwon. 2005. One Place After Another: Notes on Site Specificity. In *Theory in Contemporary Art Since 1985*, eds. Zoya Kocur and Simon Leung, 32–54. Malden: Blackwell Publishing.

Le Roy, Xavier. 2001. 4 P.M to 5 P.M. Product of Circumstances. In *Laboratorium*, eds. Hans Ulrich Obrist and Barbara Vanderlinden, 191–199. Antwerp: Dumont, Antwerpen Open, Roomade.

Lepecki, André. 2006. *Exhausting Dance: Performance and the Politics of Movement*. New York: Routledge.

Louppe, Laurence. 2007. *Poétique de la danse contemporaine (suite)*. Brussels: Contredanse.

Manchev, Boyan, Le Roy, Xavier, and Cramer, Franz Anton. 2014. Dance, the Metamorphosis of the Body. In *Danse: An Anthology*, ed. Noémie Solomon, 117–129. Dijon: Les presses du réel.

McCarthy, Paul. 2015. Barbarian God: West Coast Performance. Artist talk presented as part of the exhibition Existenz Palast, Theo Altenberg, Volksbühne am Rosa-Luxemburg-Platz, Berlin, September 6, 2015.

Molesworth, Helen. 2003. *Work Ethic*. University Park, PA: Pennsylvania State University Press.

O'Doherty, Brian. 1986. *Inside the White Cube: The Ideology of the Gallery Space*. San Francisco: The Lapis Press.

Sabisch, Petra. 2011. *Choreographing Relations: Practical Philosophy and Contemporary Choreography*. München: epodium.

Schneider, Rebecca. 2005. Solo Solo Solo. In *After Criticism: New Responses to Art and Performance*, ed. Gavin Butt, 23–47. Malden, MA: Blackwell, 2005.

Siegmund, Gerald. 2006 *Abwesenheit: Eine Performative Ästhetik des Tanzes. William Forsythe, Jérôme Bel, Xavier Le Roy, Meg Stuart.* Bielefeld: Transcript Verlag.

Solomon, Noémie. 2014. *Danse: An Anthology.* Dijon: Les presses du réel.

van Bruggen, Coosje. 2012. Sounddance (1988). In *The Studio*, ed. Jens Hoffmann, 80–83. London; Cambridge, MA: Whitechapel Gallery; The MIT Press.

Watkins, Jonathan, and Kermode, Deborah. 2001. *Oleg Kulik: Art Animal.* Birmingham: Ikon Gallery, 2001.

CHAPTER 4

Human, Non-human and Post-human Moving Together: Tino Sehgal and Alicia Frankovich

Moving through a door left ajar into a gallery space, at first the room seems empty. Then I notice someone on the floor, by one white wall. She rolls and rolls, often her back and head are on the cement floor and her legs are bent. She rolls onto her side, her weight on her shoulder, then from her shoulder she rotates onto her stomach with her legs extended. Sometimes she stays on her back, her feet stay flat on the floor and she moves her torso to the side. At other times she lies on her back as if she were sitting on a chair with her feet on the wall. She moves slowly. At one point she slides on her back away from the wall. She spreads out like a starfish, arms apart from her torso and legs more than hip-width apart. She lies there flat and a little spread. Just lying on the floor. After a while she brings her knees up towards her body in a diamond shape until they are both bent on either side like a frog. She then moves one shoulder towards one knee and uses the momentum to lift her head and body until she is sitting. She then moves back to the wall and continues a slow, aimless sort of progress around the wall and floor. Rolling and rolling. There is another component to her movements, sometimes when her head is very close to the wall she brings her legs bent up beneath herself, then, sitting on her feet with the crown of her head against the wall she brings her hands together and creates a rectangular shape with her fingers on the floor. Slowly, whilst peering through this rectangle she

V. Wynne-Jones, *Choreographing Intersubjectivity in Performance Art*, New World Choreographies, https://Doi.org/10.1007/978-3-030-40585-4_4

rotates her body around, maintaining the same orientation of head and fingers. As she moves around, she peers through the aperture of fingers, looking through it in order to see her audience. She continues to roll with the rectangle of fingers held before her face until one shoulder makes contact with the ground again and the rectangle is disassembled, her arms and hands return to the sides of her body.

The situation just described was one instance of *Instead of allowing some thing to rise up to your face dancing bruce and dan and other things* (2000) by Berlin-based choreographer and artist Tino Sehgal.[1] As art historian Dorothea Von Hantelmann explains, Sehgal does not allow any visual documentation of his work, so that direct experience, as well as oral and textual description of the kind given above, are extremely important. For as long as *Instead of allowing...* was being exhibited, every hour of every day that the gallery was open, a dancer performed, executing a choreography that involves heavy, weighted and slow rolling movements along the ground. Every now and then, each dancer was replaced by a new one who lay down taking the exact same position, continuing the movement, whilst the first dancer stood up and left. The choreography of *Instead of allowing...* physically quotes works by performance artists Bruce Nauman (*Tony Sinking into the floor, Face up and Face down; Elke allowing the floor to rise up over her, Face up* and *Wall Floor Positions*, 1968) and Dan Graham (*Roll*, 1970). Whereas the performance of attempting to sink into the floor and the assuming of certain positions between wall and floor was taken from Nauman's works, the way in which Sehgal's dancer creates the camera shape with her fingers is a reference to Graham's *Roll* in which the artist filmed himself rolling around on the ground whilst simultaneously holding a camera (Von Hantelmann 2010: 132). In quoting such works, Sehgal self-consciously engages with art history, he explicitly inserts choreography, that is a "choreographed body," into a contemporary art context. Such an insertion justifies the point made earlier in Chapter 1, that the traffic between the museum and dance is not one-way and that choreography has something to gain from the history of art. *Instead of allowing...* is a situation that unfolds in time–space, as Von Hantelmann writes "the work is the situation including the viewer." She reflects on the piece's title:

> The extra space between *some* and *thing* in the title... can be understood programmatically: the material object is replaced by a situation

between two people; while one embodies an artwork, the other observes the embodiment of the work. (2010: 133)

Von Hantelmann has referred to the shape the dancer makes with her fingers as "Sehgal's fictive camera" something that "initiates a closed circuit between the dancer and the viewer." The moment during each performance, when Sehgal's dancer frames one or more audience members with her fingers and peers through it, directly thematises a relationship between dancer/performer who embodies an artwork and beholder who observes, or art as an encounter that is intersubjective, one that involves a meeting of individuals, what Nicholas Bourriaud refers to as a "rendez-vous." Sehgal's *Instead of allowing some thing to rise up to your face dancing bruce and dan and other things* is a choreographed work that initiates a process of intersubjectivity-as-art. Where the previous chapter used Xavier Le Roy's *Self Unfinished* (1998) to explore a specific trope of artistic subjectivity as manifest by a singular artist, enacting transformations as an isolated figure within a room or enclosed space, in this chapter, the emphasis shifts to a situation between more than one person and how exactly a relational space activated by performance might function. The aim is to investigate how one might conceptualise experiencing or attending a choreographed body as an artwork, in a way that is not limited to visual or formal analysis. Although philosophical theories of intersubjectivity look at quite general encounters, each also has implications for a performer/dancer and attendee/beholder encounter. Such analyses of intersubjectivity are not merely for the benefit of a separated first person, the idea is that particular artworks might enable or arrange for experimentation and various becomings so that one might temporarily forget oneself as part of a spontaneous, intersubjective relation that is choreo-political.

This chapter turns to the reception of performed choreographies, beginning with an example of my own and going on to explore concepts of intersubjectivity, with a view to analyse what types of co-presence might be created by various artworks. Philosophical theories of intersubjectivity will be explored in order to disentangle and subsequently analyse *attending*. This section aims to rehabilitate the status of the spectator or beholder of performance so that she is more than an impoverished entity, an "other" or object to the performer's "subject."[2] According to Cvejić, activities of making, performing and being a spectator of performance are frequently unified or subsumed into the phrase "acts of communication"

(2015: 23). Tying into Von Hantelmann's proposition of *Instead of allowing...* as an artwork that is a situation that *includes* the viewer, for Cvejić a "performance of choreography" is generally approached from a unitary perspective as a live event rather than diverging into three versions of the same work, synthesised from the distinct viewpoints of maker, performer and spectator. She then goes on to argue that any binding together or synthesising of making and performing; performing and attending performance, within the term "event," needs to be interrogated.

Indeed, upon witnessing Tino Sehgal's *Instead of allowing some thing to rise up to your face dancing bruce and dan and other things* (2000) I thought about how it demanded an art historical account that could take into consideration its relational and ethical dimensions. At the core of this book is a question about how to respond to artworks that are part of a broader choreographic turn in contemporary art. Sehgal's performance produces certain kinds of orientations between performer and beholder, through proximity, movement and stillness it enacts a unique and gentle appeal to those who come upon it. One can never reduce subjectivity and intersubjectivity in art encounters down to discrete or fixed units and ingredients, therefore an expansive and interdisciplinary approach is required. Such an approach needs multiple levels of description to reflect the dynamic complexity of activities that takes place within an intersubjective art encounter. Neither cognition, nor visuality, perception, phenomenology nor philosophy can take precedence as they are all commingled within experience.

So how exactly might a relational space operate? What happens when individuals meet or encounter one another as part of a choreography or performance such as Sehgal's *Instead of allowing*? In the proceeding section I will examine selected theories of alterity, otherness or "the Other" as described by philosophers operating mostly in France after World War II and in the second half of the twentieth century. The hope is that Hannah Arendt, Emmanuel Levinas and Gilbert Simondon provide important levels of description for what implicitly happens in the meeting of two subjects, such as performer and observer. Perhaps these concepts of action, alterity and sociality can help to construct a critical framework for understanding the structure, effects and exchanges produced by choreographed works, as well as enriching a concept of intersubjectivity that might support a wider argument about intersubjectivity-as-art. According to Judith Butler, both Arendt and Levinas "take issue with the classically liberal conception of individualism" that one is only responsible for relations that have been entered into knowingly and willingly (Butler 2015: 111). For Arendt, the very condition of existence as ethical and political beings is "the unchosen character of earthly cohabitation." This discussion of coexistence and collectivity was picked up on by Simondon who, as I will explain, challenged habitual, functional relations and proposed a relation that is *transindividual*.

4.1 ACTION, ALTERITY AND ASSIGNATION: PHILOSOPHICAL ACCOUNTS OF INTERSUBJECTIVITY

At the end of the 1950s, Arendt theorised about action and what she called "the subjective in-between" (1958: 176–178). When exploring what can lie or occur between subjects she began with otherness or *alterity*. For Arendt otherness is shared, it is something one has in common with everything that is. Arendt argues that action and speech are indubitably intersubjective, it is "with word and deed" that "we insert ourselves into the human world." To act, in its most general sense is to take initiative, to begin, to set something into motion. Action, according to Arendt is a beginning, one that corresponds to natality or the fact of birth, there is a "startling unexpectedness" that is inherent in all beginnings and origins. A capacity for action means that "the unexpected can be expected," such a capacity means that one is able to perform "what is infinitely improbable." Although Arendt's thesis on action is a general one, her emphasis upon actions that are new, original, and unexpected can be interpreted as choreo-political and could easily be applied to the actions conceived and performed by artists.

Arendt argues that an act can have an "agent-revealing capacity," it is in acting and speaking that one makes an appearance in the human world and reveals who one is (175).

> This revelatory quality of speech and action comes to the fore where people are *with* others and neither for nor against them – that is, in sheer human togetherness. (180)

Arendt argues that action discloses, it can be revealing when people are with others or within what she calls "sheer human togetherness." Action always-already appeals to alterity or otherness, it "is never possible in isolation," and "needs the surrounding presence of others" (188). Action is surrounded by and in constant contact with the "web of acts and words of other men." She argues shared or common *inter-ests* lie "between people and therefore can relate and bind them together." Action as well as speech are concerned with this in-between. Arendt discusses a *subjective in-between* that consists of deeds and words that originate from "men's acting and speaking directly *to* one another." Such an in-between is intangible, yet according to Arendt "We call this reality the 'web of human relationships'" (182–184). For Arendt, the web of human relationships is the medium in which action takes place and this echoes points made in Chapter 1 about choreography as an activity of arranging relations between bodies. She states that action "always establishes relationships and therefore has an inherent tendency to force open all limitations and cut across all boundaries" (190–191). This utopic assertion is central to this book, for it argues that action changes or produces change. Action is boundless due to its tremendous capacity for establishing relationships, it has an "inherent unpredictability."

For Arendt, action is irrevocably tied to intersubjectivity, to act is to do something that is revealing, to take initiative, to do something unexpected, to set something in motion.[3] An action is something that happens when one is *with* others in "sheer human togetherness," by necessity it requires the presence of others. According to Arendt, any action is surrounded by a web of acts and words, it is concerned with the in-between, part of a larger web of human relationships. An action that challenges has the capacity to produce change. Although Arendt's theory of action and intersubjectivity is a general one, much of it can be applied to choreographed performances. At one point she posits theatre as "the political art par excellence," where the political sphere of human life might be transposed into art. Perhaps "theatre" might be replaced with "performance" so that it too might be theorised as an "art whose sole subject is man and his relationship to others."

Whereas Arendt focuses her attention on action and the way in which it might take place within a greater field of human relations, for Levinas the face-to-face encounter is the ethical encounter *par excellence* and it is his description of the face-to-face that has important implications for art as encounter. As outlined in his 1961 work *Totality and Infinity: An Essay on Exteriority*, the face of the *Other* opens up a confrontation with someone who is absolutely other, so that discourse begins. Once the face has spoken or expressed itself, a response or response-ability is obligatory (Levinas 2002). In his 1968 essay "Substitution" Levinas posited subjectivity as "being hostage" so that any "presence" is "undone by the other" and a subject is confounded by a wordless accusation for which one cannot decline responsibility (1989: 88, 110). Levinas' concept of intersubjectivity is novel and radical, he proposes that any notion of an "I" is in fact totally *dependent upon* alterity and this echoes the idea of radical intersubjectivity as introduced in Chapter 1, that the very concept of self is relational and experience is dependent upon the other.

Recalling cognitive processes of facial recognition, Levinas elaborates that any encounter starts with a process of identification, "we identify beings across the dispersion of silhouettes in which they appear" (1989: 89). Such a process is highly dependent upon the structures of language and for Levinas the way language operates means that it renders things already closed or "said" rather than "saying," unknown, or open to possibility. As an alternative, Levinas prefers to start with "sensibility inter-preted as proximity" and to seek in language "contact and sensibility." This emphasis on sensing harks back to Jenn Joy's definition of chore-ographic engagement as "sensual counter-address." Levinas posits that "proximity appears as the relationship with the other," an "absolute exte-riority" who is "incommensurable" and cannot be fixed or resolved into "images" or be "exposed in a theme." Such a figure cannot be thematised by language or in a sign, instead it signifies via contact, activating what Levinas calls the trope of "the-one-for-the-other," someone who has a surplus of responsibility for the other.

> Proximity is thus *anarchically* a relationship with a singularity without the mediation of any principle, any ideality. What concretely corresponds to this description is my relationship with my neighbour... this very relationship with the other, the-one-for-the-other. (90–91)

For Levinas, any relationship of proximity involves an "assignation by another" there is in fact "a responsibility with regard to men we do not even know." Such assignation is extremely urgent, it is also a way of being affected, a relationship that Levinas calls *obsession*. According to Levinas, obsession is "something foreign, a disequilibrium, a delirium," perhaps chaotic, destabilising and deterritorialising. Crucial to performance art is this notion of the approach, one person approaching another. Such an approach is anarchic, it is a relationship that resists thematisation by language. Levinas cautions that "To thematize this relation is already to lose it, to leave the absolute passivity of the self" (110–111).

For Levinas, consciousness is not all there is to the notion of subjectivity, although there is what he calls a "subjective condition," an identity one calls "ego" or "I." The *who* or *me* is a term within a relation, a term of "an irreversible assignation" that recurs. What Levinas calls the "oneself," "is already formed with absolute passivity," responsibility for the other means that "oneself" is irreplaceable, "incarnated in order to offer itself, to suffer and to give" (95–96). For Levinas, the self recurs in responsibility for others, responsibility for another is not an accident that happens, it precedes the very essence of a subject, it is unconditional, un-declinable and absolute. An extreme way of expressing this idea is that "the subject is under hostage," for "under accusation by everyone, the responsibility for everyone goes to the point of *substitution*." Levinas takes the title for his essay from this core concept, "a substitution of me for the others," a substitution that "frees the subject from ennui, that is, from the enchainment to itself" (104, 113).

Levinas takes care to point out that substitution has nothing to do with "moral qualities," there is a subjection to everything, a being "divesting itself, emptying itself of its being, turning itself inside out" (106). Evading the active/passive binary, substitution is a passivity incontrovertible into an act, "to be oneself, otherwise than being, to be dis-interested, is to bear the wretchedness and bankruptcy of the other, and even the responsibility that the other can have for me." One must always have "one degree more responsibility." Crucially Levinas summarises that:

> It is through the condition of being hostage that there can be in the world pity, compassion, pardon and proximity – even the little there is, even the simple 'After you sir'. (107)

Levinas likens responsibility for the other to being made hostage, he sought to de-substantiate the subject, de-reify it until it is "a pure self" oriented towards another, or a self "in the accusative" so that responsibility precedes freedom (115–117). For Levinas, intersubjectivity produces subjecthood, the self is unavoidably *subject-to*, it bears a responsibility that equates to "the weight of the universe" (118). Accordingly, any initial, ethical encounter extends itself onwards so that "the other, my neighbour, is also a third party with respect to another, who is also a neighbour," and so on and so on.

Levinas offers a unique account of the face-to-face encounter, one that is useful when taking into consideration the fact that relationality is integral to choreography. Levinas' thesis of the face-to-face is a profound exploration of radical relationality and it can be applied to that of performer and beholder. When read in conjunction with Sehgal's *Instead of allowing... a situation in which a dancer perpetually performs and is open to an encounter*, it seems fitting to me that the dancer acts as a Levinasian Other, appealing to each beholder as they enter the room. One of my own responses to this performance was that each time I visited the performance, I would always wait until another beholder arrived before leaving, as I did not want to leave the performer alone.[4] Indeed, for Levinas, a subject is dependent upon the other, a confrontation occurs and a response is obligatory. The importance of unmediated proximity, contact and sensibility is stressed rather than processes of identification structured by language. A process of assignation takes place, such as that between performer and beholder, the relationship is one that might be chaotic or destabilising. Levinas posits the self, or beholder as one who is absolutely passive, irreplaceable and unique to the point where she is hostage to the other, infinitely responsible, and completely oriented towards someone else. Levinas' account seems extreme, perhaps impossible, but it is worth noting that the example he gives of such a condition is physical, proprioceptive, spatial and generous, perhaps even choreo-political. It is the act of saying "After you, sir" occurring when one entreats another person to enter through a door before them.

One example of an artwork that manifests a relationship between a choreographer behaving as though he is infinitely and completely oriented towards someone else, is Auckland-based artist Sean Curham's *Gentle Resting on the Bonnet of a Popular Car* (2016, Fig. 4.1). This work involves the artist and an assistant inviting participants, one by one, to step up custom-built steps, onto the bonnet of a car, where they then lie down. Curham, with the aid of his assistant, proceeds to cushion the participant with bolsters and blankets behind their head, spine and underneath their arms, hands and legs, so that they can completely relax their bodies for ten minutes. He constantly asks his participant for feedback on the micro-adjustments he makes, so that he can customise the supports for each individual's body. Using restorative yoga techniques, as well as a soothing, gentle manner, Curham creates a unique time–space in which his participants can rest and relax. Curham and his assistant attend to the participant assiduously, they bend over them like a patient etherised upon

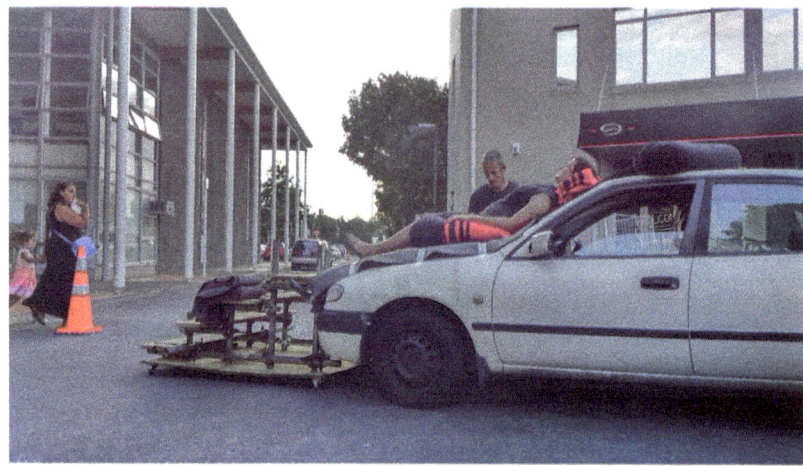

Fig. 4.1 Sean Curham, *Gentle Lying on the Bonnet of a Popular Car*, 2016 (Live performance) Performed at the New Lynn Night Markets 11th February, as part of *They Came From Far Away: Performance series*, Te Uru Waitakere Contemporary Gallery, Titirangi, February, 2016

a table, listening and touching as they make their adjustments. Once he believes the participant is totally relaxed, Curham climbs into his car and turns the engine on, so that the whole vehicle becomes a gentle massaging machine.

Another example of an artwork that manifests a relationship between beholder and an artist behaving as though infinitely and completely oriented towards someone else is Kalisolaite 'Uhila's 2018 performance *First will be last and last, first*. For this artwork 'Uhila had a plumbed sink installed in Michael Lett Gallery in Auckland, New Zealand. The artist sat before a single chair accompanied by a large basin, a jug of water, a small wooden stool, carefully folded towels, liquid soap and bottles of moisturiser. Participants were invited, one by one, to sit upon the chair at which time 'Uhila would then attend to each of them, carefully washing, cleaning, drying and moisturising their feet. As one of the participants in the performance, I waited patiently in line, though it is worth noting that not many people were eager to take part, perhaps out of a sense of embarrassment or discomfort. When my turn came, I took my place on the chair and 'Uhila invited me to place a foot on the small stool. He proceeded to wash my feet. During the process we had a brief discussion, I introduced myself and we talked about performance art in general. When queried as to his motivations to do this performance 'Uhila explained that being a Christian he was interested in the various acts Christ himself engaged in, hence the activity of washing feet. As described in the New Testament in the Gospel according to John, Jesus washed the feet of the apostles and said "If I, therefore the master and teacher, have washed your feet, you ought to wash one another's feet" (John 13:14). Inspired by this example, 'Uhila himself performs the religious rite of *maundy* or feet-washing, a moment when the master performs the role of the servant and is what Levinas would call being *subject-to*. The first is last and the last is put first. The artist sits cross-legged on the ground, his participant sits upon a chair. At the beginning of 'Uhila's performance I felt uncomfortable and vulnerable, it felt very strange placing my feet in the care of someone I had only just met, I felt a sense of guilt at being attended-to and embarrassed being observed by others. However, there was also something timeless about the experience, it felt destabilising, involving a kind of radical contact that was also very intimate and gentle. I walked away feeling oddly grateful and elated, as if the immediacy of the act was somehow rejuvenating. My experience of *First will be last and last, first* was not merely visual, it was very much about 'Uhila's orientation, his approach, proximity, sensibility, sensing, touch, human contact and kindness. It was humbling to bear witness to an artist adopting a position of servitude. There was an incongruity to an artist performing a religious rite in the space of a dealer gallery and it made me think about how secular such market-based spaces usually are.

4.2   A Relation of Relations: Gilbert Simondon's *Transindividual*

I would argue that 'Uhila's performance enacted Joy's choreographic engagement as a particular mode of attention, a positioning of oneself in relation to another as sensual counter-address. It may also have enacted a Levinasian *substitution* and made explicit a moment of what Arendt calls "sheer human togetherness." But what exactly is the relation between an individual and this sense of collectivity? Gilbert Simondon's concept of the *transindividual* explores this very relation (Combes 2013: 25–26). The transindividual is a "relation of relations," it involves both a relation interior to an individual that defines its psyche, as well as a relation exterior to it, defining the collective.[5] Similar to the way in which Levinas argues that responsibility for the Other precedes essence, and for Althusser an encounter has to have taken place for "a being to be," according to Simondon both psychic and collective individuation are problematized by *affectivity*, a relational layer that constitutes the centre of individuality, a tension or "liaison between the relation of the individual to itself and its relation to the world." It is affectivity or this relational layer that is the bridge between subject and inter-subjectivity and one reason why they are so inextricably entangled. Crucially, affectivity for Simondon "includes a relation between the individuated being and a share of not-yet individuated preindividual reality" that any individual carries with it: affectivity means "that our being is not reducible to our individuated being." According to Simondon, it is only within a collective, in relation to others, that this tension between individuated and preindividual, or that which exceeds the individual, might be resolved (32–33).

For Simondon, a unity, the domain of the collective or *transindividual* is an important milieu for any individuated being, it is a "mixed and stable home." It is the collective that allows perspective and relations:

> Relation to others puts us into question as individuated being; it situates us, making us face others as being young or old, sick or healthy, strong or weak, man or woman: yet we are not young or old absolutely in this relation; we are younger or older than another; we are stronger or weaker as well. (34–35)

Elaborating somewhat paradoxically on the subjectivity-intersubjectivity relation, for Simondon, the collective results from a specific *operation of individuation*. Of note is the example Simondon gives of a type of encounter or ordeal that allows a subject to encounter the transindividual, "a mode of relation to others constitutive of collective individuation." The encounter is between Nietzsche's fictional character Zarathustra and a tightrope walker who has been abandoned by the crowd and lies crushed on the ground before him. Zarathustra feels himself to be the brother of this man, and carries off his corpse to give it a proper burial (Coombes 2013: 36–38; Nietzsche 1969: 48).

Simondon uses this fictional encounter to contrast a transindividual relation with one that is *inter-individual*. Within the narrative, the tightrope walker is, "in fact, one of the most ordinary beings to be found." The moment when he becomes absolutely ordinary is his fatal fall, this incident strips him of his "quality of tightrope walker" so that he can become for Zarathustra "the vector of a relation of another type" rather than the inter-individual. The preindividual share or zone "remains uneffectuated by any functional relation between individuals" and it is through this that the collective arises. For Simondon, the inter-individual relation is that which links individuals, on the basis of their roles and lives within society, it involves the individual entering into a relation with others, so that she appears to herself in her own eyes as "a sum total of social images" and is part of the "constituted human community." The tightrope-walker's fall breaks the functional inter-individual relationship, that of performer and mark and it allows another subject, one stripped of his social function, to appear in his more-than-individuality. Zarathustra is then forced as a subject to become aware of what in himself is more-than-individual and to become engaged in the ordeal called forth by this discovery. Such an intersubjective event, according to Simondon is *disindividuating*, it provokes an interrogation of the subject, what Simondon calls "a momentary loosening of the hold of constituted individuality, that is engulfed by the preindividual." As synthesised by Combes: "transindividual disindividuation is the condition for new individuation."

A relation that is not inter-individual, but *transindividual* is one "whose establishment calls forth the momentary suspension of all inter-individual relations" (Combes 2013: 44). Simondon argues that there are in fact two modes of sociality, the *inter-individual* involves the enclosure of humans in their function or role and the other mode is the *transindividual relation* that, echoing Levinas, demonstrates a potential for "becoming others." *Inter-individual* relations are more likely to be choreo-policing and *transindividual* are more choreo-political. Simondon conceives of the social as a site of specific individuations, so that the relation between individual and society can be re-thought in terms of a "processual and emergent sociality." With the notion of the *transindividual* Simondon proposes a new manner of conceiving the system of relations between subject and intersubjectivity, or individual and society. He argues that the social *results from individuation*. It is only a group that has the ability to individuate, and a group is the very movement of self-constitution of the collective. Such an individuation is at once an individuation *of the group* and an individuation *of grouped individuals*.[6]

To be human, according to Simondon, is to be essentially incomplete, a bearer of potentials "of uneffectuated real possibility," the human carries within it a "charge" of preindividual reality, a "reserve of being as yet nonpolarized, available, awaiting." For Simondon, the transindividual is "an impersonal zone of subjects that is simultaneously a molecular or intimate dimension of the collective itself" (52). Accordingly, the collective is an individuation that is transindividual, it reunites the natures that are borne by many individuals but not contained in the individualities already constituted from these individuals. Only living, already-individuated beings who are subjects with a share of *apeiron* insisting in them can engage in such a transformative relation. According to Simondon, individuals in a collective exist as shares of nature or potential and it is this that means they can enter into relation with one another and constitute a collective. For Simondon, together all individuals have "a sort of unstructured ground from which new individuation may be produced" (49).

Simondon's example of the transindividual relation as an encounter between the tightrope walker or performer and the attender as Zarathustra helps to support why it is important to think of performance in terms of the subjectivity-intersubjectivity relation. From Simondon's argument can be furnished an account of an instance of performance art as an activation of the transindividual, a milieu, or relation between individual and collective. What needs to be stressed is the way in which an encounter, one that renders a performer "absolutely ordinary" might strip her of her usual existence as a term within an inter-individual relation. The inter-individual relation linking and enclosing individuals on the basis of their functions, roles and lives within constituted society might be suspended by the force of an incident and the transindividual relation can then be realised. I argue that this is what happens in 'Uhila's *First will be last and last, first* (2018) the relational layer of affectivity is activated as a transformative relation occurs. According to Simondon such an incident might render a performer like 'Uhila absolutely ordinary, appearing as more-than-individuality. Any such process of disindividuation points to the preindividual share of the individual who is no longer merely a performer, as well as that of the individual that is the beholder. For Simondon, both individuals exist as shares of nature or potential and it is this that means they can enter into a transindividual relation with one another and constitute a collective.

Simondon posits an encounter or inciting incident in which habitual roles within society might be momentarily dismissed, so that deeper, choreo-political, transindividual relations might be explored, ones that in fact dis-individuate. Levinas chooses instead to emphasise aspects of alterity barely contained within an encounter that is face-to-face, introducing radical ethical implications into such interactions. Returning to Arendt, intersubjectivity is entangled with action, something that can be unexpected and occurring within a greater field of human relations. To conclude, philosophical accounts of intersubjectivity from all of these post-World War II, Western European philosophers introduce the necessity for imaginative, critical, ethical and political considerations of the implications of any given intersubjective encounter.

It is my suspicion that as part of a mutually critical model, choreographed works have their own contribution to make to such philosophical theories, that they might inflect them in unexpected ways. In turn, philosophical accounts of intersubjectivity can be immensely generative for the broader project of exploring choreography as an emancipatory project and processes of intersubjectivity-as-art. Each account introduces novel concepts, perspectives, propositions and provides an interpretive and evaluative framework for choreographed works that goes beyond art historical analysis. It is worth noting that each of the performances I have discussed involve one-on-one encounters; a dancer frames an observer through the faux-lens of her fingers. A performer carefully cushions the body of a participant and covers her with blankets. Another artist sits directly on the ground, taking up a position of servitude as he attends to visitors and washes their feet. Perhaps it is by reducing an art encounter to something that takes place between one performer and one beholder, that artists can concentrate on exploring the choreo-political. A encounter that is reduced in complexity means that more attention can be paid to crafting and inflecting such particular instances of intersubjectivity with care, taking into consideration the ethics of such encounters and harking back to Levinas' *face-to-face* as a discrete relationship with a singularity, deliberately authoring assignation, identification, anarchic approaches, proximity, pre-linguistic sensibility and contact with an incommensurable other.

This chapter began with a description of an experience of Tino Sehgal's *Instead of allowing some thing to rise up to your face dancing bruce and dan and other things* (2000) that was elaborated upon with the aid of philosophers from the second half of the twentieth century, each with unique ways of theorising the inter-personal. But the question remains, how might twenty-first century thought re-invigorate received concepts of intersubjectivity? And what is the impact of such novel concepts on choreographed artworks?

4.3   An Unruly Mob: Swarming, Social Bonding and the Multitude

According to Helen Rees Leahy's thesis, a *performing museology* promotes the museum as a site of social and corporeal practices (2012: 2–3). As part of such a philosophy a museum might choose to temporarily "unsettle spectatorship" or deliberately change the usual script and familiar choreography of viewing. Leahy argues that the annual commissions for the Turbine Hall in the Tate Modern in London such as Sehgal's three month performance *These associations* (2012) often interrogate relationships between bodies, artworks and space. Although at first *These associations* may seem amorphous and spontaneous, it in fact realised very complex, specific and authoritative relations between choreographer/artist, his participants and museum visitors. The performance was built around an east–west pendulum movement, a response to the Turbine Hall's division into two distinct, lopsided spaces (one level, one sloping; one leading nowhere, one open-ended). The work explored processes of intersubjectivity-as-art, involving a cluster or collective of individuals, 300 in total who were chosen for "certain qualities of openness, subtlety, curiosity towards the other, and the ability to engage in reflective conversation without dominating it" (Gratza 2013: 21–22). They were also expected to sing, withstand high amounts of physical activity and move in a coordinated fashion.[7]

The participants performed free association or flow, breathing life into the hall, making it resonate with their voices, animating it with gestures, walking, jogging, running up and down, sitting, kneeling or lying down on its polished concrete floor for hours on end. One way of conceiving Sehgal's performers is as a collective or *human swarm*, a group of individuals who have been recruited and who subsequently gather (Al-Rifaie et al. 2012: 328). The work makes manifest Erin Manning's thesis of choreography as a relational assemblage. Throughout the performance, individual participants could choose to separate themselves from the group to address a visitor, couple or small group before returning to the fold. Responding to a set of questions participants were meant to ask themselves such as "When have I experienced a sense of arrival?"

these interactions between individual participants and visitors relied on a hook or arresting image to capture the visitor's imagination in an opening gambit and then progressively draw them into a conversation. Such "moments of intimacy" acted as "nodal points" in a larger work that was "conceived as a meditation on the individual in relation to the mass." The only restrictions to these conversations were that they could not discuss the work itself or art in general. Occasionally participants would holler "This piece is called *These associations* and it's by Tino Sehgal."

These associations "explores the differences between the collective or swarm and the individual, and how the two can coexist or not" (Al-Rifaie et al. 2012: 328) The way in which Sehgal's performers moved in a group, similar to the foraging or flocking behaviour of social insects and animals, demonstrated collective intelligence and interactions.such swarming intelligence challenges habitual notions of intersubjectivity, extending it to involve tacit communication, synchronisation and dispersion. There were no leaders, yet the group still functioned and behaved cohesively, demonstrating the tension between autonomy and following. The swarm-like behaviour demonstrated in *These Associations* enacted or produced intersubjectivity, evoking the way in which manipulations of rhythm, breath and movement might be utilised to create what theorist John Protevi has described as a *de-subjectivizing affect* (Protevi 2010).[8]

The unfolding of intersubjectivity into multiple dimensions, the blurring of boundaries between subjects, artworks and the location or environment of the art museum recalls some of the more complex arguments from cognitive science about the relationship between intersubjectivity and environment. Robert Pepperell argues that art can be extended to include subjects, any artistic activity involves a highly distributed process existing as a function of numerous minds, diverse materials, technologies and actions, all of which occur in a socially structured environment such as an art gallery or museum (2011). Jelle Bruineberg and Erik Rietveld detail the ways in which a particular environment, such as an art gallery might function as an "ecological niche," one that offers particular possibilities for skilled action and response (2014). Ian Sutherland and Sophia Krys Acord argue that works like *These Associations* set up conditions for interactive experiences that enable experiential knowledge to take place in a distributed manner, so that it is inseparable from the art museum or context of its production and reception (2007). Similarly, Evelyn Tribble argues that cognition might be distributed or off-loaded by some subjects onto an environment, to then be encountered by others and used as tools or prosthetics for particular cognitive activities (2005). According to theorists Pedro Silva et al., coordinated behaviours as part of a performance must be based on the formation of interpersonal synergies between performers. Coordination must be the result of collective actions executed on the basis of shared affordances or collective opportunities for action (2013). What is shared by those engaged in coordinated actions is not representative knowledge but rather affordances, the opportunities for or constraints on action and being-in-the-world.

In the face of such an entanglement of art, environment and subjectivity, the question remains of how, within the larger formation of the collective or swarm one might activate choreo-politics, mobilise one's own agency and to use a phrase from Lepecki, "move otherwise" (2013a). The performances of *These associations* explored very specific processes of intersubjectivity-as art, they were always overseen by the choreographer, maintaining his apparatus of capture. Sehgal was present, almost full-time at the start, usually somewhere in the hall or behind the scenes. Before the museum opened the artist would talk his participants through sequences, explaining what he had envisioned. Due to his personal prohibition of images, objects or texts in his works, all of his instructions or scores were delivered verbally. Participant Agnieszka Gratza noted

> The artist's presence in our midst was encouraging but it could equally be debilitating: it took me a while before I could relax into the piece without feeling self-conscious under his watchful eyes... we were, after all, only the human clay he worked with – the most brittle of artistic materials. (2013)

Although orchestrated by the artist, the intersubjective relations in *These associations* were in fact quite improvisational and spontaneous, oscillating between large collective moves and more intimate encounters. According to the artist, the whole point of the performance was to realise this tension between the singularity of specific performers and their existence within a collective swarm. Sehgal reflects that after a visitor has had a really intimate moment with a specific performer, "if you've just heard this story about their mother or something," one can no longer see them as merely part of the swarm. "Once they go back in... you've had this moment with them, with that particular person, you can't see them as being part of the collective anymore... they always stand out" in their singularity (2015). The improvisatory engine for the work was contact improvisation, a somatic technique that is centred on relational and inter-corporeal dimensions. A dance technique or mode of performance that came to prominence in the United States during the 1970s, contact improvisation's other names give a clue as to how it operates: open choreography, situation-response composition, in-situ composition, spontaneous determination, open or total improvisation.[9] The movement form involves at least two individuals who maintain a spontaneous physical exchange through sharing weight, support, common or counterpoised momentum. It deals with so-called organic bodily movement in response to physical forces like gravity or constraints that can range from surroundings, architecture or even restricted clothing or costume. There is a strong emphasis on technical ability and training, improving and expanding the existing possibilities of a body in relation to given physical forces. Crucially the "contact," between improvisers can involve physical touch as well as eye contact (Cvejić 2015: 130–131).

Another work that can be examined in relation to the question of how one might maintain or reclaim one's singularity from within a choreography is Alicia Frankovich's *Defending Plural Experiences* which was exhibited at the Australia Centre for Contemporary Art (ACCA), Melbourne in 2014.[10] This is a complex work involving video, performance and installation components. The live performance involved a crowd of participants striking various poses and performing certain movements, sometimes in unison, sometimes in small groups, or provisional clusters, sometimes in pairs and sometimes alone (Cover image, Fig. 4.2). All of the poses, movements and configurations were selected, choreographed and directed by the artist and taken from vernacular images on the internet. These included stock images, computer-generated figures, publicity photographs of musicians and models, instances of photojournalism, amateur family photos and documentation of athletic teams and individuals. Other prompts were more linguistic, there were choreographic phrases such as: "zombie legs," "airport pace" or "cat" that were used by the artist. Co-opting ubiquitous, repetitive portraiture formats, as well as tropes of the alien, zombie and avatar signals Frankovich's interest in broader categories of the human, a diversity reflected in the casting of her performers. An emphasis was placed on those who were in some way marginal, transitional or in the process of some kind of transformation and this was highlighted by the filmed component or the work taking place in the butterfly house of the Melbourne Zoo (Mathews 2014). Selected trained dancers performed alongside women who were pregnant, those transitioning from one gender to another, adolescents, bush

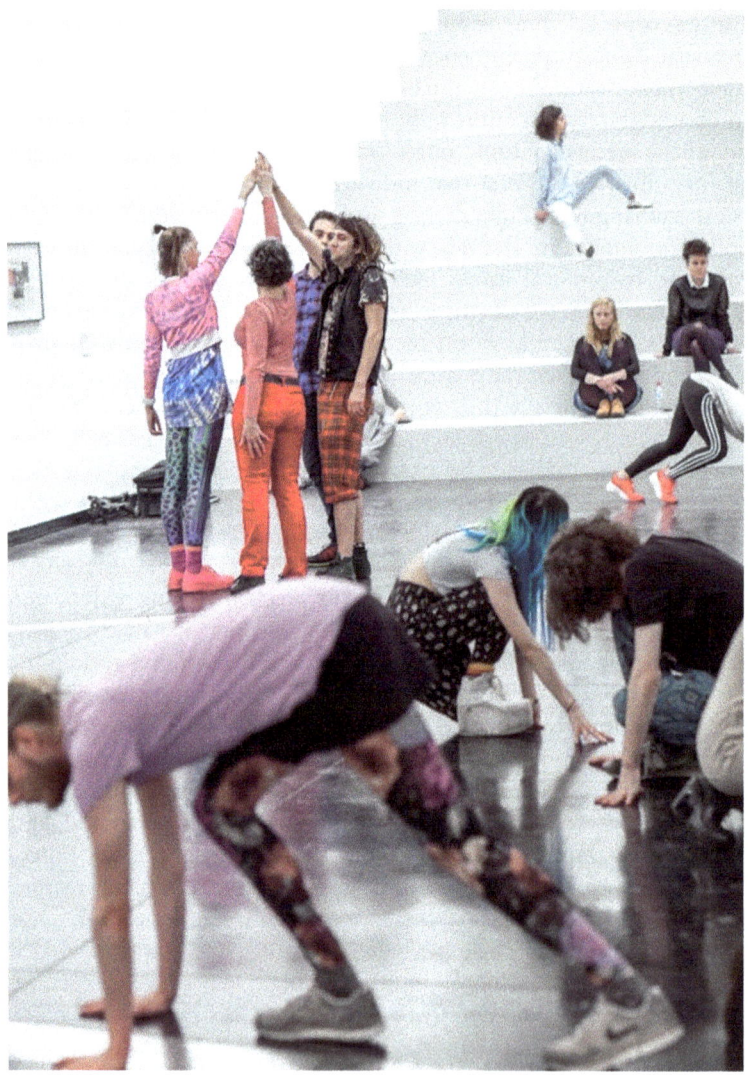

Fig. 4.2   Alicia Frankovich, *Defending Plural Experiences*, 2014. (Live performance) (*Photo* Andrew Curtis. Courtesy of the artist and ACCA, Melbourne)

doofers, menopausal women as well as members of a circus. A central "company" was supplemented with additional viewers or canned audience members who would wander through the performance, observing and occasionally participating.

In *Defending Plural Experiences* the somewhat choreo-policing convention of casting is co-opted for choreo-political ends. Frankovich puts the dissenting, somatic-political capacities of the bodies of her performers to novel aesthetic and political use, accordingly *Defending Plural Experiences* could be an instance of what Lepecki has advocated as a choreography that is *becoming-minoritarian*. There are also elements of what historian William McNeill has described as "muscular bonding," the visceral pleasure that might be gained from "moving rhythmically together in dance and drill" (1995: 11). Exploring this aspect of intersubjectivity in movement, McNeill posits that such practices can have anarchic and innovative possibilities, they can be consciousness-altering as well as develop group cohesion, solidarity and consolidation. There is the possibility that work like *Defending Plural Experiences* and Sehgal's *These associations* (2012) might evade prior structures of organisation to some degree, yet such lines of flight and instances of becoming-indiscernible or like everyone else must be approached with caution. There is a fine line between becoming like everyone else and the uniform demonstrations of subjects within totalitarian regimes. All too often choreography has functioned as a choreo-policing art of command, as Lepecki observes, such power is "genealogically majoritarian in the sense that it names a very specific masculinist, fatherly, Stately, judicial, theological and disciplinary project" (2007: 122).

Frankovich's title comes from political theorist Paolo Virno, who according to the artist posits the *multitude* as something "in-between the individual and collective," redefining masses beyond concepts of nationalism to create a more fluid group of "many individuals," ones that might be considered *minoritarian*, re-organising themselves according to their own autonomous and post-human principles (Frankovich). For Virno, intersubjectivity as a multitude signifies "plurality" or "being-many – as a lasting form of social and political existence," it consists of a network of individuals (2004: 76). Inspired by Simondon, Virno adds that the singularities within the multitude exist at a "point of arrival" they are "the ultimate result of a *process of individuation*." The individual in Virno's multitude "is the final stage of a process beyond which there is nothing else, because everything else has already taken place." Frankovich's performers enact intersubjective relations by forming provisional alliances, families and groupings, only to disperse again.

The concept of the *swarm* activates tensions between the inhuman and the post-human. Swarming is a collective activity that vibrates between subjectivity and intersubjectivity, between the swarm as a group and the crowd as a multiplicity, between bodies that subsume through contamination and bodies that might articulate.[11] Acts of swarming involve gathering, then breaking apart, becoming-molecular, only to re-group and re-form again in various configurations. Sehgal and Frankovich activate this vibration and problematize binaries of molar/molecular and majoritarian/minoritarian choreography through transversality or a passing through, so that swarming might be free from the molar/majoritarian but not be so molecularised that it is purely a stochastic indulgence.

Lepecki unravels choreographic autocracy and obedience utilising a concept of *leadingfollowing* according to which "to follow is to initiate," where "initiate" blurs and confuses "leading" and "following" (2013b). Rather than the model of an artist as author choreographing a crowd of bodies *en masse*, there might be what Lepecki describes as "a formation of an a-personal force field of actions and counter actions, emerging and dissolving as ever-multiplying actions and counter actions." So the question remains as to how the performers initiated-followed, exercised their freedom and maintained their singularity from within Frankovich's choreography or art of command.

Within the choreographed work, Frankovich's multitude moved together, sometimes performing actions in a coordinated way, sometimes acting separately. Performance theorist Kai van Eikels points out that self-induced synchronisation never leads to perfect uniformity but always retains a difference between the rhythms, the reality of "doing things together separately" is that there is the freedom of going on to do something that has already been started (2012). This is demonstrated in Frankovich's performers' frequent hesitations, the lags and pauses between each action and position. They are different ages, have different body types, levels of fitness, training and levels of discipline. They never move completely in unison, there are irregularities, different rhythms and paces as each performer takes their time, adjusts themselves, negotiate their space or territory, silently engages their partners or groups before then executing various attitudes or tableaux. Frankovich remembered that "there were diverse instances of re-embodiment or plural ways of doing things... rather than an assimilation into one mode of behaviour" (2015). Similarly, curator Hannah Mathews perceived that

> each participant/performer definitely performed their singularity ... as each instruction was open to individual interpretation even when performing in a small or dispersed group ... Each person was also chosen individually, one at a time in relation to another rather than as one block-like links forming. I think the way Alicia approached the casting reflects a real focus on the individual among the collective. The collective wasn't 'right' without each individual being 'right'. (2014)

4.4   SINGULARITY AND DISSENSUS: FÉLIX GUATTARI AND INTERSUBJECTIVITY

These ideas of moving together separately, maintaining singularity and individuality from within a broader social whole, as mentioned by both Frankovich and Mathews, tie into the way intersubjectivity was theorised by Guattari as something inextricably linked to broader political, economic and psychic structures.[12] He stresses the importance of *singularity* (2000: 31) and the cultivation of *dissensus* in the face of "an erosion of subjectivities" (50). The prospect of such dissensus is crucial to the following chapters of this book, particularly in relation to the idea of choreography as an emancipatory project. For Guattari, singularisation might be a method for distancing oneself from normal or normalised subjectivity, allowing one to obtain for oneself "a bare minimum of existential territories" (33). There is an emphasis here on action or "effective practices of experimentation" rather than philosophical speculation (translators note, 76). Guattari stresses the importance of interrogating how subjectivity is produced, so that the components of such mechanisms that might instead be utilised for the purposes of "individual and/or collective resingularization" (34–35).

Challenging oppositional structures such as subject/object, self/other, subjectivity/intersubjectivity, Guattari focuses on *ecology*, which enables a questioning of subjectivity and its accompanying capitalistic power formations. Similar to Levinas, Guattari wishes to preserve the asperity or harshness of otherness, he describes individual and collective "human modes of life," which he lists as "kinship networks," "domestic life," "family and married life" as well as "neighbourhood relations" (27).[13]

Guattari valorises relationships between subjectivity and its exteriority—be it social, animal, vegetable or Cosmic. This ties into Sabisch's point about choreography as a relational assemblage as well as Laermans' thesis of explorative associating. For Guattari, individual and collective subjective groupings are in fact "works in progress." They have the potential to develop and proliferate with the aid of practices and extending beyond the "existential territories" they have already been assigned to (40).

As part of what he calls an *ecosophy*, Guattari champions an "ethico-political" and "aesthetic" articulation between three ecological registers: human subjectivity, social relations and the environment (28).[14] What makes this articulation ethical is the responsibility and engagement required of anyone in a position to intervene in individual and collective psychical proceedings. By aesthetic, Guattari means that everything must be continually reinvented, starting again from scratch so that processes do not become trapped in a "cycle of deathly repetition" (39). Social ecosophy consists of developing specific processes and practices that might modify and reinvent the ways in which one lives in various capacities, groupings and contexts. For Guattari what is at stake is "a question of literally reconstructing the modalities of group-being," through the implementation of "effective practices of experimentation, as much on a microsocial level as on a larger institutional scale." Although Guattari warns that one must not distinguish between psychical, social and environmental actions, it is his discussion of *social ecology* and his work towards "rebuilding human relations at every level of the socius" (49) that is most relevant to this book. Guattari describes ecological practices as ones that seek out potential vectors of subjectification and singularisation, ones that "generally seek something that runs counter to the 'normal' order of things" (45). Guattari's thesis supports Bourriaud's description of artworks that engineer intersubjectivity by inventing alternative models or forms of sociability. For Guattari, a gentle de-territorialisation might enable groupings to evolve in a constructive, processual fashion. The principle specific to social ecology concerns what Guattari calls a "group Eros," a fascination with human groups of differing sizes. The emphasis is on the ways in which a given subjectivity, with its attendant mental ecology, might be reorganised in relation to intersubjective subject-groups that open broadly onto the socius and the Cosmos, rather than simple structures, stock identifications or triangulations such as me/you, she/he, father/mother/child (57, 60).

The ecological practices described by Guattari are highly relevant to a discussion of performance art, in particular the choreo-political project of re-distributing and re-inventing bodies. Guattari declares the need for "new social and aesthetic practices, new practices of the Self in relation to the other, to the foreign, the strange – a whole programme" (68) that could be read as a call to arms for artists and choreographers. Guattari hoped that so-called "new ecological practices," ones that are "micropolitical" and "microsocial" might "processually activate isolated and repressed singularities that are just turning in circles" creating "new solidarities" and a "new gentleness" (50–51). Such innovative practices should involve the creation of "alternative experiences" that are centred on a respect for singularity (59) as mentioned earlier by Kolb. Guattari posits that such ecological practices might be created in the hope that "if someone encounters creative autonomy in one domain, they might practice it in others," practices can act as a "catalyst for a gradual reforging and renewal of humanity's confidence in itself starting at the most miniscule level... to counter the pervasive atmosphere of dullness and passivity" (69).

In terms of reading Frankovich's *Defending Plural Experiences* as a choreographed work that enacts intersubjectivity and produces it for the duration of the work in ways that can affect new intersubjectivities, this is supported by Guattari's idea of practices of experimentation on a microsocial level that might develop diverse modalities of group-being, ones that might enable a distancing from normalised subjectivity through processes of singularization (2000: 27–35). Frankovich can be said to use a principle of "group-Eros" as she organises and re-organises human groupings and experiments with social configurations. Each individual who took part in the performance, possessed their own differences and singularities. Each was temporarily summoned together into a multitude or crowd, as part of a choreographed work in order to be together separately for a spell, to be managed in processes of choreography, *leadingfollowing* or being together separately.

4.5   The Posthuman: Post-Anthropocentrism, Darkness and De-familiarisation

Another novel approach to intersubjectivity can be constructed from Rosi Braidotti's post-humanism, together with choreographed works that contest the power co-opted by museums. Since the 1970s there have been many actions by artists attempting to unravel the choreo-policing, authoritative relations set up by museums, in 1971 choreographer and dancer Trisha Brown staged *Walking on the Gallery Wall* at the Whitney Museum.[15] As part of this "equipment piece" Brown's dancers stood, walked and ran parallel to the floor along two adjacent walls, whilst suspended in special harnesses, rigged on cables to trolleys and on industrial tracks along the ceiling (Anderson 2011). Thus the very act of walking around the gallery was interrupted and altered, also changing the very orientation of the performers in relation to spectators. This instance of performance art or intersubjectivity-as-art saw Brown play with proximity and orientation in order to question the habitual forms of behaviour expected by art institutions.

However, posthuman thought can challenge the very theoretical foundations of such institutions. In the museum or art gallery, artists and visitors find themselves within inherited structures of authority that exert their influence on art, bodies, subjectivity and intersubjectivity (Bennett 1995). As argued by Bennett in Chapter 2, the institutional thinking of the museum or art gallery is made up of certain presuppositions and implicit values, it also requires allegiance to certain undeclared and implicit presuppositions about the human. Although what it means to be human or a subject is often understood to be "natural," evolutionary and normal, it in fact masks political, ideological traditions that favour the white, imperialist male, corresponding to the earlier points made by Rose and Rothfield in relation to geography and phenomenology. As art institutions were built to celebrate the human and his achievements, questioning their conception of the human is one way their authority can be contested.

Humanism is a view predicated on eighteenth and nineteenth-century renditions of classical Antiquity and Renaissance ideals. A belief in "man as the measure of all things" promotes a very specific and restricted sort of "human" (Braidotti 2013: 13) The dominant cultural model of universal humanism, re-perpetuated by museums as the motor for their cultural logic, is the binary of identity and otherness. Central to the museum's "universalist" pose is a binary logic recalling Kojève's master/slave dialectic with what Braidotti refers to as a positioning of "difference' as pejoration" (2013: 15). Such association of difference with inferiority impacts upon the subject-intersubjectivity relation, there are "essentialist and lethal" connotations for those who are branded as others:

these are the sexualised, racialized and naturalized others, women, indigenous peoples and animals who are reduced to the less than human status
of disposable bodies. (2013: 26)

This specific concept of the human is instrumental to intersubjective
practices of exclusion and discrimination. Such an argument has particular resonance for decolonising choreographies as discussed in Chapter 7.
Humanism spells out a systematised standard of recognisability or sameness, by which all others can be assessed, regulated and allotted to a
designated social location.

Braidotti explains that since the 1960s, various types of Anti-
Humanism have sought to de-link the human agent from such a univer-
salistic posture, they have committed to working out the implications of
post-humanism for shared understandings of the human subject. "Man"
as male, white European, handsome and able-bodied was recognised as an
historical construct, contingent to values and locations (24). Rejecting the
unitary subject of Humanism means replacing it with a more complex and
relational subject framed by embodiment, sexuality, affectivity, empathy
and desire. Because it is impossible to speak in a unified voice about
women, indigenous peoples and other marginal subjects, the emphasis
falls on diversity and difference that are now positively defined. Braidotti
argues that over time, each emancipatory movement has marked a crisis
of the former humanist centre or dominant subject position. Each has
been driven and fuelled by the resurgent or structural "others" of modernity involving movements for women's rights, anti-racism, decolonisation,
anti-nuclear and the environment. Echoing Rothfield's emphasis on
approaching lived bodies on pluralised terms, (Rothfield 2010) Braidotti
argues for a political economy of difference, an intersectional analysis that
argues for the methodological parallelism of gender, race, class and sexual
factors, investing politically in their complex interactions. Alternative ways
of conceiving of the human, from a more inclusive and diverse angle,
produces a so-called "crisis of the majority" (37). Ecology and environ-
mentalism is a major source of inspiration for critical post-humanism, due
to the way in which they rely upon an enlarged sense of inter-connection
between self and others. An ecological post-humanism raises issues of
power and entitlement and calls for self-reflexivity on the part of the
subjects who occupy the former humanist centre.

Braidotti argues that the posthuman predicament stems from the
Anthropocene, the current historical moment in which "the Human"

has become a geological force capable of affecting all life on this planet. This necessitates a re-thinking of the basic tenets of interaction with both human and non-human agents, on a planetary scale. For Braidotti, the critical condition of humanity means that a "qualitative shift in thinking" is required, in particular thinking about the *human*, or "the basic unit of reference for our species, our polity and our relationship to other inhabitants of this planet."[16] What is envisaged instead is a transversal inter-connection, or an assemblage of human and non-human actors. Braidotti's definition of a critical posthuman subject, within an eco-philosophy of multiple belongings, a relational subject constituted in and by multiplicity, recalls both Sehgal's *These Associations* (2012) and Frankovich's *Defending Plural Experiences* (2014). For Braidotti, climate destabilisation and the realities of contemporary bio-genetic capitalism highlights the global, mutual interdependence of all living organisms, including those that are non-human. This has only been further heightened by the global pandemic of Covid-19. Human interaction is therefore re-conceived as an affirmative bond locating the subject in the flow of relations with multiple others. Braidotti argues that critical post-humanism is linked to a move beyond anthropocentrism.[17] A concept of life is thereby expanded towards the non-human. An ethical bond is promoted, a post-human ethics for a non-unitary subject proposes an enlarged sense of inter-connection between self and others, including non-human or "earth" others, rejecting self-centred individualism.

But the question is, how does post-humanism reconceive intersubjectivity? How might choreography situate itself not only in re-performing the museum, but re-performing the human museum? How can choreography perform the posthuman—thereby escaping the limits of traditional humanism and its baggage of normative assumptions? And how might it be utilised to dissolve the authoritative relations created by museums with visitors, choreographers with their dancers, or participants with each other? A central tenet of Braidotti's post-humanism is positing the universe as monistic, or made up of intersections of affective relations and raw cosmic energy. This thesis originates with Netherlandish philosopher Baruch Spinoza (1632–1677) and was re-habilitated during the 1970s by scholars including Althusser and Deleuze. According to Braidotti, there is a direct connection between *monism*, the unity of all living matter, and post-anthropocentrism as a general frame of reference for contemporary subjectivity. Spinoza's argument is that matter, the world and humans are not dualistic entities structured according to principles of internal or external opposition. Matter is one, driven by the desire for self-expression and ontologically free.

One way in which artworks indicate the monism of the universe, challenging the oppositions, hierarchies and categories enforced by the museum, is by confusing unitary identity and blurring the boundaries between individuals. Such techniques could be considered part of the bio-experimentation of *body without organs*, due to the ways in which they unhook separated individuals from their points of subjectification. The choreographed works discussed in this section utilise such techniques in order to probe the subject-intersubjectivity relation. A monologue flows through different performers within the video work *Gaps* (2014) by Australian artist David Rosetzky (2014).[18] In this work four dancers, Dimitri Baveas, Lee Serle, Jessie Oshodi and Rani Pramesti share a monologue previously delivered by one person. Towards the beginning of the looped film, Rani describes her experiences engaging with other young women who come from very different socio-political backgrounds. The first time this is heard as a voice-over, during which the footage shows Rani as well as another dancer Jessie, stretching. At a later point in the film all four dancers sit in a row on a studio floor. Three are on their knees, one has his legs bent in triangles beneath him. They all look towards the camera with their hands placed straight on the ground in front of them, their fingers extended forwards. Moving from left to right, beginning with Rani, the performers use their hands to create a mechanical sequence of movements, each part interlinks with that of the person beside them and flows across from one side to the other. Hands make movements back and forth along the floor, passing from one dancer to the next. Lee begins to say the same monologue recited by Rani earlier: "And there were gaps in experiences. Most people have never been through a revolution, and most people..." The monologue continues, spoken sometimes by one performer, then by another or by two at the same time, it continues:

Rani:	have never witnessed the things that I...
Rani and Jessie:	thankfully got to witness.
Jessie:	Some of which have left me, um there's some horrible things as well
Jessie and Dimitri:	that happened,
Dimitri:	it wasn't just all inspiring. But there was this gap, you know,
Dimitri and Lee:	between me

Lee:	and the other girls in that they hadn't had to go through that so recently. You know? What that means when there's complete
Jessie:	social and political upheaval, and people hoarding food from the supermarket, and you know, not being sure
Rani:	if your parents were going to come home from the day. And riots breaking out
Rani and Dimitri:	and the city burning around you, you know like
Lee:	most of those girls have never been through that, and I wouldn't wish that on them. But there was this
Lee and Dimitri:	gap, you know
Dimitri:	in experiences and
Rani and Jessie:	formation of self.
All:	Yeah.

The way in which dancers perform a sequence of movements chore-ographed by someone else, in this case not the artist but choreographer Stephanie Lake, and deliver words as part of a script collectively written by them, in collaboration with a writer Anna Zagala; the way in which move-ments, sequences of action and dramatic narratives are executed, shared and repeated, all point to the way in which bodies might act as vessels for shared words and deeds, or in other words complicated intersubjective relations.

Choreographed works explore processes of intersubjectivity-as-art in various ways, in Rosetsky's film, bodies instantiate previously spoken sentences. Identity and boundaries are blurred by a confusion of where bodies begin and end in the film *It is raining and I am unconscious in the living room* (2012) by Auckland-based artists Juliet Carpenter and Dan Nash.[19] This work problematises individual bodies, and almost literally illustrates the complexity of the subject-intersubjectivity relation through costuming, movement and video composition. The visual mate-rial of this work is made up of two performers, Kaya Campi and Marina Anne-Fergusson engaging in contact improvisation. In the video there are moments when the two performers bodies are so enmeshed and clothed in the same illusionistic black and white fabric, that one cannot see where one body ends and the other begins. The two become an undif-ferentiated mass or assemblage and there is an evasion of individuation, providing temporary relief from categorisation. Interestingly this occurs through joint co-operation in an act of improvisation and conformity to the artist's instruction. Reconsidering the ways in which figural relations can be staged through different imaginings of reciprocity and movement, in this video the figure is a shape whose boundary might be distorted and unbalanced; whose limits are open to question, open to negotiation and shaped by inner drives, peculiar capabilities and points of contact with others. For Sabisch, choreography can be used to critique the notion of separated bodies, positing contamination as the body's power to assemble and be assembled. This thesis is realised in the moment of Carpenter and Nash's film when one can no longer distinguish how many bodies are present. Via acts of filming, framing and contact improvisation, the boundaries between bodies are blurred so that the singularity of the body, and the relations between bodies are broken down and elaborated so that intersubjectivity, ways of physically relating as well as boundaries might be re-conceived.

Braidotti's thesis of post-anthropocentrism has also been explored in various choreographed works. As part of German artist Ann Imhof's work *Forever Rage* (2015) performed at Berlin's Hamburger Bahnhof, six performers took turns introducing tortoises into the performance space.[20] Walking slowly, they knelt and carefully placed each one onto the floor throughout the performance, until by the end nine tortoises were roaming around the gallery space amongst the six performers and their audience. According to Braidotti, once a species hierarchy is displaced, "in the ontological gap thus opened, other species come galloping in" (67). For Braidotti, animals present other modes of embodiment, ones that are normally kept as either a familiar, cherished "other" or cast out on the side of "monstrosity and bestiality." The point is that such an intersubjective relationship is generally an unequal one, "framed by the dominant human and structurally masculine habit of taking for granted free access to and the consumption of the bodies of others" (68). Braidotti posits a new intersubjectivity or mode of relation that has a more ethical appreciation of what animal bodies can do, recognising the complexity of contemporary non-human animals with a "zoontology" of their own (70). Braidotti wonders aloud whether the human–animal interaction might be deterritorialised and replaced with a recognition of a vital bond, one based on the reality of sharing a planet together and there is the possibility that such ideas are alluded to in performances that involve animals.[21]

Another instance of a choreographed work that demonstrates an inter-section of dance with post-anthropocentrism is American film-maker Cameron Jamie's *Massage the History* (2007–2009). This colour film, shot on 35 mm film, depicts a private performance of two amateur dancers in a middle-class, suburban living room in Alabama. As part of their dance they explicitly engage with their surroundings, utilising the soft furnishings and living room furniture as partners in their eroticised and tender dances.[22] In a ritualistic and trance-like way, the dancers thrust their pelvises back and forth, straddle chairs, caressing table legs and plush carpet floors. In a kind of foreplay, the young men seem to re-familiarise or perhaps de-familiarise themselves in tandem with the everyday objects. Completely uninhibited, they appear to react and take pleasure from the everyday domestic surroundings, the different textures and objects that surround them.[23] Further de-centring their identities, their clothing is uniform and they take turns mirroring each other's movements. *Massage the history* images the way in which the displacement of anthropocentrism can result in a restructuring of intersubjective relations between humans and objects. The video harks back to observations made by Bruno Latour regarding the importance of non-human actors. For him objects are "par-ticipants" that perform actions as "*any thing* that does modify a state of affairs by making a difference is an actor... or actant" (2005: 71). According to Latour, things might "authorize, allow, afford, encourage, permit, suggest, influence, block, render possible, forbid and so on" (71–72, 85). The actions of objects are varied, their influence is ubiquitous, their effects ambiguous and their presence is distributed. *Massage the history* also relates to Laermans' concept of *choreography in general* as discussed in Chapter 1, in which human and non-human elements are brought together and explored.

Echoing Deleuze and Guattari's theories of becoming-animal and molecularisation, (Deleuze and Guattari 2008) Briadotti extends this thesis further, from becoming-animal, to becoming-object towards becoming-earth, that is a planetary, geo-centred perspective. A *posthuman becoming-earth* involves reconfiguring and extending intersubjectivity as a relationship with a complex habitat rather than mere nature, so that humans are "geological agents" (83). Conceiving of our planetary dimen-sion, earth becomes a middle and common ground, a milieu for human and non-human alike. For Braidotti, the scale of environmental issues activates the possibility for a change in perspective, one rich in alter-natives for a renewal of subjectivity, hence intersubjectivity. Braidotti's aspiration involves an enlargement of the frame and scope of subjectivity along transversal lines of post-anthropocentric relations. The idea is that subjectivity, or indeed intersubjectivity is not "the exclusive prerogative of *Anthropos*" it can be an assemblage that includes non-human agents. Braidotti entreats "We need to visualise the subject as a transversal entity encompassing the human, our genetic neighbours the animals and the earth as a whole" (82). A posthuman and post-individualistic notion of the subject is marked by a monistic and planetary relational structure.[24] This relates back to becoming-animal as well as the concept of the swarm, an intersubjective configuration utilised by flocking birds and foraging insects.

Bradotti's post-humanism has implications for choreography as an emancipatory project. One strategy for involving critical distance from the dominant vision of the subject is the involvement of de-familiarisation, a loss of familiar habits of thought in order to make room for creative alternatives and as new intersubjectivities. This ties into what Guattari calls "pragmatic entrances into Unconscious formations" (1995: 68). According to this argument, a choreographed work might act as "a poetic-existential catalysis" one with the

> capacity to promote active, processual ruptures within semiotically struc-
> tured, significational and denotative networks, where it will put emergent
> subjectivity to work. (19)

Dis-identification from the familiar, as well as normative values, is part of a move towards a process of becoming-minoritarian and transforma-tion. For Braidotti, with her accompanying thesis of monism, such a transformation, a becoming-earth implies "open-ended, inter-relational, multi-sexed and trans-species flows of becoming through interaction with multiple others" (89). Many aspects of Braidotti's posthuman becoming-earth are realised in the choreography of Alicia Frankovich's performance *World is a Home Planet* (2016).[25] Similar to the works by Rosetzky and Carpenter, in Frankovich's choreographed work, activities and words circulate through performers. It takes place in darkness as a way of discouraging hierarchies, then tableaux and situations are lit by a torch, a mechanism by which the gazes of audience members can be directed (Frankovich 2016). The performance begins with a shared situation of darkness, oranges are circulated, these are eaten by the performers and some of the audience members anonymously in the darkness, so that juice drips and peels fall to the floor and their scent pervades the space. Lepecki has argued that darkness functions as "full potentiality," it allows a freeing of perception and is a means "by which a some*thing* else can be brought into visibility, audibility and sensation" (2016: 55–57).

In the next sequence, flashlights are used to illuminate performers holding up pieces of fabric dyed with natural juices from fruits and vegetables. One by one a performer is lit up, holding a piece of fabric for twenty seconds. Each provides a commentary: "This is a red apple... Das ist ein See... This is purple carrot" however in each instance all that can be seen are what appears to be images of celestial landscapes. A series of "body images" follow that are made up of all the bodies of the performers together. In perhaps the most pertinent moments in which intersubjectivity is enacted, the dancers create what is called "circle hands – global unity" a pose in which one performer kneels and extends her hands before her to create a curved line. Four other performers extend this curve with their hands until it forms a circular, spherical, planet-like shape framing her face (Fig. 4.3). The dancers also construct the shape of a house by

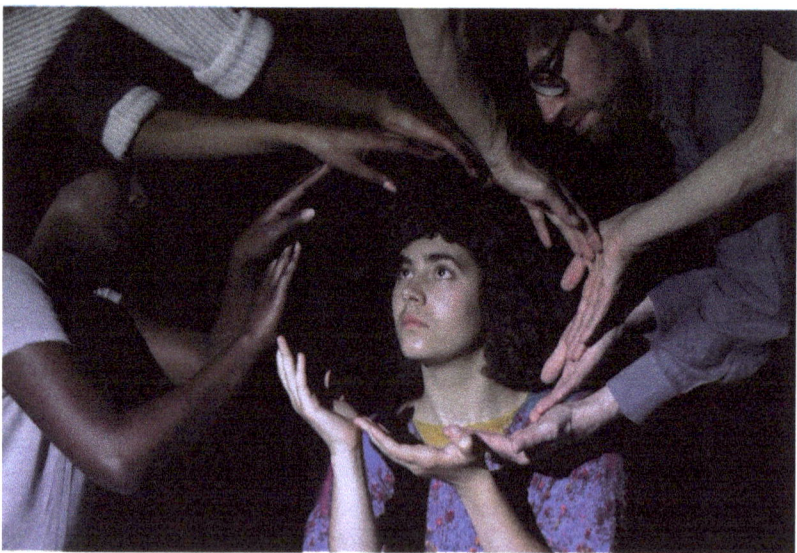

Fig. 4.3   Alicia Frankovich, *World is a Home Planet*, 2016. (Live performance). Performed as part of *Trans-corporeal Metabolisms*, Art Fair Basel 2016

making a negative space with their hands, it has a tilted roof, walls and a floor. The shape of the house creates a shadow. Just as in Rosetzky's work, person by person they recite the words "World... is... Home... Planet." Planetary relations and forms are constructed in a myriad of ways in this work, in both subtle and explicit ways. The small spheres of oranges recall the shapes of planets, their vestiges in stains, pips and scattered peels on the floor of the space appear like a constellation. Each of the pieces of fabric makes a comparison between a galaxy and a much smaller entity, a vegetable or a lake. And the performers themselves make up the forms of a house, a place for dwelling as well as a planet, with their hands and bodies.

Perhaps darkness can operate with choreo-political force, it is a technique that allows de-familiarisation and an interrogation of the subject-intersubjectivity relation is also utilised by Sehgal in his work *This Variation* performed in 2012 at Documenta 13 in Kassel, Germany.[26] Contained within the Bode-Saal of the Grand City Hotel, the work involved entering a dark room already populated with around a dozen performers. At first disorienting, eventually one's eyes adjust and the shadows of performers, along with other spectators can be seen. One critic described the way in which people created currents of air as they moved around and that they could be identified by their different smells (Searle 2012). Vocalisations were made by the performers, at first short, then longer, playful, in call and response with each other. As the rhythm builds the sounds and rhythms intensify into a "concert." If spectators speak, their words can be taken up by the performers, repeated and riffed upon until they become scat-like songs. As the rhythm of sounds builds, movements are also made. Sometimes there are vigorous dances that jostle the spectators around. The voices make beat-box-like sounds, imitating various instruments and re-creating pop-songs, unaccompanied by music. The performers dance around the space. At another point a performer uses a dimmer to illuminate the room and the music comes to an end. Discussion about economics ensues, a "talking game," a pondering of income, production and consequences. This is repeated in English and in German, sometimes in other languages too. Personal, confessional anecdotes are also told by the performers. The discussion tends to be about money, income, consumerism and family relationships. A performer gives the title "Variation, January 2009," they then press their ears to the wall and slide to the ground.

In terms of intersubjectivity, rather than a direct, face-to-face, dyadic encounter between performer and spectator what is created by this choreographed work is what Sehgal has called a "vibe in the room" (2015). *This Variation*, like Frankovich's *World is a Home Planet* uses darkness to evade processes of facial recognition as well as the limited identification described by Levinas. Evoking Levinas as well as Joy's "sensual counter-address" is the way in which choreographies in the dark stress the importance of the approach and proximity in a way that is dehabitualising, due to the fact that no one can be seen. Such darkness also corresponds to the disindividuation of the *transindividual* posited by Simondon. According to Sehgal, any connections made are not individualised, there is instead "a kind of collective reverberation of that movement, or a connection with yourself somehow." *This variation* has been referred to by the artist as an opening up to a particular "vibe-space," one that evades the dominance of the eyes and an accompanying sense of judgement and criticality. One aim was to activate "another modality," an entering "into something else."

NOTES

1. I encountered this work as performed at St Paul St Gallery as part of the Fourth Auckland Triennial from 12 March to 20 June, 2010.
2. According to Simone de Beauvoir "the Other" is a primordial category, part of the duality of Self and Other, "Thus it is that no group ever sets itself up as the One without at once setting up the Other over against itself." For de Beauvoir, human relations are often viewed as a series of contrasts or oppositions, via Hegel she argues that "we find in consciousness itself a fundamental hostility towards every other consciousness, the subject can be posed only in being opposed – he sets himself up as the essential, as opposed to the other, the inessential, the object" (1977: 16–17).
3. This proposition of unexpected action can be applied to instances of performed choreographies such as Seghal's *Instead of allowing*. Indeed museum visitors who encountered the work have been observed to be irritated, confused, frightened and insecure. Some visitors expressed their concern to the dancers themselves or else reported to the front desk that they thought something was wrong (Von Hantelmann 2010: 132).
4. In doing so I also unconsciously mirrored the moment when the performers change over.

5. Combes points out that Simondon wishes to think of the psyche and the collective in a way that is anti-substantialist, i.e. without appealing to substances such as the "soul" or "society."

6. For Combes it is arguments like this that enable Simondon to conceive of the political as something *outside* the horizon of the legitimization of sovereignty, legitimating the State.

7. I have only experienced Sehgal's *These Associations* (2012) through documentation and supplemented this through an interview with the artist. Tino Sehgal, Personal Interview, Berlin, 17 September 2015.

8. Protevi theorises that rhythmic marching, singing and the shouting of war cries may have been used to trigger berserker rage and mindless frenzy in Viking warriors. His thesis suggests that musical pulse, rhythm and breath might be manipulated to create collective, de-subjectivizing states.

9. Contact Improvisation came to prominence in the US during the 1960s and 1970s with practitioners such as Steve Paxton, Nancy Stark Smith, Lisa Nelson and Simone Forti. Officially founded in 1972 it is a style of dance composition based on personal and bodily experience (Cvejić 130–131).

10. I myself experienced the installation, including the video component as part of the exhibition *Framed Movements* (2014) at ACCA Melbourne, Australia. I only experienced the live performance via documentation and consultation with the artist.

11. For choreography that creates relations of articulation and contamination see Sabisch (2011).

12. Guattari is not strictly a twenty-first century philosopher, the texts I reference were written in the 1990s, however English translations emerged in the 2000s and it was not until after that they they began to have an impact on Anglo-American scholarship and artistic practice.

13. Guattari has a *transversalist conception of subjectivity*, proposing an interface between "existential territories" that are personal, singular, idiosyncratic, sensible and finite and "incorporeal Universes" that are non-dimensional, non-coordinated, trans-sensible and infinite (2000: Translator's note, 75–76).

14. Although Guattari adds that "it is quite wrong to make a distinction between action on the psyche, the socius and the environment."

15. Hans Haacke critiqued the social system of art institutions in conceptual and cognitive terms with works such as *Shapolsky et al. Manhattan Real Estate Holdings, a Real-Time Social System, as of May 1, 1971*, an exhibition of a series of photographs and documents with which he drew attention to the commercial interests that supported the museum's institutional structure. However more embodied critiques include Acconci's 1970 *Proximity Piece* which involved the artist visiting the Jewish Museum

in New York City and standing near another visitor, intruding on his or her personal space.

16. The profound transformations described by Braidotti include: climate destabilisation, lone-wolf shootings in everyday environments, the increasing use of drone warfare, the extreme exploitation of homogenous crops and cattle as well as advancements in biotechnology and artificial intelligence.

17. The "body humanism" of dance is critiqued in Laermans (2008).

18. I first viewed this work when it was exhibited at ACMI (Australian Centre for Moving Image), Melbourne, Australia in 2014.

19. Exhibited as part of *touch light silk screen* (2012) at Gloria Knight, Auckland, New Zealand.

20. Ann Imhof's *Forever Rage* (2015) was included in the Preis der National-algalerie 2015 where I saw it at the Hamburger Bahnhof – Museum für Gegenwart in Berlin.

21. Another theorist who has studied this topic in more depth is US-based scholar Matthew R. Calarco. See *Exploring Animal Encounters Philosophical, Cultural, and Historical Perspectives* (2018).

22. Cameron Jamie, *Massage the History*, (2007–2009). Film, colour 35 mm film with Dolby Digital stereo, soundtrack by Sonic Youth, 10 minutes.

23. This engagement with objects also recalls theories of object-oriented ontologies and new materialism as described in Jane Bennett's *Vibrant Matter: A Political Ontology of Things* (Bennett 2010). Such theories currently enjoy great popularity with contemporary artists.

24. Yet crucially, it is not undifferentiated in terms of the social coordinates of class, gender, sexuality, ethnicity and race. Although the post-human as becoming-earth seeks to challenge oppositional structure of sameness and difference as pejoration, power differentials are still "enacted and operationalized through the axes of sexualisation/racialization. Questions of difference necessarily lead back to power, the politics of locations and the necessity of an ethical–political theory of subjectivity, one that resists the neutralisation of difference" (Braidotti 2013: 86–87).

25. Alicia Frankovich *World is a Home Planet* 2016 (Volkshaus Basel as part of Transcorporeal Metabolisms, The 12th Performance Project of LISTE Art Fair, Basel, curated by Eva Birkenstock).

26. Tino Sehgal *This Variation*, 2012. Produced by Frank Willens, Louise Höjer; music director: Ari Benjamin Meyers. Courtesy Marian Goodman Gallery, New York, Paris. Commissioned and produced by Documenta (13). Grand City Hotel Hessenland (Bode-Saal).

REFERENCES

Al-Rifaie, Mohammad Majid, John Mark Bishop, and Suzanne Caines. 2012. Creativity and Autonomy in Swarm Intelligence Systems. *Cognitive Computation* 4: 320–331.

Anderson, Laurie. 2011. *Laurie Anderson, Trisha Brown, Gordon Matta-Clark: Pioneers of the Downtown Scene, New York 1970s*. Munich; New York: Prestel.

Arendt, Hannah. 1958. *The Human Condition*. Chicago: The University of Chicago Press.

Bennett, Jane. 2010. *Vibrant Matter: A Political Ecology of Things*. Durham: Duke University Press.

Bennett, Tony. 1995. *The Birth of the Museum: History, Theory, Politics*. London; New York: Routledge.

Braidotti, Rosi. 2013. *The Posthuman*. Cambridge: Polity.

Bruineberg, Jelle, and Erik Rietveld. 2014. Self-Organization, Free Energy Minimization, and Optimal Grip on Affordances. *Frontiers in Human Neuroscience* 8: 1–14.

Butler, Judith. 2015. *Notes Toward a Performative Theory of Assembly*. Cambridge, MA; London, England: Harvard University Press.

Combes, Muriel. 2013. *Gilbert Simondon and the Philosophy of the Transindividual*. Trans. Thomas LaMarre. Cambridge, MA; London: The MIT Press.

Cvejić, Bojana. 2015. *Choreographing Problems: Expressive Concepts in European Contemporary Dance and Performance*. Houndmills; Basingstoke; Hampshire: Palgrave Macmillan.

de Beauvoir, Simone. 1977. *The Second Sex*. Trans. H. M. Parshley. Harmondsworth, Middlesex: Penguin Books.

Deleuze, Gilles, and Félix Guattari. 2008. *A Thousand Plateaus*. Trans. B. Massumi. London: Continuum.

Frankovich, Alicia. 2015. Defending plural experiences. Email communication with the author. 18 November 2015.

Frankovich, Alicia. 2016. Hi there! Email communication with the author. 30 September 2016.

Gratza, Agnieszka. 2013. Conversation Pieces: Taking Part in Tino Sehgal's These associations. *Frieze* 152: 21–22.

Guattari, Félix. 1995. *Chaosmosis: An Ethico-Aesthetic Paradigm*. Bloomington: Indiana University Press.

Guattari, Félix. 2000. *The Three Ecologies*. Trans. Ian Pindar and Paul Sutton. London; New Brunswick: The Athlone Press.

Laermans, Rudi. 2008. 'Dance in General' or Choreographing the Public, Making Assemblages. *Performance Research* 13.1: 7–14.

Latour, Bruno. 2005. *Reassembling the Social: An Introduction to Actor Network Theory*. Oxford; New York: Oxford University Press.

Leahy, Helen Rees. 2012. *Museum Bodies: The Politics and Practices of Visiting and Viewing*. Farnham, Surrey; Burlington, VT: Ashgate.

Lepecki, André. 2007. Choreography as an Apparatus of Capture. *TDR: The Drama Review* 51: 119–123.

Lepecki, André. 2013a. Lepecki, Susan Manning, Janice Ross, Rebecca Schneider, Noemie Solomon, Stefanie Miller. *Dance Research Journal* 45: 3–28.

Lepecki, André. 2013b. From Partaking to Initiating: Leadingfollowing as Dance's (a-personal) Political Singularity. In *Dance, Politics & Co-Immunity* eds. Gerald Siegmund and Stefan Hölscher, 23–40. Zurich: diaphanes.

Lepecki, André. 2016. *Singularities: Dance in the Age of Performance*. New York: Routledge.

Levinas, Emmanuel. 2002. *Totality and Infinity: An Essay on Exteriority*. Trans. Alphonso Lingis. Pittsburgh: Duquesne University Press.

Levinas, Emmanuel. 1989. Substitution. In *The Levinas Reader*. Trans. Alphonso Lingis. Ed. Seàn Hand, 88–126. Oxford: Basil Blackwell.

Mathews, Hannah. 2014. Framed Movement—Alicia Frankovich. Email communication with the author. 13 November 2014.

McNeill, William Harvey. 1995. *Keeping Together in Time Dance and Drill in Human History*. Cambridge, MA: Harvard University Press.

Von Hantelmann, Dorothea. 2010. *How to Do Things with Art*. Zurich; Dijon: JRP Ringier; Les Presses du Réel.

Nietzsche, Friedrich. 1969. *Thus Spoke Zarathustra*. Trans. R. J. Hollingdale. London: Penguin Books.

Pepperell, Robert. 2011. Art and Extensionism. In *Situated Aesthetics: Art Beyond the Skin*, ed. Riccardo Manzotti, 148–170. Exeter, UK: Academic Imprint.

Protevi, John. 2010. Rhythm and Cadence, Frenzy and March: Music and the Geo-Bio-Techno-Affective Assemblages of Ancient Warfare. *Theory & Event* 13: 3.

Rosetzky, David. 2014. *David Rosetzky: Gaps*. Melbourne: Australian Centre for the Moving Image.

Rothfield, Philipa. 2010. Differentiating Phenomenology and Dance. In *The Routledge Dance Studies Reader*, eds. Alexandra Carter and Janet O'Shea, 303–318. Abingdon; New York: Routledge.

Sabisch, Petra. 2011. *Choreographing Relations: Practical Philosophy and Contemporary Choreography*. München: Epodium.

Searle, Adrian. 2012. A Piece of Performance Art Set in Darkness Made Me See the Light. *The Guardian*. https://www.theguardian.com/artanddesign/2012/jun/14/tino-sehgal-this-variation. Accessed 15 June 2016.

Sehgal, Tino. 2015. Personal Interview, 17 September 2015.

Silva, Pedro, Júlio Garganta, Duarte Araújo, Keith Davids, and Paulo Aguiar. 2013. Shared Knowledge or Shared Affordances? Insights from an Ecological Dynamics Approach to Team Coordination in Sports. *Sports Medicine* 43: 765–772.

Sutherland, Ian, and Sophia Krzys Acord. 2007. Thinking with Art: from Situated Knowledge to Experiential Knowing. *Journal of Visual Art Practice* 6: 125–140.

Tribble, Evelyn. 2005. Distributing Cognition in the Globe. *Shakespeare Quarterly* 56: 135–155.

Van Eikels, Kai. 2012. From 'Archein' to Prattein'—Suggestions for an Uncreative Collectivity. In *Rehearsing Collectivity: Choreography Beyond Dance*, eds. Elena Basteri, Emanuele Guidi and Elisa Ricci, 5–21. Berlin: Argobooks

Virno, Paolo. 2004. *A Grammar of the Multitude: For an Analysis of Contemporary Forms of Life*. Trans. Isabella Bertoletti, James Cascaito, and Andrea Casson. Los Angeles; New York: Semiotexte.

CHAPTER 5

From Elsewhere to Here: Rebecca Hobbs' Networked and Post-Internet Choreographies

An isolated individual dances unabashedly, in the midst of a London shopping centre for 25 minutes, in the video work *Dancing in Peckham* (1994). English artist Gillian Wearing filmed herself on a camcorder dancing with abandon in a public and commercial environment, to the bewilderment of passers-by, who become spectators despite themselves. *Dancing in Peckham* captures Wearing's pre-planned act of rebellion and non-conformity, rather than ambulating around the mall and making purchases, she stays in one spot and dances. Recently, Wearing revealed a practice version, *Rehearsing for Peckham* (1994) in which she filmed herself on VHS in her bedroom, in preparation for the public performance. The artist reflected, "when I look at the work now it feels like a film on YouTube" (Wearing 2014). *Rehearsing for Peckham* evokes private processes of research, rehearsal and improvisation before proceeding on to dance in public and to camera. Wearing sought to capture the spontaneous, improvised movement common to kinds of social dancing that might take place in a club, or when letting loose in the privacy of one's own home. Yet taken together, these two works provide a precedent for recent artworks involving choreographies performed to camera, ones that are self-taught and subsequent to viewing dance content uploaded to the internet, from dancers across the globe. In such

© The Author(s), under exclusive license to Springer Nature
Switzerland AG 2021
V. Wynne-Jones, *Choreographing Intersubjectivity
in Performance Art*, New World Choreographies,
https://doi.org/10.1007/978-3-030-40585-4_5

situations, the kinds of relations between those who conceive of particular movements or steps and those who might come to perform them,
is diffuse and complex, far from the authoritative relations between a
singular choreographer and his dancers as described in Chapter 2.

In 2011, New Zealand-based artist Rebecca Ann Hobbs created two
video works: *Otara at Night* and *Mangere Mall* and both capture choreographies with content taken from the internet. The process is similar
to Alicia Frankovich's use of stock images as choreographic prompts in
Defending Plural Experiences and the way Cameron Jaimie found inspiration for his *Massage the History* in dancers seen on YouTube. Hobbs'
works also fit within a broader narrative about "post-internet" art and
"post-digital" aesthetics in contemporary art. In fact, a whole host of
contemporary performance artworks engage with the internet and digital
technologies. These include recent works by Shahryar Nashat and Adam
Linder as well as Anne Imhof's *Faust* at the German Pavilion of the
2017 Venice Biennale. Dance also featured predominantly in Hito Steyerl's video *Factory of the Sun* (2015) as well as Cao Fei's narrative video
Asia One (2018). Historically, dance has always enjoyed a special relationship with the internet, one of the first videos to become immensely
popular or "go viral" at the end of the 1990s was an animated, dancing
baby known as "Baby Cha-Cha" (Lovink 2012) and dance continues to
be central to material shared by amateurs and professionals alike on social
media platforms like TikTok and YouTube. In the wake of lockdowns and
stay at home orders during the global pandemic of Covid-19, even established, professional dance companies have been forced to stream more
and more performances and content online.

Theorist Melissa Gronlund has posited that contemporary art explores
how new technologies can both mediate and communicate the relationship between "here" and "elsewhere" in the context of the internet
(2017: 120). The dancers in Hobbs' videos demonstrate that solace
and inspiration can be taken from prior choreographies that have been
shared with the aid of contemporary information technology (Wynne-
Jones 2017). Various dance genres from very specific locales, such as
dancehall in Jamaica or vogueing in the United States, have their own
stories and struggles, these can be re-visited and re-embodied in another
time-place in order to create novel choreographies. With *Otara at Night*
and *Mangere Mall* Hobbs presents *networked choreography*, the dancers
in both of these videos instrumentalise what dance theorist Harmony
Bench has referred to as online "movement archives" to learn new ways of

moving and to engage with responses to struggles from a whole range of different peoples around the world (2017). In the process of making such works, space is indeed *matrixial*, as proposed by Brown in Chapter 2. Just like Wearing's *Rehearsing for Peckham* and *Dancing in Peckham*, Hobbs' videos were shot in shopping malls. They are firmly rooted in the specificity of idiosyncratic architectural features and embodied encounters with these built environments, using particular forms of popular dance.

How exactly might the intersubjective relations involved in artworks like *Otara at Night* and *Mangere Mall* be described? Both video works involve a complex array of interactions that can be difficult to untangle. They can be conceived as what French theorist Bruno Latour has called *actor-networks*. For Latour, any given interaction overflows with elements from another time and place and is a "terminus point" of a great number of various different agencies and informal associations. Therefore, one way of analysing an action is to ask who else is acting and how many agents are also present. For Latour there is always an uncertainty about the origin of action, it can often be overtaken, or "other-taken," carried out and then distributed to others (2005: 45).

Additional questions are raised by the kinds of subjectivities present in Hobbs' videos. I will argue that they are *cyborg-subjects* who enjoy an intimacy of mind, body and tool. Choreo-political projects involving the re-distribution and re-invention of bodies is taken to a whole different level. Thanks to their electronic devices, they participate within highly distributed forms of knowledge and art, they have the ability to readily connect with others and confuse the polarity of public and private. They enjoy unique intersubjective relations with innumerable others across the globe. Though they may be amateurs, they can learn from each other as well as more practiced performers from the past and present. They can then test or try out various choreographies and ways of moving, permuting them and re-enacting them for their own ends. In a never-ending oscillation of voyeurism, repetition, edification, rehearsal, presentation and exhibition, a multitude of identities with their accompanying sets of knowledge and particular histories can be re-visited, reperformed and re-choreographed.

5.1   Rebecca Hobbs' "Otara at Night" (2011)

It is night-time. A series of large, concrete, zig-zagging steps lead up to a row of three shops. The shopfronts have old-fashioned, painted signs and all three are covered with roller doors to prevent burglaries. Music starts, the soundtrack is a reggae song with a distinctively Jamaican-sounding male voice and a low-fidelity, synthesiser back-up track. Dancer Amelia Lynch stomps into the locked-off frame in very high-heeled shoes. Lifting her feet up high before firmly planting one in front of the other, one hand clicks fingers to the beat. Exaggeratedly swinging her hips from side to side she steps up to the stage, positions herself in the centre of the frame, and with her back to the camera begins to dance. Shimmying her torso forwards and making a waving motion with both upper arms from the elbow, she drops into a wide squat position. With her arms lowered, inner wrists just above each knee, she performs a *wine* or isolations of her hips back and forth and from side to side, in time to the music. Dressed as though she just came from a night club, Lynch is heavily made-up, wearing fitted leggings, a silver-sequinned top, elaborate jewellery and hoop earrings. Whilst dancing she generally orients herself with her back to the camera or in profile, whatever angle affords the best view of a particular sequence of movements.

Hobbs is originally from Black River in Far North Queensland. At the time *Otara at Night* was made she was living in Otahuhu and teaching at the Manukau Institute of Technology (MIT) in Otara. Both Otara and Otahuhu are suburbs in the South of Auckland and *Otara at Night* is part of *South* a series of works Hobbs made in South Auckland spaces influenced by dance cultures. This work was intended to be a celebration of the style of dance known as dancehall and the way in which it has been interpreted by certain bodies and specific sites in South Auckland (Hobbs 2011b). *Otara at Night* was included in the exhibition *WWJD?* curated by Auckland-based Fijian curator Ema Tavola, at Otara's Fresh Gallery, which is located just a few doors down from where the video was shot. The title of the exhibition *WWJD?* plays with the popular 1990s phrase "What Would Jesus Do?" evoking instead Tavola's mentor, Cook Islands curator Jim Vivieaere (1947–2011). Tavola's exhibition was structured around Hobbs' *Otara at Night*, partly because she was involved in the process of its making and partly because of her own interest in dancehall culture and movement. For Hobbs herself it was important that the work be exhibited in "the same community that it was made in and for" (2016). Tavola's *WWJD* is integral to the specific context of Hobbs' video work. This video runs for two minutes but is looped so that it appears continuous, with Lynch entering just left of the camera and exiting to the right, only to enter from the left again. Lynch's solo was filmed in one continuous, unedited shot, on Otara's Fair Mall stage. As is the case with other works in Hobbs' *South* series, such as *Mangere Bridge: 246 Metres* (2010) and *Mangere Mall; Otara at Night* was inspired by the ways communities use specific architectural or built environments. Utterly site-specific, all three videos were shot in response to Hobbs' observation of the embodied relationships various communities have with particular places. The location is one that would be familiar to many Aucklanders as it is close to the mall's carpark where a large market is held every Saturday morning.[1] However, departing from the familiarity and bustle of Otara on a Saturday morning, Hobbs' work was filmed at night. With this videoed performance, Hobbs attempts to reclaim the darkened space at a time when it is deserted. Crucially she does this via a female, dancing body. By locating Lynch's movements in the mall, at night, Hobbs images a feminist occupation of such a space. This location and spatiality means that Lynch's movements in *Otara at Night* are in fact, a choreo-political exercise of freedom.

Lynch's dance occupies a space which is convivial and welcoming during the day, yet at night might seem deserted and threatening. Spaces within a city at night are also heavily gendered, even masculinised, according to feminist geographer Gillian Rose. Rose points out that spaces "are not necessarily without constraint" and spatial freedom is something "only white heterosexual men usually enjoy" (Rose 1993: 34). Indeed, "[s]exual attacks warn women every day that their bodies are not meant to be in certain spaces" (34). For this reason, it is common for women to experience an unease and fear of public spaces, particularly at night. Citing feminist geographers Gill Valentine and Rachel Pain, Rose further argues that "women's sense of security in public space is profoundly shaped by our inability to secure an undisputed right to occupy that space" and, on some occasions, even to move through that space (34). In poet June Jordan's words:

> This holds throughout the world for women and literally we are not meant to move about in the world freely. If we do then we have to understand that we may have to pay for it with our bodies. (quoted in Rose 1993: 34)

Within Hobbs' *Otara at Night*, Lynch not only demonstrates mobility within such a potentially dangerous nocturnal space, she dances. Moving on from its spatial context, the video involves Lynch's performance of a very specific kind of choreography, that of dancehall repertoire, one that she has a very specific knowledge of (Hobbs in Gago 2012). When Hobbs was working in Otara, she used to meet Tavola and Tanu Gago, a fellow film-maker and dancer, at Fresh Gallery. Hobbs explained that from there, the friends would often go to clubs such as Matafaga, which was just across the road. Patronised almost exclusively by locals with Pacific Island heritage, English was rarely heard, and it was in these spaces that dancehall repertoire was performed (Hobbs 2017). Having previously taught herself the style by watching YouTube video clips—observing the moves, practising, and putting them together—Hobbs enjoyed going out to clubs and performing them in a social setting.

During pre-production of *Otara at Night*, Hobbs used word-of-mouth throughout the dance community to find a dancer who was confident with dancehall, and it was through this call that she found Lynch. A teacher of urban dance in Auckland's central city, Lynch had also learnt dancehall through online videos. According to Hobbs, those in Auckland who participate in dancehall are "internet savvy," using online platforms "effectively and with clarity" (Hobbs 2016). In the accompanying artist statement, Hobbs indicates that her intention was for *Otara at Night* to be a "celebration of dancehall and the reinterpretation of culture through site" (Hobbs 2011b). As part of a broader investigation of specific dance styles from abroad, Hobbs' interest is in how dance translates geographically, is manifested locally, and the ways in which styles maintain their integrity yet also change their flavour and take on new forms (Hobbs, quoted in Gago 2012).

Dancehall culture has a long and complicated history, as traced by Caribbean studies scholar Sonjah Stanley Niaah. The dancehall scene originated in Kingston, Jamaica and it is one aspect of Jamaica's popular performance culture (Stanley Niaah 2010, xv). Elaborating on what I would argue is a possible temporal context for *Otara at Night*, media theorist and film-maker Julian Henriques explains that in Jamaica "a dancehall night out means precisely that, a night in the open air, under the stars, out on the street" (Henriques 2010, 61). Henriques theorises that in most popular cultures the "cycle of pleasurable activity is synchronized with that of the working week" (61). In Auckland, Friday and Saturday nights are the most popular nights to out, but in Kingston, the main night

is Wednesday and this, together with the way dancehall sessions traditionally go until dawn, suggests for Henriques a "Jamaican disavowal of the
work ethic that some would attribute to origins in the slave plantation"
(2010, 16).

In the same way that Hobbs has described *Otara at Night* as depicting
a South Auckland dancehall queen claiming Otara as a stage to perform
her nocturnal dance, Stanley Niaah asserts dancehall events involve such
a "central female persona" (2010, 138). A marked ascendency of female
figures in the dancehall scene accompanied what Stanley Niaah calls a
"maturation of Jamaican cultural expression in the years after independence of women in the context of dancehall, and during the 1970s,
dancehall queens emerged as informal community celebrities." Stanley
Niaah observes that after 2000, economic activities such as street-vending
meant that women had achieved some degree of independence and as a
result began to attend events on their own. With less of an emphasis on
partner dancing, women began to attend events with friends rather than
partners, and there was an "element of free play among women in particular as new levels of economic and social independence were reached"
(141). The interrelationship between dance and gender is explored by
Stanley Niaah who explains the way in which dancehall performers might
be classified according to their particular kinaesthetic emphasis. For
example, classically female dances are those "in which the essential point
of articulation is the rotation or thrust of the pelvic girdle" (142). This
articulation is seen in Lynch's *wine* at the start of her dance.

Lynch's performance in *Otara at Night* is lively and infectious, and
this ties into Henriques' argument that the "sharing of appreciation and
expression of rhythm" are key elements of dancehall (Henriques 2014,
80). Rhythm is a means of communication as well as an "energetic
patterning process" (80). Henriques theorises that the three elements
of the performance techniques of rhythmic embodiment are: amplification, inflection and transduction. Rhythmic inflections occur when certain
beats in a regular periodic meter are selected for additional emphasis.
One way Lynch emphasises certain beats in the accompanying music via
choreography is by standing with one foot in front of the other and
quickly *dipping* or bending herself back at the waist and flicking her head
and long ponytail backwards. Transduction is a "transformation process
whereby the patterning of signal, wave or disturbance in one medium is
translated into another medium" (82). One example Henriques gives is
of a dancer "hearing a rhythm in her ears and over her body and then

transforming this into a dance move" (82). *Otara at Night* can be read as Lynch's response to an audible rhythm, and the transformation of such rhythms into improvised dance moves using dancehall repertoire.

Within its locked-off frame, *Otara at Night* captures and realises diverse enthusiasms and interpersonal relations. On a personal level, there was a friendship between Tavola and Hobbs, both of whom were heavily invested in facilitating art of and for South Auckland communities. There was also the collaboration between Hobbs as an artist with dancer Amelia Lynch, supported by Tavola, Gago and others. In terms of the relationship between artist Hobbs and dancer Lynch, it is important to emphasise the fact that Lynch herself choreographed the dance she performed in *Otara at Night*. And finally there was the auto-didacticism of Hobbs and Lynch, who taught themselves dancehall moves by watching videos on the internet posted by other dancers and choreographers. Hobbs' video extends the relations between performance, choreography and the gallery to include the internet. It is important to note here that the internet makes the ongoing project of choreography as an emancipatory project more rich and complex. Although *Otara at Night* was performed upon a stage within a very specific site, shot with a fixed camera and presented on a single screen, any further unfolding of the work necessitates an analysis of choreographies that are self-taught from dance content uploaded to the internet, by dancers across the globe. Such choreography, that is networked, enacts or makes manifest digitally mediated relations between bodies.

5.2   Networked Choreographies, Subjectivity as Network

To bring into the discussion networks of dancers and choreographers means focussing upon what Foucault referred to as ideas of "extension" rather than mere "site" (1986: 23). In the second half of the twentieth century, Foucault described what he perceived as an "epoch" of "simultaneity," "juxtaposition," "the near and far," the "side-by-side" and the "dispersed" (23). Such an experience of the world, for Foucault, is "less that of a long line developing through time than that of a network that connects points and intersects with its own skein" (22). When describing the way that social media has impacted upon intersubjective relations more than three decades later, media theorist Geert Lovink argued that the social is now manifest as a network, the network is its "actual shape" (Lovink 2012).

This idea of the social as network-shaped, made up of interconnected points or nodes and referring back to itself ties into arguments made within dance studies by Bench. For Bench, digital networks are increasingly important in the creation and distribution of choreography. Platforms such as the video-sharing website YouTube produce and proliferate performances, as well as enabling dances and choreographies to become "archivable content" (Bench 2017: 155–156). What Bench refers to as "movement archives" act as "generative repositories of the present and recent past for contemporary audiences" (166). Such movement archives could be interpreted as a broader choreo-political project, on a global scale the significance of which is still being figured out. It is arguable that at this point in the twenty-first century, there is more of an emphasis on archival records than on live dancing bodies and that dances which permeate dance pedagogy are kept in digital archives (160). Dance practices, according to Bench, operate as part of digital culture so that "dancing *like* the archive" and "dancing *for* the archive" have become strategies of dance production (156 emphasis added). This is seen on TikTok, a mobile device app in which users frequently perform short dances that were previously posted on the same app or sometimes from the online video game Fortnite. These micro-dances are usually oriented to the front, in order to be captured by a self-timer. Due to the portrait format of mobile devices these dances tend to involve isolated movements of the upper body, arms and hands whilst lip-synching to popular music tracks. The point is that the format of the archive dictates the form of the dancing.[2]

As a dancer learning dancehall from online videos, Lynch interacted with movement archives before going on to perform the archive for *Otara at Night*. Her performance then returned to the archive as the dancevideo was uploaded to Hobbs' personal YouTube channel for all to see. Bench points out that popular dance styles such as dancehall have become heavily mediatised, so that the reach and circulation of its choreographies has dramatically increased (160). According to Gronlund, the internet has transformed the notion of public as a mass audience to one of dispersed strands of niche interest such as, for example, those interested in dancehall (Gronlund 2017: 121). Indeed for Gronlund the very structure of the internet with its search engines and algorithms means that it tends to privilege subcultures rather than mainstream pop culture.

Dancehall has thereby become part of various different cultural repertoires via re-enactment, restaging and reperformance. Bench argues for a
logic of circulation, one that is enabled by a unique and specifically "asyn-
chronous relationship between performer and viewer," as performances or
dances can be viewed online, in multiple locations and at multiple times
(159). Such circulation allows choreographies to persist regardless of any
distinction between the live and the recorded, or the performed and the
archived.

Digital movement archives have become a crucial meeting place of
amateur and professional dancers and choreographers, as well as a place
for dance performance and pedagogy. It is common for dancers who have
mastered a choreography, and sometimes the choreographers themselves,
to "share" dances in online tutorials, demonstrating choreographed
routines or teaching popular steps to viewers (162). Online videos have
become a significant mode of teaching and transmitting movement. For
Bench, such archives demonstrate a departure from earlier models of
dance pedagogies with their emphasis on body-to-body transmission of
knowledge (156). Therefore, platforms such as YouTube, which act as
digital archives of dance, create a broader context of training and rehearsal
alongside performance and its documentation (160). Bench points out
that learning choreography from a video maintains a bodily separation,
"replacing physical intimacy between teacher and learner in a shared
space with dancers' anonymity and instructor's distance" (160). There
is a transmission of movement and a "circulation of mediatized gestures
which maintain a separation between bodies not likely to share a physical space," such as dancehall dancers in Jamaica and dancers based in
Aotearoa New Zealand. Importantly, choreographies are kept in circulation by those like Lynch learning and restaging them, adding their own
performances to the mix, so that movement archives support modes of
learning, and then performing or re-performing choreography (164).

Otara at Night makes manifest complex networked relations as it
plugs into patterns of collective transmission, reception and performance.
The unfolding of the interpersonal into multiple dimensions, the blurring of boundaries between subjects, artworks and the location of display,
whether it be a webpage or the art museum recalls certain arguments
from cognitive science about intersubjectivity, particularly those of situated cognition as mentioned in Chapter 1. These include the thesis of
extension, as interdisciplinary scholar Robert Pepperell argues that art
can be extended to include subjects, so that any artistic activity is a

highly distributed process existing as a function of numerous minds, diverse materials, technologies and actions which then go on to occur in a socially structured environment such as an art gallery or museum (2011). Another researcher of *distributed cognition*, Evelyn Tribble has argued that cognition might be distributed or off-loaded by some subjects onto an environment to then be encountered by others and used as tools or prosthetics for particular cognitive activities (2005). Tribble's theory can be easily applied to the way in which videos of choreographies are uploaded onto social media platforms to then be encountered by many other people and used to their own ends.

In the case of *Otara at Night*, artistic activity exists as the function of various minds, bodies and digital formats in the environment of the world wide web and domestic environments as well as the art gallery. Movement is distributed and re-distributed in processes of research, mimicry, rehearsal and repetition as well as improvisation, public performance, filming and exhibition. The kinds of relations between those who originally conceived of particular movements or steps, such as in this case Dancehall dancers and those who might come to perform them, such as Lynch is complex. These kinds of diffuse intersubjective relations hark back to Latour's argument about how action is also distributed, so any given interaction "here" has already been affected by actors who might be "elsewhere" or faraway, both temporally and spatially. Using Latour's argument a dancer like Lynch choreographing herself from various filmed dances viewed on the internet is a specific actor-network, a form of agency involving techno-bio-morphisms, one informally associated and connected with a wide range of other agents and entities.

In his effort to unravel the interpersonal, French theorist Latour cautions against appealing to the term *social*. Instead he champions *actor-network theory* (ANT), a critical sociology of associations, one that can even encompass non-human actors, so that they might also have agency rather than mere causality (2005: 10). As seen in Chapter 4 this idea is especially pertinent to post-humanism. For Latour, the social is "a provisional movement of new associations," it cannot bind together elements in a way that is straightforward or unproblematic. Concerning himself with action, Latour poses the following questions "When we act, who else is acting? How many agents are also present?" (43–45). Action is far from transparent, it is "a node, a knot, and a conglomerate of many surprising sets of agencies that have to be slowly disentangled." For Latour action is

overtaken or *other-taken*, it is taken up by others and shared. It is myste-
riously carried out and at the same time distributed to others. For Latour
an *actor* is:

> the moving target of a vast array of entities swimming toward it... to use
> the word 'actor' means that it's never clear who and what is acting when
> we act since an actor on stage is never alone in acting.

Action is dislocated and far from a "coherent, controlled, well-
rounded, and clean-edged affair." Action is "borrowed, distributed,
suggested, influenced, dominated, betrayed, translated." It is what Latour
calls an *actor-network* that "represents the major source of uncertainty
about the origin of action" (46).

For Latour, agency is "the most difficult problem there is in philosophy," too often it is conceived as an anthropomorphic figure, when
many different entities, not just humans can exercise agency (51, 53).
Agency is important for this book due to the way in which subjects have
the ability to produce intersubjectivity and choreographed works realise
complex and special forms of social relations that actually interrogate what
it means to be a subject or agent. For ANT the "figuration of agency"
might involve "*ideo-*, or *techno-*, or *bio*-morphisms," agency need not be
restricted to an "actant" as a "single individual" (54). Elaborating on
the phrase *actor-network theory*, a network, according to Latour is "an
informal way of associating together human agents." Tracing a network
involves connecting entities with other entities (103). What is highlighted
are "connections, vehicles and attachments" (220). Importantly Latour
points out that an *actor-network* can capture a wide variety of states,
entities and collections: "With Actor-Network you may describe something that doesn't at all look like a network – an individual state of mind,
a piece of machinery, a fictional character..." (142). Returning to relations, Latour points out: "Stretch any given inter-action and it becomes
an actor-network" (202).

> It is perfectly true to say that any given interaction seems to *overflow* with
> elements which are already in the situation coming from some other *time*,
> some other *place*, and generated by some other *agency*... action is always
> dislocated, articulated, delegated, translated. (166)

Of great importance to figuring out connections is the recognition of what Latour calls a "networky shape." According to Latour, telling an actor-network story involves being able to capture "centres of calculation" with their star-like shapes, emphasising the network (178). For Latour, a network is "what connects actors together with indirect, yet fully traceable connections" (180). Latour prefers to focus on what he calls "connectors" rather than context or interaction, highlighting the "work of assembling, collecting and composing."[3] According to Latour, face-to-face interactions are "constantly *interfered* with by other agencies... action is dislocated, diffracted, re-dispatched and redistributed." Latour sets out a series of statements about interactions, such as:

> What is acting at the same moment in any place is coming from many other places, many distant materials, and many faraway actors... places that are acting on one place....

Latour is sceptical of emphasising "intersubjective interactions" due to the fact that objects, relations with objects or *inter-objectivity* introduces into any local interaction "some fundamental dislocation." Any tracing of social connections or associations reveals that they are star-shaped, and that templates and formats are circulating. Latour goes on to explain that interactions may involve hidden parties: "Very few participants in a given course of action are simultaneously visible at any given point... many others are acting as well, only there is no way to sum them up." Interactions are far from *homogeneous*, they often involve a "crowd of non-human, non-subjective, non-local participants" gathering "to help carry out the course of actions and transport it through channels" and "all of them are associated together" (201). The complexity of interaction is increased exponentially by digital technologies. By Latour's account, interactions cannot be contained, they "overflow in all directions," a "bewildering array of participants is simultaneously at work" within them, dislocating any neat boundaries, "redistributing them away and making it impossible to start anywhere that can be said to be 'local'" (202).

5.3   POST-INTERNET OR POST-DIGITAL
ART AND PERFORMANCE

Latour's actor-network theory is useful in going some way to capture the complexity of the interpersonal relations activated by works such as Hobbs' *Otara at Night*. But to return to an account or history of contemporary art, as I mentioned in the introduction to this chapter, the way in which this artwork instrumentalizes choreographies learnt from online tutorials and videos means that it, together with *Mangere Mall* are examples of art that is engaged with the internet and digital technologies or what is sometimes referred to as "postinternet art." Although there is scepticism about the term amongst some art historians, there is a substantial difference between new media art or net.art produced before 2000 and what has been produced since then (Tribe and Jana 2006). In the first two decades of the twenty-first century, digital culture has had a profound effect on the production, reception and circulation of contemporary art. According to curator Lauren Cornell and critic Ed Halter, it is this generation of artists that responded to the internet

> not as a new medium, but rather as a true *mass medium*, with a deeper and wider cultural reach, greater opportunities for mass distribution and collaboration, and advanced corporate and political complexities. (Cornell and Halter 2015: xv)

The prevalence of hand-held electronic devices and personal computers connected to the internet means that tools and technology for a large amount of functions, interactions and services—whether it be chatting with friends, finding a date, creating a standing grocery order or signing into an app that provides casual employment—are readily available 24/7. Accordingly, Latour's theory of the network as a star-shaped and informal association of human agents and entities, together with Foucault's proposition about an epoch of extension, simultaneity, dispersion and interconnected nodes, are well positioned to furnish a theoretical context for aesthetics and practices which are *post-internet* or *post-digital*, a milieu that Hobbs' artworks exist within. Ideas about art that is post-internet and post-digital might also be fruitful for those within dance studies to consider. There is no doubt that the internet and digital technologies have moulded contemporary subjectivity and the ways in which one interacts with others. Perhaps inevitably, the internet has also greatly affected the creation of art. Online networks have expanded the possibilities of art-making exponentially with their capacity to act as a tool for self-imaging and interpersonal communication, as well as research, exhibiting and archiving. As media theorist Geert Lovink explained, the existence of the social web means that *prosumers* can upload and download content relatively easily and the existence of mobile devices means that they can do so almost anywhere and at any time (2012).

By 2021, post-internet practice has become somewhat historicised, roughly starting with "pro-surfer" groups, performances and conceptual art projects by artists and educators, like US artist Marisa Olson who participated in Rhizome, a platform for the discourse and exhibition of digital art, affiliated with the New Museum in New York City. First using the term in an art context in 2006, Olson described "a process of making art *after* using the internet" (Gentles 2015: 112–113). According to art historian Tim Gentles, post-internet art responds to the banality of the internet, as a feature of everyday life and art. Similarly, the heterotopic and matrixial space of the internet has become important as a distribution context for art and the ubiquity of computing technology has re-oriented the art world around the screen. Art writer Michael Sanchez pointed out that "Art is no longer discovered in biennials and fairs and magazines, but on the phone" (quoted in Gentles: 113) Post-internet art is "consciously created in a milieu that assumes the centrality of the network" and is "art that reflects an internet state of mind." Crucially, it is also a reaction to and identification with the communicative conditions of global, networked capitalism. As summarised by Gentles it is a way of thinking about art in "broadly technologically deterministic terms."

To situate Hobbs' work further, in hindsight, two exhibitions appear to have marked zeniths of post-internet art practice, *Surround Audience*, the third New Museum Triennial, curated by Lauren Cornell and Ryan Trecartin, which opened in February 2015 and the Berlin Biennale, curated by DIS collective in the summer of 2016. In terms of how to delineate practices that are post-internet, I would argue that these are artworks of any media that co-opt the logics, formats and operations of the internet and digital technology, such as surfing, scanning, searching, coding, going viral, memes, GIFs, copy and pasting, looping, reality television, polling, competitions, advertisements, spam, viral content, surveys, video tutorials, chatting interfaces, image databases, video archives, filters and live streaming. Artists like Hito Steyerl, Ryan Trecartin and Simon Denny have been prominent in post-internet art practice. *Grosse Fatigue*

(2013) a video work by French artist Laure Provost in which the universe seems to be created via a multitude of pop-up windows, tabs, video and image files, is a post-internet artwork *par excellence*.

So where does the term *post-digital* come in? According to theorist Florian Cramer, the term "post" can be used to mean a "continuation of" but also "beyond" (2014, unpaginated). Cramer argues that the term *post-digital* describes "either a contemporary disenchantment with digital information systems and media gadgets, or a period in which our fascination with these systems has become historical." There certainly are moments within most post-internet artworks that are more pessimistic and post-digital, in fact it is often such moments that give them complexity and depth. Although online networks mean that performances might easily reach large audiences across vast distances, it is also important to remember that the social web is not accessible to all people everywhere, users or members of such networks require access to infrastructure, hardware, electricity, power as well as internet service providers (Butt 2008: 31). As Lovink has already explained, the social web, web 2.0 or what he refers to as an "Empire of the Social" was enabled by the neoliberal 1990s, facilitated by growing computing power, storage capacity, internet bandwidth, as well as easier interfaces on smaller and smaller mobile devices (2012). According to Lovink, currently intersubjectivity involves an "empowering of loosely connected individuals in networks." However, as mentioned by Butt, such networks are unevenly distributed and far from utopic. The post-digital disenchantment mentioned by Cramer might be considered to have started with, or at least was exacerbated by, revelations of the extent to which governments used telecommunications networks to surveil users by CIA employee Edward Snowden in 2013. As part of what she calls the "content industrial complex," commentator Dena Yago has pointed out the ways in which everything put online is "quantified and instrumentalized" (Yago 2018: 3). Yago explains that any user-generated content is in fact always-already policed, scanned, recognised, mined, indexed and aggregated as data to be bought and sold. Therefore an aesthetic that is post-digital is one that is less naïve and more knowing of the inequity and exploitation built into the very structures of internet and digital technologies.

5.4   BECOMING-MACHINE AND CYBORGS

With the aid of the internet, artists like Hobbs, Frankovich and Jaimie have created choreographed works that explore and probe contemporary post-digital realities and relations. These artists, along with countless others, mobilise the prosthetics of hand-held electronic devices, personal computers, editing software, camera equipment, websites and online video archives, to explore how such techno-social forms of extension affect the ways particular, highly networked subjects might choreograph and exhibit themselves as well as figure out new ways of moving politically. It is worth noting that these performances make evident or even explicit the various ways in which bodies are layered and extended to include prosthetic devices.

According to Braidotti, the contemporary context has witnessed a dissolution of the asperity of the human and machines, or the previously "technological other" to the point where there are now "unprecedented degrees of intimacy and intrusion" between them (2013: 89). Braidotti proposed the concept of a post-human, *becoming-machine* to account for the ways in which contemporary subjectivity, like the production of art, is highly distributed and extended across a myriad of devices and networks. This concept of *becoming-machine* is highly indebted to the concept of the *cyborg* as theorised by Donna Haraway in the early 1990s, just before the so-called dot.com boom. In her "Cyborg Manifesto" Haraway sought to undermine the opposition between subjects/objects and bodies/machines and explore subjectivity as shaped by technologies with the concept of the cyborg as "a cybernetic organism, a hybrid of machine and organism, a creature of social reality" (Haraway 1991: 149). Haraway's *cyborg* can be read as a choreo-political project, the idea was that as an "imaginative resource" the concept of the cyborg has the capacity to suggest "very fruitful couplings." As a feminist exercise, Haraway explores and elucidates the concept of the cyborg, in the hope that it might challenge choreo-policing, dissolve patriarchal foundations and challenge hierarchical oppositions. Haraway observed:

> By the late twentieth century, our time, a mythic time, we are all chimeras, theorized and fabricated hybrids of machine and organism; in short, we are cyborgs. The cyborg is our ontology; it gives us our politics. The cyborg is a condensed image of both imagination and material reality. (150)

Haraway explicitly argued for "pleasure in the confusion of boundaries" as well as "for responsibility in their construction." The distinction
between organism and machine is complicated whilst at the same time the
ubiquity of devices one uses to access the internet mean that machines are
everywhere and at the same time invisible (152). Mind, body and tool
are thus "on very intimate terms," a description that is very fitting for
the kinds of relationships many people currently have with their mobile
devices (165). Haraway describes the way in which machines or prosthetic tools can become "us," our "intimate components," part of our
processes and embodiment until one becomes hybridised with communication devices (178–180). Championing extension, Haraway's question
of "why should our bodies end at the skin?" (178) presages Andy Clark's
thesis of extended mind, according to which external environmental
supports or tools aid in processes of cognition (Clark and Chalmers
1998). Even in the early 1990s, one can detect something of the post-
digital disenchantment in Haraway's observation that cyborgs, like the
internet are "the illegitimate offspring of militarism and patriarchal capitalism" (165). Communication technologies depend on electronics, as
well as modern states, multinational corporations, military power, welfare
states, apparatuses, satellite systems and political processes.

Haraway's description of the cyborg anticipates post-internet aesthetics
and post-digital relations. The cyborg is "needy for connection," she has
the capacity to be both "oppositional and utopian," and has the ability
to confuse the polarity of public and private (151). Haraway describes "a
polymorphous information system" in which identities "seem contradictory, partial and strategic" (155, 161). In terms of subjectivity, the cyborg
is thus "a kind of disassembled and reassembled, postmodern collective
and personal self" (163). Haraway's cyborg world is "about lived social
and bodily relations" in which people are unafraid of joint kinship with
animals, machines, as well as partial identities and contradictory stand-
points. It is a place where boundaries are transgressed, potent fusions
take place and "dangerous possibilities are explored" (154). Communications technologies are therefore tools that "embody and enforce new
social relations," Haraway argues:

> I prefer a network ideological image, suggesting the profusion of spaces
> and identities and the permeability of boundaries in the personal body
> and in the body politic. 'Networking' is both a feminist practice and

a multinational corporate strategy – weaving is for oppositional cyborgs. (164)

More than three decades after Haraway's manifesto, Braidotti pondered how a post-human self might be both enfleshed, extended and relational, simultaneously harbouring a "desire to be wired' as well as pride in being flesh" (2013: 90). Harking back to Haraway's cyborg, with its combination of imagination and material reality, Braidotti advocates *becoming-machine* as a "playful and pleasure-prone relationship to technology that is not based on functionalism" (91). There seems to be the hope that technology could be co-opted for choreo-political means. A similar relation seems to have been anticipated and performed in Jim Allen's *Poetry for Chainsaws* (1976) when he playfully recited poetry and moved around the buzzing machines. For Braidotti, the contemporary machines of information technology are "engines or devices that both capture and process forces and energies, facilitating interrelations, multiple connections and assemblages." They stand for radical relationality, delight and productivity. Such devices allow a *becoming-machine*, an actualisation of "the relational powers of a subject that bears a privileged bond with multiple others and merges with one's technologically mediated planetary environment." For Braidotti, to be post-human is to be part of a radical relationality on many levels, including the social. The way in which the contemporary context is globalised and technologically mediated is one more aspect of post-anthropocentrism.

In tandem, Braidotti and Haraway theorise intersubjectivity that is intimately intertwined with machines, within a technologically mediated environment, whilst at the same time being playful, critical and self-aware. Indeed throughout twentieth century performance art, artists have explored technologies pertaining to the body as they developed in order to critically probe machine-body relations and cyborg subjectivities. Works that dealt with physical extension and prosthesis include Gutai artist Atsuko Tanaka's *Electric Dress* (1956) and Nam June Paik and Charlotte Moorman's *TV Bra for a Living Sculpture* (1969). There were also works that explicitly explored the immediacy of performing directly to film and video, rather than using them as a means for performance documentation. Although this is exemplified in often discussed works such as Nauman's studio films and Vito Acconci's *Centers* (1971) there are also many examples of female-identifying artists using film and video technology and performing to camera, in order to critique the various ways in which images of women's bodies were generally presented by patriarchal mass media such as Yvonne Rainer's *Hand Movie* (1966), Valie Export's *Body Tape* (1970), Joan Jonas' *Vertical Roll* (1972), Marina Abramovic's *Art Must Be Beautiful, Artist Must Be Beautiful* (1975) and Martha Rosler's *Semiotics of the Kitchen* (1975).

Gronlund summarises this phenomenon well, taking her cue from Rosalind Krauss' 1975 essay "Video: The Aesthetics of Narcissism." In the 1970s artists used the camera to explore themselves, tracing their bodies and using the instantaneous feedback of video to explore the gap between self and representation and focussing inward into one's own psychology (Gronlund 2017: 155). Whereas in the post-internet art of the 2000s–2010s artists no longer conceive of themselves as a psychologically coherent whole, their identities are constructed through a social field and the specific conditions of interacting on the internet. In this "on-line imaginary" identity is conceived as "fungible, shaped by images and commodities, with a dispersed authority and authorship" (158). By Gronlund's argument, subjects appear as externally constituted characters, living autonomously on platforms like YouTube so that their thoughts and the artworks they produce circulate beyond their control, as they circulate through everyday internet consumption, in which response and recirculation are implicit.

5.5   PUSHING MOVEMENT ARCHIVES INTO THE BODY: THE INTERNET AS A LIBRARY OF DANCE

Theorist Boris Groys has observed that the internet offers "an alternative possibility for art production and distribution" so that "anyone can put any texts or visual material of any kind on the internet and make it globally accessible." The internet creates a vast field of "total visibility, accessibility and transparency" (Groys 2013) and it is due to this accessibility that online video repositories such as YouTube hold immense amounts of content. Hobbs' *Otara at Night* is just one work that reflects a *networked choreography* and the way in which artists and choreographers are currently influenced by dances that have become available to view on what Bench has called the "movement archives" of the internet. These movement archives enable seeking and experimenting with movement to operate on an unprecedented level. Online libraries act as another kind of prosthesis or tool of extension for art-making. Curator Hans Ulrich Obrist observed that

Whenever I talk to choreography or dance students, I notice that a big part of their education comes from YouTube where you can find a whole history of dance from Isadora Duncan to Jérôme Bel. (2013: 169)

Berlin-based, New Zealand choreographer Joshua Rutter takes this concept of the internet as "the first public library for dancers" a step further, writing: "I often find myself watching a video on YouTube.com with the desire to somehow emulate or reproduce its contents, faithfully or not, for the purpose of a staged performance" (2015a: 1). Rutter describes this propensity as a "remote voyeurism (of people, animals and things in action) oriented towards exhibitionism."

The internet as a library of dance takes Charmatz's *dancing museum* almost literally. For Rutter, YouTube in particular is "a kind of archive, a reservoir of potential mass-culture or potential physicality" (3). Such content can act as choreographic fodder as "anything recorded and uploaded to YouTube has the potential to be mass-produced as it is now available to anyone (or any algorithm)." As Bench surmised earlier, these movement archives can be very generative and each of their particular formats can have an impact on the kinds of choreographies that are created for them, or in response to them. Rutter views material on movement archives as "found movement" similar to the *objet trouvé* in Surrealist sculpture. Such a process, for Rutter involves "the act of copying or learning a movement with one's own body," the choreographer "hosts the movement object in their body" before a subsequent re-contextualisation of a found movement, a re-performing or display as part of a presentation in a theatrical stage-space in the presence of an audience. Importantly, for Rutter any repetition or iteration of movement found online might be permuted as an "imperfection or unconscious alteration and conflation of form, feeling or rhythm may occur. An artist busy with found movements will likely generate unexpected and novel movement artefacts." Rutter demonstrated his co-opting of found movement as a choreographic device in a recent performance that included what appeared to be: a beheading, a dog video, an energetic dance step, robotic movements in slow motion as well as yoga positions. Throughout the performance Rutter indicated:

This is from the internet... and this... is also from the internet. This was from the internet. But I changed it, yeah... This is on the internet...

because I uploaded it. This will be connected, soon enough. I like to think, and the sooner the better. (2015b)

Obrist's reflection and Rutter's desire to reproduce what he sees online ties into a broader argument made by Lepecki, that returning to the performances of past dancers "paradoxically becomes one of the most significant marks of contemporary experimental choreography" (2016: 117). Lepecki introduces heavily loaded arguments from performance studies and theories about the implications of re-enactment and the concept of the archive.[4] Important points to be taken include Lepecki's proposition that responding to prior movements or choreographies in the present indicates "a capacity to identify in a past work still non-exhausted creative fields of 'impalpable possibilities" (120). Rutter's will to re-perform what he sees in online archives of movement recalls a description by Martin Nachbar, another Berlin-based choreographer of his attempts to "visit the storehouse" of the archive as well as his attempt to push his body into it, Lepecki describes this as a process of:

> pushing the body into the archive and pushing the archive into the body –a mutual metamorphosis conjuring up, creating, secreting, excreting, inflecting critical points where virtuals and actuals exchange place. (127)

It must be pointed out that one way in which the internet departs from the archive as described by theorist Jacques Derrida, is that its practice of storing, housing and retaining is no longer a matter of what artist Myriam Van Imshoot has called the commanding force of "patriarchal conservatism" that archives (2014: 41). And as Groys explains, one of the reasons why the internet is so likable is because "it is not selective- or at least much less selective than a museum" (2013).

This phenomenon of the internet as a less selective archive is articulated by Berlin-based artist Hito Steyerl who describes the way in which images, including moving images are circulated. For Steyerl, the internet is a circuit for "image circulation," one that multiplies possible points of transfer. Images are therefore:

> nodes of energy and matter that migrate across different supports, shaping and affecting people, landscapes, politics and social systems. They acquired an uncanny ability to proliferate, transform and activate. (2014: 31)

Contemporary information technology as *becoming-machine* means that the relationship between subjectivity and intersubjectivity is even more entangled. Images and videos can be "copied and dispersed at the flick of a finger" and "data, sounds and images are now routinely transitioning beyond screens into a different state of matter" such as being copied, learnt and reperformed by performers. As Bench argued, these movement archives allow for endless instances of creation and production, as well as distribution and proliferation. Steyerl anticipates this when she describes the way in which images might become "incarnate," they "materialise" and "spread through and beyond networks, they contract and expand, they stall and stumble, they vie, they vile, they wow and woo." This is evident in Frankovich's use of stock and vernacular images in *Defending Plural Experiences* (2014). When such images are re-virtualised or "walk off-screen" as described by Steyerl, when they are iterated, copied, learnt or reperformed as part of a choreography they "become real" and are "substantially altered. They get translated, twisted, bruised and reconfigured." They are "dilapidated, incorporated and reshuffled." All of these active verbs point to the ways in which artists and choreographers, as part of an immense intersubjective network, utilise movements taken from online sources. Rutter takes this a step further arguing that:

> the artist will probably be affected by the movement as they choose, learn and consider it, as the medium of expression is her own body, and changes or actions in the body can affect one's immediate appearance, felt experience and self-perception. (2015a: 2)

Another example of an artwork that explores the complex interrelations of contemporary subjectivity and art production is Swiss artist Alexandra Bachzetsis' live performance *From A to B via C* (2014) which has been performed in Central America, the United States as well as at the Tate Modern where, somewhat appropriately, it was streamed online as part of the BMW Tate Live performance room, an initiative that allows audiences from all over the world to watch a livestream of performances as they take place in the gallery. Previous live-streamed performances have been watched by audiences of up to 330,000 people.[5] Bachzetsis explains that *From A to B via C* "is a work composed from a set of online tutorials. All the existing material in the piece was learned from the internet, appropriated, and finally embodied on stage" (quoted in Howe, 2015: 85). These processes of learning, appropriation and embodying content taken from the movement archives of online video repositories and subsequent incorporation of material into a choreography, or performance artwork, echoes Rutter's desire to emulate and reproduce content seen on the internet. For Bachzetsis, online, dance-based fitness classes are what Lepecki would call "non-exhaustive fields of possibility" she de-virtualises them and re-virtualises them so that there is a circulation from screen and video to live performance and back to video again. There is no doubt that *From A to B via C* is a post-internet performance, one that uses the logics, structures and formats of the internet such as: speaking *to camera*, the tutorial, the instructional video as well as rewinding and re-playing movement.

Like Hobbs, Bachzetsis is interested in dance genres as "structures and mechanisms of established systems" as well as online formats and the way in which such gesture vocabularies and styles are chosen and realised. Bachzetsis also interrogates the ways in which various dance genres might be learnt from the internet or the ways in which choreographic instruction takes place via uploaded videos. Its use of instruction harks back to the Bouillon Group's *Religious Aerobics*. Just as the museum was described as performing a pedagogical function for those who visited it, (Bennett 1995) such online choreographic instruction is a novel, auto-didactic, intersubjective and often choreo-policing relation that manages bodies and encourages conformity. Bachzetsis explains: "I'm interested in how you can educate yourself with these new forms of learning online, where instructions are shared with a wide audience."

Explicitly repeating the form of the online tutorial, *From A to B via C* covers a wide range of movement styles taken from online tutorials from tennis manoeuvres, sign language, to classical ballet to hip-hop.[6] At the beginning of the performance one performer stands and speaks to camera so that her face appears on a monitor facing the audience. She enthusiastically reads her script aloud from a pile of paper and her utterances are quickly repeated by the two other performers, placed centre stage. A mediated, intersubjective relationship of viewing and mimicking, call and response is set up: "For the next little while, it's going to be you and me together alone. I want you to lock the door and turn the phone off and really concentrate on what we're going to do. We're going to start with some of my favourite exercises." The false gaiety and high-energy verbal delivery of the performers is where the sense of post-digital disenchantment comes in, the whole exercise is enthusiastic and entertaining, yet also somehow hollow and false, it is up to the audience to decide whether the gestures and dances performed really do provide healthy models for doing and being.

5.6 Rebecca Hobbs' "Mangere Mall" (2011)

It is daytime. A series of locked-off shots from different perspectives show the empty expanse of a covered mall in Mangere, Auckland. The music is tinny, beginning with a synthesised, marimba-like melody. Six young dancers strut into the space, four of them scatter themselves around the central space whilst two enter it and squat, heads lowered, hands touching the ground, facing outwards and away from each other. The squatting two rise, waving their bodies sinuously and making contrasting wave like forms with their arms and hands. Unlike *Otara at Night, Mangere Mall* (Fig. 5.1) is heavily edited, cutting from mounted camera to camera, in time with the music, and allowing the dancers' movements to be captured from multiple angles. The dancers alternate between facing outwards, towards the four different sides of the space, and turning inwards and facing each other. The duet becomes a dance of four as two more dancers enter the central space and join in. Intriguingly, the dancers never seem

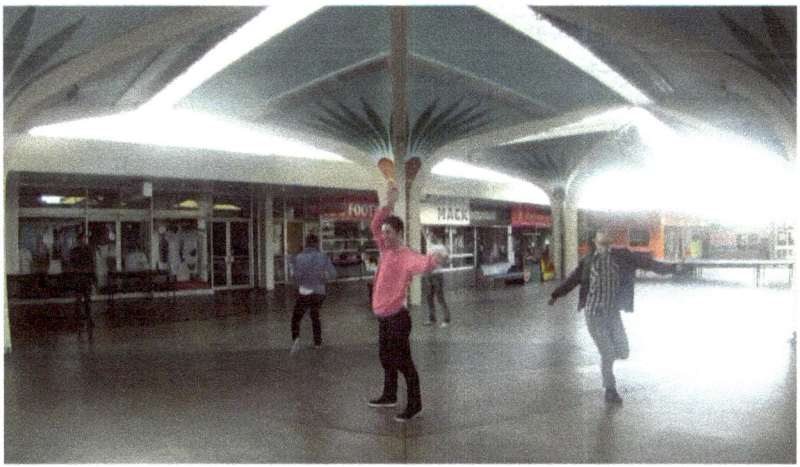

Fig. 5.1 Rebecca Ann Hobbs, *Mangere Mall*, 2011 (Single-channel HD video, colour with sound, 4 minutes 28 seconds, looped)

to be performing to camera, either dancing to each other or to the empty mall around them.

The mall of the title is located near an industrial centre, and it is one of several developments the New Zealand government instigated during the 1970s, as part of a state housing programme (Hobbs 2011a). During the late 1970s and 1980s, the area saw an influx of immigrants from the neighbouring Pacific Islands who came to work in the surrounding industrial areas and settled there.[7] Originally an open-air mall, the community designed the canopy structures and skylights so that they could gather and move between shops without being affected by inclement weather. The result is a covered mall that is nonetheless spatially expansive and filled with light, which streams through skylights. These are a feature in themselves, supported by distinctive structures that resemble tree trunks and are painted with palm motifs. Beyond the visual aspects of the architecture, what interests Hobbs are the embodied relationships to place and the way communities use the space for their own ends (Hobbs 2017). This community is partially represented in the voguers' fluid groupings and dispersals, which contrast to the vast architectural space. Similarly, their undulating movements also contrast with Hobbs' balanced and symmetrical framing, which creates an ultra-wide, almost detached perspective, almost as if we were at the theatre. We might see this group but we are not part of it, unlike the more intimate, invitational style of *Otara at Night*.

For this environment, Hobbs decided to use a dance troupe from the Waikato, an area just south of Auckland. Even though the VOGUE crew had been winning competitions, they experienced resistance from dance communities due to their decision to engage with the popular dance style of vogueing (Hobbs 2017). Nevertheless, the collective was breaking new ground, learning the popular dance style from videos seen online. Videoing whilst the mall was closed, six members of the crew danced their own choreography whilst being recorded by nine cameras simultaneously. In order to capture the mall's vast architectural features, Hobbs made the decision to use go-pro cameras with their built-in, wide-angle lenses, each mounted to the mall's architectural elements. Recording simultaneously meant that Hobbs could later edit the performance, cutting between the many angles afforded her by the multiple mounted cameras, all evenly spaced, at the same height, and maintaining symmetrical framing of the architecture. The music was created by colleagues Cat Ruka and Joshua Rutter. Hobbs was assisted again by Tavola, her mum did the catering and the dancers were surrounded by their supportive families. Hobbs recalls it was "a family sort of affair" (Hobbs 2017). Vogueing is a style of dance that originated in the Harlem ballroom scene in New York City during the 1980s. In one of the earliest scholarly accounts, Marcos Becquer and Jose Gatti explain that vogueing is in fact a subculture, a dance that was practised casually in gathering places, nightclubs, subway cars and more formally at events called balls. Vogueing brings together poses from the magazine of the same name, breakdancing moves and gestures represented in Egyptian hieroglyphics (Becquer and Gatti 1991: 66).[8] The genre itself is characterised by syncopated movements, angular, linear, rigid poses or "interruptions" which are then choreoegraphed into dynamic runway walks or sashaying that can then include dips backwards and drops to the ground. For Becquer and Gatti, vogueing as a dance form is *syncretic*, meaning it is a tactical articulation of different elements. Importantly, syncretism involves a signalling, an historicised interchange between elements based on a complex play of differences and affinities (70). Becquer and Gatti also proposed that the Egyptian hieroglyphic element in vogueing is a link to African heritage, yet also one that connects to a white gay tradition of self-display through the exotic and flamboyant re-enactment of narratives. Breakdancing elements connect vogueing to black Hispanic gays of hip-hop culture which emerged in the South Bronx during the 1970s. That tradition valorised verbal and physical dexterity as well as sublimating "fight into dance," "conflict into contest" and "desperation into style and a sense of self-respect," all these hip-hop elements can be seen in vogueing (74). Vogueing involves a repositioning of breakdancing elements by re-situating them within an emergent history of black and Hispanic gay pride, critiquing hip-hop's heterosexist currents.

Contemporary vogueing, like dancehall, migrated to Aotearoa New Zealand first through documentary films such as Jennie Livingston's *Paris is Burning* (1990) and more recently through online videos and tutorials. Hobbs' intention for *Mangere Mall* was to celebrate "the movement and reinterpretation of culture," specifically the way various dance forms alter as they manifest in new locations (Hobbs 2011a). Unlike *Otara at Night*, *Mangere Mall* has enjoyed quite a wide distribution as an artwork, being exhibited in many galleries nationally as well as internationally.[9] Just as the dance form of vogueing circulated from its original context via online videos, tutorials and feature films to make it to New Zealand, it has then been re-articulated by a Waikato-based dance collective before being enacted as part of a dancevideo which has then re-circulated in various exhibitions throughout the world as well as being accessible online through Hobbs' YouTube channel.

As I mentioned in the introduction to this chapter, art historically, Hobb's *Mangere Mall* harks back to Gillian Wearing's 1994 works *Dancing in Peckham* and *Rehearsing for Peckham*. Also playing with the idea of privately rehearsing, then dancing in public, *Mangere Mall* is heavily edited, presenting multiple viewpoints so that the various members can be seen from the most advantageous viewpoint and shot times are dictated more by the accompanying music.

To reiterate Steyerl's proposition of circulation and Bench's arguments about choreography and the internet; digital or movement archives such as YouTube have acted as generative repositories for the Waikato-based VOGUE dance crew who have learnt to dance from, and ultimately for, the archive. Vogueing subculture has extended its reach and circulated through networks, infiltrating cultural repertoires as it is re-enacted, restaged and reperformed. Through the pedagogies of online movement archives, choreographies have been transmitted, circulated between bodies that have vast geographical and temporal distances separating them. Movements and movement styles have been learnt through processes of research, training and rehearsal, before going on to use the same platforms for performance, documentation and dissemination. These endless cycles of watching, learning, training, rehearsing, repetition, performance and documentation are reflected in the way in which *Mangere Mall* is edited. Hobbs' strategy of multiple camera angles recording simultaneously, enabled her to edit the footage in a playful and rhythmic manner. Recalling Henriques' point about dancehall transduction, Hobbs frequently responds to the rhythm of the music by marking it with abrupt alternations of angles and cuts in the footage, as well as making them correspond with the dancers' actual movements. This style of editing itself echoes the play-back, pausing and slowing down afforded by online movement archives.

Vogueing is "a site of interaction for the categories of race, class, gender and sexuality" (Becquer and Gatti 1991, 65). Whereas *Otara at Night* focused upon the population of a stage in a particular socio-economic and suburban setting, at night as a feminist gesture, *Mangere Mall* can be read in terms of the way in which it engages with queer identities and dis-orientations. Queer choreographies will be explored in greater detail in the following chapter, however at this point it is worth noting that according to Stanley Niaah, the dominant homo-phobic tendencies in much of Jamaican culture mean that dancehall is explicitly hetero-normative, with male and female heterosexual identities visible in partner dancing through amorous display and sexually provoca-tive or explicit dance styles (Stanley Niaah 2010, 141). This means that the dancehall queen typically manifests heterosexuality. In contrast, as mentioned by Becquer and Gatti, the subculture of vogueing has its origins in flamboyant, queer self-display.

The performers in *Mangere Mall* used online movement archives that distributed or circulated the popular dance style of vogueing, in order to author their own dance, as part of a post-digital choreographic process. However it is also important to note that ever since the 1980s vogueing has been instrumentalised to challenge received ideas about gender. Theorist Judith Butler observed that gender is often performed "under duress" "tenuously constituted in time" and "instituted through a stylised repetition of acts" (Butler 1988, 519–520). The ways in which the perfor-mativity of gender is limited is particularly relevant for the performers in Hobbs' dancevideos as, often, youths in Maori and Pacific communities are constrained by the socially conservative and heteronormative ideals of Christian and Mormon churches and the ubiquity of Christianity as the effects of the missionisation of the Pacific. Their bodies are constrained by a very specific form of choreo-policing, one that encourages confor-mity to specific norms in terms of clothing and bodily deportment. The dominance of Christianity is what Tavola alluded to with her evocation of the phrase "WWJD?" or "What Would Jesus Do?" Moving on, Butler's emphasis on the specific, corporeal acts by which gender is constituted means that there is also the possibility for cultural transformations of gender through choreo-political acts. It is the performative character of any gender identity which means there is the possibility for contesting its reified status.

Importantly, for Butler, if conceptions of gender are constituted, they are then capable of being constituted differently. Butler describes the "performative fluidity of gender" (528) meaning that gender becomes something that is "put on," it is playful and "basically an innovative affair" (531). I would argue that instances of gender transformation take place in vogueing as the ways in which the movements and poses of fashion models are co-opted and exaggerated to the point where such a perfor-mance of upper-class femininity becomes a subversive repetition. One example is a certain flourish, or "swish," the way in which the dancers in Mangere Mall frequently hold a slightly bent arm away from the body whilst doing an exaggerated runway walk in a rhythmic manner. The wrist is relaxed, moving from side to side with the motion of hips and feet. This strutting or sauntering, seen as the dancers move around the central space, in and out of frame, involves a bounce in the step, a sauntering, a swishing and swaying back and forth of the body.

Since the making of *Mangere Mall*, and due to the ongoing efforts of Tanu Gago, vogueing has grown in popularity around Auckland (Gordon-Smith 2016, 68). In October 2012, together with Pati Solomon Tyrell, Gago founded FAFSWAG (a conjunction of fa'afafine and swag) as a platform for Pacific LGBQTI+ or "Rainbow Pasifika" youth to connect. Since its founding, the FAFSWAG annual ball, itself modelled after the Harlem vogueing balls, has become a fulcrum for the community, leading to increasing popularity of the form. Since the inception of these balls, which now occur more and more frequently throughout Auckland, ten years after Hobbs' *Mangere Mall*, it seems difficult to divorce Rainbow Pasifika with their struggles for body sovereignty from the queer choreographies that are performed at such events.[10] Such issues will be un-packed in more depth as part of discussions of queer choreographies in Chapter 6, and decolonising choreographies in Chapter 7.

NOTES

1. In fact, the markets themselves often serve as a stage for artworks. For example, Jeremy Leatinu'u filmed his performance *Public Observations II* (2010) there and Australian artist Keg de Souza ran workshops there one market day during the 13th Auckland Triennial in June 2013.
2. Tik Tok has a unique choreo-politics all of its own. As Tik Tok users and even celebrities encourage one another to certain challenges, re-performing and perfecting dances, the play between freedom and conformity continues and is extended through one-upmanship and increases in difficulty.
3. For Latour, any given location has always-already been affected by the power of local mediators who have made such a place, "you are thoroughly framed by other agencies brought silently on the scene" (195–196).
4. Contemporary art and exhibition making have also be enamoured with the idea of the archive, see Hal Foster "An Archival Impulse" *October* 110: 3–22. Susan Hiller's installation *From the Freud Museum* (1991–1997) is

a good example. In dance studies work and discourse from choreographer Meg Stuart has addressed the phenomenon of body as archive.

5. http://www.tate.org.uk/join-support/corporate-support/sponsorsh ip/bmw.

6. This deadpan quotation and repetition of the kinds of movement seen in hip-hop music videos ties into Bachzetsis earlier video work *Gold* (2010) in which the artist performs hip-hop moves as well as the kinds of dance performed by strippers in a gold bikini, filmed from the neck down and using her trademark technique of providing crudely written on pieces of paper piled high so that are revealed to the camera one by one as a kind of commentary. In this work Bachzetsis performs the movements over-enthusiastically and often violently so that she often seems to be injuring herself in the process.

7. For more see Chapter 7.

8. This sampling of poses and attitudes from Vogue magazine anticipates the way images are used in post-internet performance.

9. The work was included in Hobbs' 2012 solo exhibitions, *Mangere Mall*, at Sutton Gallery in Melbourne, and *Waack, Whine, Pop and Roll* (2012) in Christchurch's Dog Park Art Project Space. It was included in the curated group exhibition *In Spite of Ourselves* (2012) at St Paul St, Auckland and The Dowse Art Museum, Wellington and as part of the *Transoceanic Visual Exchange* (2015) Video Art Network Lagos, Nigeria and at Fresh Milk, St. George, Barbados.

10. Vogue culture has been more and more commonly seen in contemporary art contexts. One example was the exhibition of FAFSWAG member Pati Solomona Tyrell's *Fāgogo*, 2016 (single-channel HD video) in the 2018 Walters Prize at the Auckland Art Gallery. Across the Tasman work from the *House of HMU* series by French artist Frédéric Nauczyciel was included in the exhibition *UA NUMI LE FAU* (2016) by Léuli Eshraghi at Gertrude Contemporary, Melbourne.

REFERENCES

Becquer, Marcos, and Jose Gatti. 1991. Elements of Vogue. *Third Text* 5: 65–81.

Bench, Harmony. 2017. Dancing in Digital Archives: Circulation, Pedagogy, Performance. In *Transmission in Motion: The Technologizing of Dance*, ed. Maaike Bleeker, 155–167. New York: Routledge.

Bennett, Tony. 1995. *The Birth of the Museum: History, Theory, Politics*. London; New York: Routledge.

Braidotti, Rosi. 2013. *The Posthuman*. Cambridge: Polity Press.

Butler, Judith. 1988. Performative Acts and Gender Constitution: An Essay in Phenomenology and Feminist Theory. *Theatre Journal* 40.4: 519–31.

Butt, Danny. 2008. Local Knowledge and New Media Theory. In *The Aotearoa Digital Arts Reader*, eds. Stella Brennan and Su Ballard, 30–35. Auckland: Aotearoa Digital Arts and Clouds.

Clark, Andy, and David Chalmers. 1998. The Extended Mind. *Analysis* 58: 7–19.

Cornell, Lauren, and Ed. Halter. 2015. *Mass Effect: Art and the Internet in the Twenty-First Century.* Cambridge, MA: The MIT Press.

Cramer, Florian. 2014. What Is Post-Digital? APJA A Peer-Reviewed Journal About Post-Digital Research. http://www.aprja.net/what-is-post-digital/. Accessed 8 November 2014.

Foucault, Michel, and Jay Miskowiec. 1986. Of Other Spaces. *Diacritics* 16.1: 22–27.

Gago, Tanu. 2012. "WWJD Curated by Ema Tavola." YouTube, July 3, 2012. https://www.youtube.com/watch?v=5QqJYHN92B4.

Gentles, Tim. 2015. Between Here and Nowhere: A survey of Post-Internet Practices among New Zealand Artists. *Reading Room: A Journal of Art and Culture* 7: 110–125.

Gordon-Smith, Ioana. 2016. Make Space: The Rise of the FAFSWAG Art Movement. *Art New Zealand* 158: 68–73.

Gronlund, Melissa. 2017. *Contemporary Art and Digital Culture.* London and New York: Routledge.

Groys, Boris, 2013. Art Workers: Between Utopia and the Archive. *e-flux Journal* 45. https://www.e-flux.com/journal/45/60134/art-workers-between-utopia-and-the-archive/. Accessed 18 November 2015.

Haraway, Donna J. 1991. *Simians, Cyborgs, and Women: The Reinvention of Nature.* New York: Routledge.

Henriques, Julian. 2010. The Vibrations of Affect and their Propagation on a Night Out on Kingston's Dancehall Scene. *Body & Society* 16.1:57–89.

Henriques, Julian. 2014. Rhythmic Bodies: Amplification, Inflection and Trans-duction in the Dance Performance Techniques of the 'Bashment Gal'. *Body & Society* 20.3&4: 79–112.

Hobbs, Rebecca Ann. 2011a. Mangere Mall Statement and Full Credits. Rebecca Ann Hobbs. http://rebeccaannhobbs.com/works/video/. Accessed 19 October 2016.

Hobbs, Rebecca Ann. 2011b. Otara at Night Statement and Full Credits. Rebecca Ann Hobbs. http://rebeccaannhobbs.com/works/video/. Accessed 19 October 2016.

Hobbs, Rebecca Ann. 2016. Hi there! Email communication to the author. 4 November 2016.

Hobbs, Rebecca Ann. 2017. A question… Email communication to the author. 9 November 2017.

Howe, David Everitt. 2015. Dance in the Ruins: Tajal Harrell, Adam Linder and Alexandra Bachzetsis on Their Work, Its Institutionalization, and the Art World. *Mousse* 50: 76–89.

Latour, Bruno. 2005. *Reassembling the Social: An Introduction to Actor Network Theory.* Oxford and New York: Oxford University Press.

Lepecki, André. 2016. *Singularities: Dance in the Age of Performance.* New York: Routledge.

Lovink, Geert. 2012. What Is the Social in Social Media? *e-flux Journal* 40. https://www.e-flux.com/journal/40/60272/what-is-the-social-in-social-media/. Accessed 18 November 2015.

Obrist, Hans Ulrich. 2013. Hans Ulrich Obrist in Conversation with Mathieu Copeland. The Fragility of Exhibitions Stroll in Hyde Park, London, 31 October 2011. In *Choreographing Exhibitions*, ed. Mathieu Copeland, 192–199. Dijon: Les presses du réel.

Pepperell, Robert. 2011. Art and Extensionism. In *Situated Aesthetics: Art Beyond the Skin*, ed. Riccardo Manzotti, 148–170. Exeter, UK: Academic Imprint.

Rose, Gillian. 1993. *Feminism & Geography: The Limits of Geographical Knowledge.* Minneapolis, MN: University of Minnesota Press.

Rutter, Joshua. 2015a. Finding Movement in Cyberspace. Master in Solo Dance Authorship (SODA), Hochschulübergreifendes Zentrum Tanz (HZT) Berlin.

Rutter, Joshua. 2015b. SoDa 202 Research showing 16.04.2015, as part of a Master in SODA at HZT Berlin.

Stanley Niaah, Sonjah. 2010. *Dancehall: From Slave Ship to Ghetto.* Ottawa: University of Ottawa Press.

Steyerl, Hito. 2014. *Hito Steyerl: Too Much World.* Berlin: Sternberg Press.

Tribble, Evelyn. 2005. Distributing Cognition in the Globe. *Shakespeare Quarterly* 56: 135–155.

Tribe, Mark, and Reena Jana. 2006. *New Media Art.* Köln: Taschen.

Van Imshoot, Myriam. 2014. Rests in Pieces: On Scores, Notations, and the Trace in Dance. In *Danse: An Anthology*, ed. Noémie Solomon, 41–54. Dijon: Les presses du réel.

Wearing, Gillian. 2014. Gillian Wearing: Rehearsing for Peckham. Nowness. https://www.nowness.com/story/gillian-wearing-rehearsing-for-peckham. Accessed 19 October, 2016.

Wynne-Jones, Victoria. 2017. Wine and Swish: Rebecca Ann Hobbs' Dancevideos in the Mall. *Performance Paradigm* 13. https://www.performanceparadigm.net/index.php/journal/article/view/198.

Yago, Dena. 2018. Content Industrial Complex. *e-flux Journal* 89. https://www.e-flux.com/journal/89/181611/content-industrial-complex/. Accessed 11 November 2020.

CHAPTER 6

Articulating Alternatives: Val smith's Queer Choreographies

How exactly might one summon the courage to disobey, misbehave or find other ways of moving? Such a question is central to this book: it asks whether or not it is possible to evade authoritative structures in some way, even if it is only for a brief period of time. The question ties into a political project described by theorist Judith Halberstam as a "quest to articulate an alternative vision of life" before putting such a vision into practice (Halberstam 2011: 2). According to Halberstam, artists, amongst others, can act as "radical utopians" who "continue to search for different ways of being in the world and being in relation to one another than those already prescribed for the liberal and consumer subject" (ibid.). Earlier on in this book Jordan Wolfson's metallic marionette *Colored Sculpture* (2016) served as an emblem for *choreo-policing*, for bodies made docile by the authority of museums and choreographers. However, as Laurent Goumarre proposes, it is Pinocchio, another puppet, a disobedient wooden boy who is not yet finished but already has no respect for his father, who is an appropriate representative for the *choreo-political* and artworks that realise intersubjective encounters that might undermine authority (2014: 275–277). This chapter turns to choreographies performed by those categorised by what Tony Bennett calls the "exhibitionary complex" (1995) and its binary logic as sexualised: choreographies that are queer. I will argue that queer choreographies make

© The Author(s), under exclusive license to Springer Nature Switzerland AG 2021
V. Wynne-Jones, *Choreographing Intersubjectivity in Performance Art*, New World Choreographies,
https://doi.org/10.1007/978-3-030-40585-4_6

up a counter-hegemonic, political project similar to that proposed by Halberstam; they propose alternatives through disobedience, actions that misbehave, other ways of moving and being, ways that deviate.

Various different encounters or permutations of intersubjectivity are explored, ones that disorient and are queer. The works discussed in this chapter act as a critique of the often heteronormative environments of exhibition spaces and museums that frequently create modes of address directed towards traditional nuclear families. Queer choreographies present identities that are provisional and contingent, rather than fixed and coherent. They introduce novel collectivities, presenting what Halberstam calls a "difference in form" as a "possibility embedded in the break from heterosexual life narratives" (2011: 70). This is another reason why the emblem of Pinocchio is so apt: he is a wooden boy crafted by an elderly man who wishes for a son. Choreographies that are queer can challenge the habitual consumerist interactions of the exhibitionary complex, as well as participation in what Alexandra Kolb has previously described as an experience economy of self-display and self-promotion (2013). Choreographies that can be considered queer can include a presentation of effeminisation, "swish," embodiments of flamboyance and contrived or exaggerated ways of moving.

Central to this chapter are works by val smith, a choreographic artist currently based in Auckland, New Zealand. smith's performances often involve toying with audiences, a manipulation that begins to unravel the choreo-policing of bodies within exhibition spaces. Throughout their oeuvre what is stressed are the ways in which particular spaces are gendered, oriented and the ways in which such spaces might be performed so that they become confused, uncanny or seen from a different slant.[1] smith takes up positions strategically, frequently these involving lowness or challenges to vertical and normative axes. Intersubjective relations of pride and shame are activated so that they might then be interrogated and diffused. Through their small movements, actions and contact, smith challenges the stability of identities. By donning costumes they evoke creatures that are indeed queer and post-human, ones that successfully enact failure and in doing so create lightness, humour and entertainment in the face of the machinations of power.

According to the cultural logic of humanism, difference is situated as pejoration, and accordingly, Rosi Braidotti argues, there are those branded as "others" due to their sexual orientation (2013: 13). Queer theory, a field that emerged in studies of the humanities during the

1990s, focusses on these so-called "other" practices, sexual and gender practices that cannot be reduced to either homosexuality or heterosexuality (Corber and Valocchi 2003). In the words of gender theorist Eve Kosofsky Sedgwick, in general Western culture is "epistemologically cloven," harking back to Kojève's master/slave dialectic (2008: 12). Therefore, in the case of homo/heterosexual categorisation the opposition is a "pseudo-symmetrical" one in which the sanctity and dominance of the first term are "kept inviolate" (Kosofsky Sedgwick 2008: 67, 82). In the field of queer studies the term *queer* is not a shorthand for "lesbian, gay, bisexual and transgendered." Instead:

> "queer" names or describes identities and practices that foreground the instability inherent in the supposedly stable relationship between anatomical sex, gender and sexual desire. (Corber and Valocchi 2003: 1)

Accordingly, the category of queerness rejects the humanist notion of the subject. Instead, it embraces "non-normative forms of identity" or what humanism with its limited structures of sameness/difference denigrates to the "other." Queer takes up such otherness or strangeness, deliberately and wilfully appropriating the term and its position. Another crucial concept to queer studies is that of *heteronormativity* or "the set of norms that make heterosexuality seem natural or right and that organise homosexuality as its binary opposite" (Corber and Valocchi 2003: 4). Such binary logic is undermined by queer studies scholars who claim that desires, practices and identities do not line up as neatly as lesbian and gay studies scholarship previously implied. For these scholars, lesbian and gay identities are provisional and contingent, rather than fixed and coherent. Kosofksy Sedgwick proposes:

> the open mesh of possibilities, gaps, overlaps, dissonances and resonances, lapses and excesses of meaning when the constituent elements of anyone's gender, of anyone's sexuality aren't made (or can't be made) to signify monolithically. (1993: 8)

Sedgwick extends this concept of queer further so that it might include various identity-constituting and identity fracturing discourses, including those of race, ethnicity and "postcolonial nationality" (ibid.). In this chapter I will discuss various artworks in order to address the question:

how might *queer* be performed, choreographed and received in contemporary art? It is important to note that accounts of intersubjectivity taken from dance studies often emphasise somatic attention, a concept used to analyse encounters between and amongst performers/dancers and spectators/beholders. The trouble is that such bodily based attention can also be structured around heteronormativity and the oppositions mentioned above.

So, what exactly is somatic attention? Somatics is derived from the Greek word *soma* meaning "the living body in its wholeness" (Brodie and Lobel 2012: 6). It refers to processes that are inclusive of one's entire being—body, mind and the environment in which one coexists. The soma is a changeable, fluid entity that responds to both external and internal stimuli. Somatics emphasises physical sensation and the fundamentally unique embodied experience of each person. Paris-based academic Isabelle Ginot, who takes a thoroughly critical view of somatic practice, states that the criterion of all somatic methods is, in any interaction, to generally aim to be conscious and considerate of a whole person (2010: 16). Attention is given to self-awareness, the improvement of coordination and certain movement qualities so that movement is reversible and mild. A foundational principle is that of alteration or the virtue of variation (2010: 20).

Confusingly, there seems to be an entanglement of concepts of somatic awareness, empathy and attention. California-based dance theorist Edward C. Warburton writes that *somatic awareness* is a bodily based sensing of one's own and another's experience as *somatic empathy* (2011: 71). Anthropologist Thomas J. Csordas described what he called *somatic modes of attention* that can be identified in a variety of cultural practices (1993). Central to Csorda's thesis is the importance of *attention* and *situation*. Csordas defines attention as a "consciously turning toward" someone or something. This is combined with further consideration and anticipation of the characteristics of the object of attention (Alfred Schutz quoted in Warburton 2011: 138). Unfolding the role of attention in the very constitution of subjectivity and intersubjectivity as bodily phenomena, Csordas argues that this notion of "turning toward" implies bodily and multisensory engagement rather than mere visual perception. Somatic attention provides an account of how one might attend to oneself as well as the performers, dancers or fellow participants within a choreographed work in a way that is: conscious and considerate of a whole person, a multisensory engagement and an attending with and through one's entire body rather than just one's eyes. The issue here is that such attention is always-already culturally and politically inflected and is therefore at risk of operating with an unconscious bias, and it is highly likely that somatic attention is heteronormative, racialised and choreo-policing. Australian dance theorist Philipa Rothfield points out that bodily acts of perception, described as forms of *somatic attention*, involve firstly an attending with or through the body, with the caveat that each body's mode of attention is culturally, socially and intersubjectively formed (2010: 311). Inter-corporeal understandings and kinaesthetic sensibilities are embedded in forms of practice; there are links between the embodied rituals of everyday life, ethics and aesthetics (315). Similarly for Csordas, sensory engagement to and with the body in the immediacy of an intersubjective milieu might be culturally elaborated. Attending to aspects of others' bodily forms, positions, or movements can be visceral and might involve erotic, moral, or aesthetic sensibilities (1993: 139–140). Crucially Csordas holds that there is a cultural patterning of bodily experience and an intersubjective constitution of meaning through that experience, attending to and with the body involves "culturally constituted somatic modes of attention" (140–141).

Sharing Rothfield's concerns about somatic modes of attention being culturally constituted, Ginot points out that somatics acts as a normative system. It is an ideological construction or ISA that demands conformity and as such must be examined critically:

> Behind the insistence on the singularity of each corporeality, most somatic methods have as a backdrop a homogenous, universal, ahistorical and occidental body... an essentialist ideal of the body reasserts itself, one that brings with it illusions of the natural and organic. (23)[2]

Pulling out what is relevant to the possibility of queer choreography, Ginot encourages a de-naturalisation of somatics so that it might take into account the complexity engaged each time something changes in the relation of a subject to its physical, symbolic, social, economic and political environment. Ginot asks whether somatics might deal with processes of decolonisation, prosthetics or cyborg bodies, queer practices, as well as politico-pharmaceutical or hormonal experiments. Attention to and with a body, as well as the aim of conscious consideration of a whole person, is thereby complicated and problematized. As argued by Rothfield, and in the tradition of Foucault, bodily experience is culturally patterned, embedded in forms of practice and embodied rituals of everyday life, ethics and aesthetics. If one perceives and understands the world in a culturally specific manner then this will affect somatic attention as the manner by which one engages with another. After Ginot, one must be critical of somatic practices as they are always-already ideologically constructed and often champion normativity. Therefore any concepts of bodily based attention must be interrogated so that the complexity of various physical, symbolic, social, economic and political environments can be taken into consideration, and somatic modes of attending to and with queer bodies can be found.

6.1   On the Possibility of Queering Choreography

What are some examples of performances that might activate somatic modes of attending to and with queer bodies? Following Ginot's argument, such artworks or performances might involve queer practices that situate complex bodies in relation to specific environments or places. One strategy that performances which champion non-normative forms of identity might take is to emphasise instability in reference to Kosofsky Sedgwick's point about the queer operating in terms of possibilities, gaps, overlaps, dissonances, lapses and excess. Another strategy in response to an "epistemologically cloven" culture that queer practices might adopt is to align themselves to the second-terms of Kojève's master/slave dialectic, appropriating difference rather than sameness, the contingent rather than the fixed, so-called low art rather than high, bodies that are untrained rather than trained or the nightclub rather than the concert hall. Clare Croft has stated that one of the broader goals of queer dance is "that social dance and concert dance hold equal import" (2017: 4). Such a strategy was taken up recently in *Moving Backwards* by artists Pauline Boudry and Renate Lorenz at the Swiss Pavilion of the Venice Biennale in 2019. This exhibition saw the pavilion transformed into a nightclub that audience members entered so that they emerged backstage, upon a slick-black stage decked with tinsel curtains. As Boudry explained, the work was set in a nightclub as "a space that allows us to experiment with different forms of desire."[3] The video element of *Moving Backwards* involves dancers moving in slow motion and walking forwards whilst wearing their shoes backwards, undermining the backwards/forwards opposition, and the impetus for progression as advancement and improvement.

Returning to a work discussed earlier in this book, the way in which Xavier Le Roy temporarily evaded or undermined the position of the white, cis-gendered, male, solo performer through his technique of *effeminisation* might be one example of destabilising the male/female opposition as well as performing queer. In *Self Unfinished* Le Roy used theatrical or illusory means such as costume and perspective in order to present another body and assume a subordinate relation to a male majority utilising the minoritarian feminine as an active medium of becoming. An earlier example from the history of art might be the way in which Andy Warhol (1928–1987) performed in a feminine or dandified manner that he referred to as "acting swish" (Jones 1998: 68). Warhol's equivocal self-imaging as seen in Christopher Markos, *Portrait of Andy Warhol* from his "Altered Image" series (1981), his combination of wigs and make-up that could be read as feminine with conservative masculine suiting or leather jackets were, according to the artist, part of an overall strategy of un-hinging the dominant, Pollock-like masculine figure of the action painter. A more kinaesthetic evocation of the *swish* has been described by Melbourne-based artist and writer Jeremy Eaton:

> Certain movements derive from celebrity quotation and act as coded moments of communication evoking cultural occurrences and corpses to elaborate on facets of queerness that are unwritten. They are also reclamations of movements that have derogatorily been used to frame and marginalize certain men and women as attributable to sexuality; limp wristedness as a sign of weakness being one such movement. (Eaton 2018: unpaginated)

It is this "limp-wristedness" that Warhol evoked in his account of "acting swish," in contrast to the strident, hyper-masculine grip and brushstroke of the abstract expressionist painters. Indeed, Eaton's account involves what he calls "lineages of gesture," recurrent motifs that occur in drag as well as queer acts. For Eaton, gestures such as a fluttering hand, the throwing back of the hair and a hand on a hip evoke queer histories, particularly those from performance vocabularies from the US ballroom scenes in the 1980s.[4] Eaton elaborates:

Through an indexicality of movements performers can elicit challenges to
gender, class, sexuality while simultaneously reflecting on social struggles
and figures. These gestures, repeated, generate a lineage that talks to an
alternative inheritance beyond reproductive normativity by claiming modes
of performance that create relations by re-tracing past sexualities, in all
their heterogeneity. (ibid.)

Another kinaesthetic iteration of the *swish* can be seen in Mark Bradford's 2005 film *Niagara* in which the camera follows a young, African
American man with a particular swish or bounce in his step as he saun-
ters down a dilapidated pavement in South Central Los Angeles (Lord
and Meyer 2013: 226–227). The title of the work alludes to a film in
which the camera lingers on a view of Hollywood actress Marilyn Monroe
(1926–1962) from behind as she walks away. Bradford has described his
film as a protest piece involving the swishing and swaying back and forth
by a particular kind of man taking public space, "owning it for himself,
using it as a runway" (2008). For this work Bradford was inspired by a
"walker" in his own neighbourhood, one known "for his fearless embodiment of flamboyance within an especially tough public sphere." *Niagara*
also relates to the Vogue dancers in Hobb's *Mangere Mall*, who also take
turns performing swish and walking as though on a runway.

Pablo Bronstein, an artist mentioned in Chapter 2, combines mechanisms of dance, architecture and queer politics with a focus on the
impacts and significance of social codes and stereotypes. As part of
the performance that accompanies Bronstein's installation *Magnificent
Triumphal Arch in Pompeian Colours* (2010), an architectonic arch is
placed in the centre of the gallery. The arch has a disruptive effect: when
performers step through it their movement changes from the pedestrian
or apparently every day to something more grandiose and mannered.
The arch politicises space, standing in for the neoclassical architecture
favoured by imperialist and colonial buildings such as art museums. An
element taken from greater structures of power, such built structures "are
comparable to learnt codes of behaviour that are perceived as natural
– 'normal' gender-specific behaviour or mannerisms" (Rosenthal 2010:
18). Bronstein's choreographed work provides an exploration of processes
of intersubjectivity-as-art with a body that performs affectation, echoing
the ways in which it might be modelled by intersubjective structures of
architecture, dance conventions and decorum.

The movements of Bronstein's dancers span a history of movement, from the Baroque to contemporary dance. The kinds of seemingly natural, prosaic and everyday movements they begin with have been favoured by dancers since the postmodern dance of choreographers such as Yvonne Rainer and Steve Paxton. However, the flourishes they go on to perform, after passing through the arch, belong far back in the history of dance, dating back to the aristocratic deportment of courtiers in the sixteenth century. Elegant courtly attitudes or *sprezzatura* conform to a canon of precise rules yet also aim to seem natural and uncontrived.[5] The contrast of these two forms of movement activates the tension between what appears to be natural or artificial, mannered and contrived and demonstrates how such judgments are constructed and arbitrary. According to Bronstein, the *swish*, affectation or "body politics of *sprez- zatura* would be codified as queer politics now." According to curator Stephanie Rosenthal, *Magnificent Triumphal Arch* serves to give choreo- graphic form to wider manipulative strategies. For Rosenthal the arch is a threshold. It marks a transition from one form of behaviour to another; it is an "indicator of change or being different." A disruption in action is caused by the power of a choreo-policing, architectonic form. Both Bronstein and Bradford contribute performances of walking, behaving, or transitioning that is queer, beginning to create a kinaesthetic queerness. For both artists, walking, perambulation, moving from one point in space to another is appropriated and then literally mobilised. Walking or passing through space with difference is one strategy that can be interpreted as a queering of choreography. This manipulation of walking, making it deviant and strange, harks back to Trisha Brown's *Walking on the Gallery Wall* (1971).

Bradford, Bronstein and smith begin to create kinaesthetic queer- ness that is also spatialised, echoing Sara Ahmed's argument about the subject-intersubjectivity relation, orientations and the "spatiality of sexual desire" (2006: 543–545). For Ahmed, orientation is a matter of "how one inhabits spaces and who or what one inhabits spaces with" (551– 553). Summarising her phenomenology of bodily orientations, Ahmed argues that each body is a "point from which the world unfolds," using Husserl's attendance to the lived body and the intimacy of touch. The importance of "hands that reach" is stressed as well as proximity, what or who can be sensed and touched. Bodies make and leave impressions, they are something touching that is also touched. Orientations are therefore tactile, they involve at least a two-way approach or the "more than one" of an intersubjective encounter. Ahmed surmises that bodies take shape through being oriented towards each other so that an orientation may be experienced as the cohabitation or sharing of space. Taking this a step further, bodies are shaped by contact with others, who is near enough to be reached, tendencies are important, as these dictate what kinds of bodies one might tend towards.

Thus orientations are "the effects of what we tend toward" (554). To be oriented sexually, according to Ahmed, is to dwell on something, to linger, orientations take time. An atmosphere of compulsory or dominant heterosexuality necessitates an orientation *around*. For Ahmed, a queer subject within straight culture has no choice but to *deviate*. From this point of view, the queer body is a "failed orientation." For Ahmed, to be queer is to challenge the normative line or axis, heteronormativity is a straightening device, one that encourages a very specific trajectory. To be out of line is to destabilise these axes, to be oblique or slanted. Ahmed posits "queer moments' as moments of dis-orientation." When things come out of line the effect is "wonky" and Ahmed embraces these queer or wonky moments (562).

Due to the way in which the dominant structures of the world, including heteronormativity, are already in place, queer moments occur when things "come out of line," or are "fleeting" (565). According to Ahmed, "the 'what' that flees is the very point of disorientation." Ahmed makes explicit that she utilises the term *queer* to describe non-straight sexual practices, particularly lesbianism as a form of social and sexual contact. An appeal is made to the root of the word that is from the Greek for cross, oblique or adverse and extended to mean odd, bent or twisted. Ahmed highlights the queer potential of the oblique to make things queer is "certainly to disturb the order of things." To point out the contingency of bodies, coming into contact with bodies creates a disorientation in how things are normally arranged, even a series of uncanny effects. In summary, a queer politics for Ahmed involves a commitment to a certain way of inhabiting the world "at the point at which things fleet" (566, 569). Ahmed's concepts of queerness as disorientation, the oblique, slanted, wonky and fleeting have the possibility of being choreo-political and contributing towards a conception of *queer choreography*.

6.2   VAL SMITH: QUEER AUTHORITY
AND SHIFTING OFF SHAME

As part of their final *duotones* (2014) performance, val smith played a recording of a seductive-sounding disco song.[6] In a distorted and deep voice they repeatedly intoned the word "Forward... Forward... Forward" into a microphone whilst making a beckoning gesture with one raised hand that seemed to say "come forward, towards me." Audience members obeyed, they got up from their seats and slowly moved towards the artist, paying close attention to the ways in which smith altered hand movements, like a police officer on point duty directing traffic. Choreo-policing, smith literally manipulated audience members around the room, herding them like sheep, dividing them into groups, beckoning with their hands to make them crouch, kneel, sit, jump. At one point smith had coerced the audience out of the gallery into the foyer whilst remaining inside the central space, only the artist's arm was visible from the door-frame, still signalling, as if to say "move back." At that moment we were all huddled together by a wall as far back as we could possibly go. Appealing through strange verbal cues, confusing hand gestures and sometimes more direct bodily intervention, smith moved participants, commanding, separating, dividing, controlling and directing. A partic-ular body, one that enjoyed a certain amount of authority, manipulated the bodies of others. The aim was to give an indication or suggestion of a possible movement, manipulating spectatorship through instructions and gestures to the point where such instruction becomes confusing for audience members as well as for the artist (smith 2016a).

smith's instruction, direction and domination ties into the main points about subjection, docile bodies, surveillance, self-regulation and control covered in Chapter 2. The way in which smith positions themselves intersubjectively as a choreographer demanding the obedience and acqui-escence of their audience members echoes the authoritative relations between art institutions and those who visit them; between choreogra-phers and dancers and between performers and participants. *Duotones* is therefore a choreographed work that explores very specific processes of intersubjectivity-as-art, ones that are manipulative as well as arbi-trary. It can be argued that it demonstrates *queer choreographic authority* or an instance of choreo-policing that is in fact choreo-political, once again challenging the binary. It is worth reiterating that historically art museums have presented very specific bodies, ones positioned within certain configurations of imperialist power, to be viewed by those at the summit of an exhibitionary order of things, in other words, the dominating gaze of a white, bourgeois, metropolitan and male eye. An examination of the relations between choreographer and dancer indicates a traffic of bodies and ideologies, the command of docile bodies and subjects who must yield to the instruction of a previously decided sequence of actions. As I have argued, choreographic commands can be perpetuated by religious, salutary, professional, psychoanalytic and artistic authoritative structures in order to dictate action and behaviour. smith repeatedly performed instruction until such authoritative structures seemed absurd, even arbitrary. As someone who attended the performance, I found myself becoming fatigued, exasperated, even a little bored. I began to wonder how long I was expected to obey the instructions and what would happen if I ceased to. When smith finally stopped moving us around, and the performance ended, I felt an immense sense of relief that the ordeal was over, and a certain pride in the fact that I managed to support the artist by obeying them and helping to make the performance a success.

smith's performance *Gutter Matters* (2014) begins with the artist lying face down in the gutter outside of an art gallery "as a kind of dance practice" (smith 2015). A helper stood above the artist with a sign that says "Gay Shame Parade" inviting passers-by to lie on the footpath with smith, to examine what is in the drain below with the aid of a torch. The performance inhabits an area that houses what is abject, forgotten and discarded from the city. It investigates the gutter as a place of sculptural interest rather than a space of lowness that merely channels detritus and waste. smith's horizontal placement of themselves and their participants in the gutter challenges the normative vertical axis, recalling Ahmed's conception of the queer as disorientation and a disturbance in the usual order of things.

smith has written of their interest in "mapping a politics of queer pride and shame" (2016b) and indeed the binary opposition of pride and shame tends to characterise and form queer identities, as stated by gender theorist Sally R. Munt. (2000: 533). Shame is also deeply relational, argued US-based psychologist Silvan Tomkins (Nathanson 1997: 107–138). Given that one's psyche develops in an interpersonal or relational context, for Tomkins shame is an innate affect that is triggered by some kind of stimulus. Often shame is caused when there has been an external impediment or inhibitor of interest and enjoyment which then becomes an impediment to further positive affects. Importantly, according to Tomkins, affect tends to amplify whatever has triggered it, thus shame begets shame: "Each affect is therefore a compelling stimulus for the production of more of that same affect" (Nathanson 1997: 122). For Munt shame is internally violent and contagious:

> we are ashamed of our shame, and then those around us catch it they flush and blush in awkward sympathy, vacillating, they turn their gaze upon another. (Munt 2000: 541)

Shame can refer to feelings of inferiority and discouragement. Relevant to the deliberate position of lowness adopted by smith in *Gutter Matters*, Tomkins gives physical responses to shame such as: the lowering or tilting of one's head in defeat, lowering the eyelids as well as decreased activity in facial and neck muscles. For Tomkins, everyone experiences the affect of shame at some point in their lives, for it is inevitable that desire outruns its fulfilment. "I want, but…" is the condition for the activation of shame (130).

I would argue that *Gutter Matters* produces an affect of shame so that it may be overcome and neutralised. So although shame might be something familiar to those persecuted within an intersubjective environment of compulsory heterosexuality, it can also be used as a methodology for creating choreographies. Note that Munt describes a "choreography of shame," one that involves the delivering of a gaze that deflects or cuts so that the subject is forced to turn away from the source of shame in the hope that one might be "*lost from view*" (Munt 2000: 541). If shame is embodied primarily in the face and gaze, then a transformative moment can involve turning back and looking at the other right back in the eyes. Indeed, for smith the aim is to increase visibility of this state and "make friends with shame" in order to take the power out of it (2016b). It is no coincidence that participating in smith's parade of shame involves a joint examination of gutter rubbish or what is cast away because, due to the way that the pride/shame opposition functions, abjection and shame go hand in hand. Shame is a kind of "social abjection," both are the result of rejection and repudiation, both operations attempt to separate and put people and things into their place. Yet abjection and shame can both be re-worked: in Munt's writing she notes that previously much homosexual discourse has repressed shame when really its ambivalent effects need to be revisited so that potential alliances can be explored and greater agency can be gained. For Munt shame is contradictory in nature, on the one hand, it functions to produce conformity, but on the other, it can "liberate new grammars of gender" (2000: 536). Shame has destabilising properties, thus its performance, invocation and citation can produce a "confrontational momentum" so that shame "becomes a statement of being" until paradoxically "the shame is shifted off" (538). The idea is that an intervention occurs in Tomkins' cycle of "stimulus-affect-response" (Nathanson 1997: 131) so that, via performance, responses to the affect of shame can be creatively altered and even co-created.

It is important to note that this definition of the affect of shame, the one used by Tomkins, Nathanson and Munt comes from the discipline of psychology. Generally historians of contemporary art tend to adopt philosophical theories of affect derived from Spinoza via Deleuze and Guattari. In her own discussion of various choreographic works, theorist Bojana Cvejić turns to theories of affect due to a contempt for theories of so-called authentic movement and kinaesthetic empathy (2015: 165). Such concerns relate to Rothfield's argument that any somatic mode of attention or way of attending is in fact a process that has been culturally and politically constituted, chiming with Ginot who sees a need for the normative systems of somatic practices to be de-naturalised, in the hope of finding somatic modes of attending to queer bodies, for example. As an alternative, Cvejić describes a particular expression of movement that is accounted for by a composition of affects and sensations. Wishing to detach movement from its subject Cvejić is interested in demonstrating:

> how the composition of movement relies on another understanding of expression, one that does not belong to the individual self of the performer, or to its attender, or to the relation between these two terms, but that instead arises in performance in and for itself and has an existence of its own. (2015: 285)

This idea of affect as something that arises from the performance itself with an existence of its own recalls what Deleuze and Guattari refer to as unnatural participation (2008) or an *affectability* that is no longer that of mere subjects, destabilising the subjectivity-intersubjectivity opposition as an "interstitial event" (168). Affectability is therefore un-hooked or delinked from individual subjects. Cvejić's concept of affect is highly indebted to Spinoza's distinction between *affection* as a state of an affected body that implies the presence of an affecting one and *affectus* or "affect" as the transition from one state to another felt by the affected body. For Cvejic, empathy is in fact affection because it involves imagination as well as an identification or imitation of affects. Cvejić quotes Spinoza:

> By affect I understand affections of the body by which the body's power of acting is increased or diminished, aided or restrained, and at the same time, the ideas of these affections. *Therefore, if we can be the adequate cause of any of these affections, I understand by the affect an action; otherwise, a passion.* (166)

Spinoza's concept of affects that might "approximate or coincide with adequate ideas of the mind, or actions" is useful for dance scholars and contemporary art theorists alike who might wish to posit performances as what Lepecki calls "an exchange of affects" (2006: 128). Cvejić takes Spinoza's thesis of active affects conceived by the mind and argues that these might also be produced by a performer's body. For Cvejić, affects can result from a choreography that is "a rational construction, which problematizes emotional expression through experimenting with ways of composing affects from bodily motion" (166–167).

From theorist Brian Massumi, Cvejić co-opts a concept of *affect* that emerges as an autonomous relation between resonating sensations and multiple senses that participate with one another, it is *synesthetic*. Affect is a capacity, a "measure of a living thing's potential interactions" and its "ability to transform the effects of one sensory mode into those of another" (174). Affect is a "matter of synesthetic transversal and transformative power of intensity." Recalling Jenn Joy's account of choreography as sensual address, Massumi's synesthetic affect is useful for accounts of choreography as a composition of affects because it is not limited to visual perception.

Coming back to smith's *Gutter Matters*, I propose that theories of affect are useful in that they may provide a way of attending to queer bodies that are less normative and culturally or politically constituted in an unhelpful way. If a de-linking of affect from subjects is indeed possible, then perhaps a performance or citation of shame as affect might enable it to be taken away or out of the intersubjective equation, to be acknowledged but then ejected. Rather than focussing on problematic theories of so-called authentic movement and smooth exchanges of empathy from idealised bodies to viewers as perfectly receptive vessels, a performance might be conceived as an experiment with ways of composing affects with the aid of bodily motion, or as Lepecki would argue, stillness. Affect as a transition from one felt state to another, something that enables one's power of acting to be increased or diminished and transform the effects of one sensory mode into another, is a useful tool for examining queer choreographies like *Gutter Matters* with less of the biases that have previously shaped discourses of dance and performance criticism.

In *Gutter Matters* a deliberate invitation is made to activate an affect of shame. smith deviates, performing a low and failed orientation, they challenge verticality, destabilising the normative axis of the upright figure. The artist is horizontal in an effort to be placed as low as possible, before crawling, maintaining horizontality in order to enter the gallery space in an unusual way.

The next phase of the performance involved crawling up two flights of stairs from the street up to the pristine white cube of the art gallery. According to smith "This is a Pride Parade of my own design. I finish with a slow-motion pompom routine on the floor." It is here that smith activates the other element of the pride/shame dichotomy, according to Munt pride involves "claiming a place in society – coming out in order to be entered in" (Munt 2000: 533). It is worth noting that the "pride" segment comes after that of shame and involves an entering into the space of the art gallery, smith proceeds from the gutter to the white cube, entering with pride as opposed to the abject which is ejected from spaces, cities and bodies. Such a transition is neither easy nor straightforward, smith must laboriously crawl from the space of shame to that of pride. Throughout the performance the artist, still soiled from their sojourn on the street is dressed in gold, wearing a long shaggy wig with gold tinsel wrapped around their neck and gold and blue foil pom-poms. Once inside smith performs what appears to be a cheerleading routine, a manipulation of pom-poms whilst lying on their back on the floor (Fig. 6.1). smith summarises that *Gutter Matters* "investigates the relationship between city drainage systems, ecological thinking, and a queer politics of pride and shame." smith evokes the convention of the very public gay pride parade with its relations of spectacular display and exhibitionism, though this is choreographed to be oblique or offline, performed with the artist lying horizontally on the gallery floor whilst others are standing upright. The intersubjective dynamic of pride/shame is activated and problematised so that it might then be interrogated and diffused; the opposition is complicated. It takes a certain amount of pride to decide to join smith's

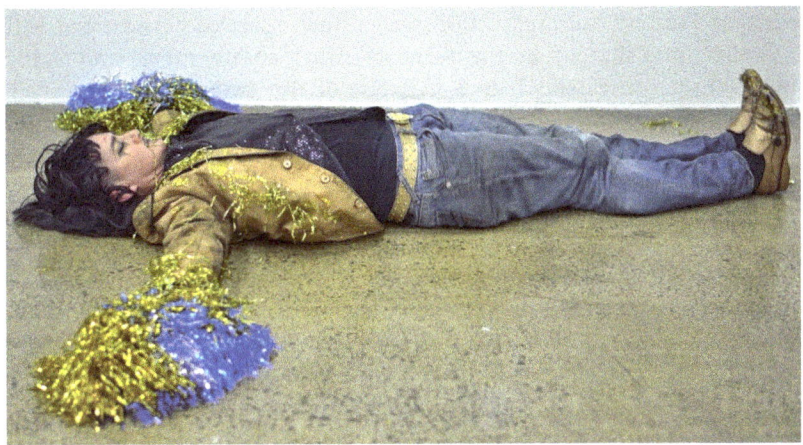

Fig. 6.1   val smith, *Gutter Matters*, 2014 (Live performance). Artspace, Auckland

"Gay Shame Parade" and there is a poignancy to the shabbiness of a slow-motion pom-pom routine delivered whilst lying on the ground.

Attending to smith's body as they deliberately assume positions of lowness, struggle, perseverance and celebration, however idiosyncratic, meant attending to affects of pride and shame that were delinked from a subject. The base materiality of the gutter was overwhelming and repellent. As smith climbed the stairs they were contaminated by its filth, as it matted their clothes, skin and tinsel wig, the very materiality smacked of dirt and shame. smith's experiments with composing affects of pride and shame then progressed to an unabashed celebration of freedom, one that was crooked, deviant and above all queer. They manipulated their pom-poms diligently, in slow motion, whilst remained faithful to an idea of positivity and cheer.

6.3   VAL SMITH: TRANSITIONING AND TRANSFORMATION

It is within liminal, threshold spaces that smith uses movement, action, proximity and contact to challenge the stability of identities. Two works by smith, *Meiosis* and *Homoshamanism*, both from 2016, took place outside the toilets of art galleries. Concerning shame and how it can be spatialised, Munt has noted that toilets are "the principal shame spaces of Western culture" (2000: 537). Such spaces are associated with "morality, punishment in the form of ritual chastisement, and sexual anxiety/indecipherability." It is in front of the two doors traditionally marked "male" and "female" that smith interacts with a fellow performer attempting to dissolve into their very identity. smith dons a costume to evoke the homoshaman, a queer and post-human creature, successfully enacting failure and creating lightness, humour and entertainment in the face of the machinations of power.

Earlier, in Chapter 2, I mentioned the possibility of activating an "other space," one that is heterotopic, a place for an individual whose behaviour deviates from norms. Via performance, the more customary, masculine, Newtonian and measured conception of space can be complicated, even queered. In *Meiosis* and *Homoshamanism* smith firmly positions their own body and those of their audience members within such a space. Borrowing from Halberstam I would add that the areas in and around public toilet facilities are simultaneously exterior and interior spaces, in and out, to perform before them activates a heterotopic space of affect and becoming. By situating themselves here as well as performing and labouring, smith indicates the use and materiality of such places and in doing so challenges the way that such spaces as heteronormative are generally associated with cleanliness and hygiene, whereas for queer communities, they can be spaces of cruising and gathering (2011: 113).

Continuing this discussion of queer spatiality, for Ahmed, "orientations matter" because they affect what bodies can do and *where* they might do it. Ahmed describes the queer world as "a space of entrances, exits, unsystematised lines of acquaintance, projecting horizons, typifying examples, alternate routes, blockages, incommensurate geographies" (Berlant and Warner quoted in Ahmed, 565). For Ahmed, being oriented in different ways matters because of the ways in which spaces are already oriented around the straight body. The city street is therefore "normally a heterosexual space," its appearance is produced by the "repetitive performances of hegemonic asymmetrical gender identities and heterosexual desires" that go on to "congeal over time" (563). Even more so than the street, public toilets are facilities that reinforce such identities and desires. Such spaces have become something of an obsession for smith, and part of their research has been examining "bathroom experiences for transgender, non-binary and gender non-conforming folks" (smith 2016c: unpaginated).[7] This also ties into wider concerns about proposed laws that would make it a crime for a person to enter a single-sex public restroom that does not match the person's "biological gender."[8]

Interrogating how spaces are oriented around straight bodies, it was on a wooden bench outside the public toilets of Auckland's Te Uru Waitakere Contemporary Gallery that smith chose to stage *Meiosis* (2016) with fellow dancer Kristian Larsen.[9] Similar to works previously mentioned by Rosetsky, Carpenter and Nash, *Meiosis* involved a process of enacting a unique intersubjective relation as an attempt to commingle or dissolve identities. This transitioning is gradual, unlike the discrete transition enacted by Bronstein's arch. In the words of smith, the aim of the performance was to engage in a four-hour process "of comprehensively transitioning to become each other" (smith 2016d: unpaginated). A disclaimer was added: "val smith and Kristian Larsen are in no way stable identities, rather they are in a constant and fluid state of reinterpretation of themselves through daily acts of sexual repetition." Rather than transitioning from one gender to another, smith attempts to transition into someone else, their fellow performer. Due to the way it activates the gap in between smith and Larsen, one that they attempt to bridge, *Meiosis* relates to Cvejić's ideas about affect as something delinked from or in-between subjects. With the aid of Deleuze, Cvejić extends this idea so that affect is "purely transitive" and "experienced in a lived duration that involves the difference between two states" (Deleuze quoted in Cvejić 2015: 168). Emphasising duration, for Deleuze affect is "a transition between two states of affection" (169). Affects are not feelings, they do not arise from the affection of the subject "Instead, active affects arise from the subject's increased power of acting (*puissance*), of forming compositions or *agencements* in which they emerge." It is this very *agencement* or becoming, this attempted composition that is activated in smith's *Meiosis*.

Both smith and Larsen were dressed in a similar way, both sported short-cropped haircuts and wore plaid shirts, crudely cut blue denim shorts, white sneakers and a wrist-watch. smith noted that prior to the performance they anticipated the need for an "embodied listening practice… drawing on a kinaesthetically focused practice of empathy to comprehend the subjectivities" of Larsen. smith also conjured the notion of osmosis and the possibility for the identification of impressions that "might emerge through an osmotic process of sensing, listening and tuning." The performance itself involved:

sensing and talking. Sensing through touch, closeness, being-with; talking through noticing, awareness and the sharing of insights and embodied experiences.

Parts of the performance involved touch, smith and Larsen mapped or touched parts of each other's bodies, sometimes with the same parts, wrist on wrist, elbow on elbow, in a kind of tactile mirroring or correspondence in close proximity. However, there were a lot of non-touch interactions such as closeness, conversation, shared experiences of the space and relations with people who sat with them in the gallery. On reflection, smith noted that although they entered the performance with the belief that they could actually become Larsen, afterwards they became concerned about the ethical implications. smith and Larsen moved through the various spaces of the galleries, from outside the toilets to the exhibitions and café, they also participated in various other performances that were occurring simultaneously. smith wrote of the experience

> Unfortunately, I truly failed to become Kristian, yet I feel like I know him in my body a little more microperceptually and intimately, which I think is, in itself a small success ;). (smith 2016d)

smith reiterated "I failed the brief. I failed it utterly," and reflected that even though they failed to become Larsen, in the attempt they had managed to feel more of themselves through the process. Similar to Ahmed's conception of queerness as something wonky, not quite there or offline, is a concept of queer failure.[10] Failure, like shame, is an intersubjective relation smith deliberately courts in their choreographies. Indeed, it is what Halberstam refers to as the "queer art of failure" that "offers more creative, more cooperative, more surprising ways of being in the world" (2011: 2). Just as *Gutter Matters* questioned the role of pride in relation to shame, in its failure, *Meiosis* challenges the hegemony of success. For Halberstam.

> Resistance takes the form of investing in counterintuitive modes of knowing such as failure and stupidity; we might read failure, for example, as a refusal of mastery, a critique of the intuitive connections within capitalism between success and profit, and as a counterhegemonic discourse of losing. (Halberstam 2011: 11–12)

Homoshamanism is a series of performances in which smith dresses in a costume constructed from wigs that covers their entire face and body. In early performances the wigs were naturally coloured brown and blonde hair. In a later iteration they were crafted from bright red, clown-like wigs, referencing the artist's grandmother, who was a red-head, as well as evoking the "mysterious power" red-heads are meant to possess (smith 2016a).[11] smith has referred to this costume as a form of drag, but rather than altering the appearance of gender, it is instead a form of drag in which they might become more themselves. Similar to Le Roy, smith utilises costume to allow a transformation to take place and to create a body that is de-familiarised. The invocation of the word 'shaman' also indicates the techniques of transformation utilised by such figures. Harking back to Cvejić, the affect of smith's homoshaman is synesthetic: it is at once colour, visual stimulus and haptic, tactile, a person that is all synthetic hair, one that moves, touches, manipulates, writes and communicates, recalling Massumi's definition of affect as "matter of synesthetic transversal and transformative power of intensity" (Cvejić 2015: 174).

Homoshamanism (2016) was performed outside the public toilets within the Gus Fisher Gallery at the University of Auckland (Fig. 6.2).

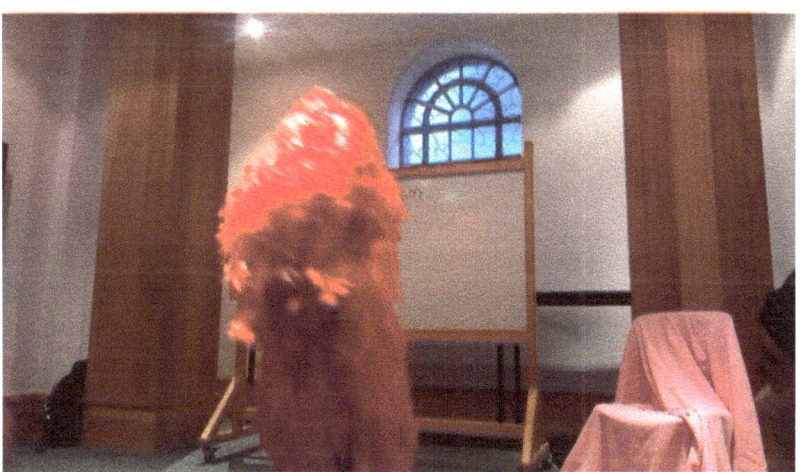

Fig. 6.2 val smith, *Homoshamanism*. 2016 (Live performance). Gus Fisher Gallery, University of Auckland (*Photo* Victoria Wynne-Jones)

There were two pieces of furniture, a whiteboard and a chair. The performance began with smith writing the heading "Homoshamanism" upon the whiteboard. The artist then undressed and put on the bright red costume. They then performed a series of actions, each announced by a heading written on the whiteboard beforehand. The headings read "Faux Falls, Contemporary Dancer, Artist Talk, Energy Healing, Gay Shame Parade, Femme Realness and Single Fitted Pink Sheet." At the end of the performance smith made two columns beside the headings, one reading "real" the other "fake." They set up an intersubjective relation of evaluation, beckoning to the audience to decide whether each component was "real" or "fake," and perhaps also "failure" or "success," marking each with either a tick or a cross.[12] The personage of smith's homoshaman appears without gender and with an indeterminate humanity, half yeti or abominable snowman. "It" has no real face, undermining intersubjective and automated systems of facial recognition and empathy. Appearing as a body without a face the figure provides a counterfactual to Deleuze and Guattari's "facialisation:" the very human system of organisation that bestows subjectification (O'Sullivan 2012: 190). smith's adoption of the homoshaman persona ties into an observation made by Croft that it is common for queer dance to involve a sensibility that embraces the "pleasures and difficulties of moving between multiple, layered identities" (2017: 1). In the last section of the performance, the homoshaman sits upon a chair and cocoons itself inside a pink-fitted sheet so that all that can be seen is an ovular pink cocoon shape with a hairy red centre. In making itself object-like, there is no doubt that the homoshaman is an utterly post-human figure. Although it is de-familiarising, they are also completely entertaining, activating intersubjective relations that are light and comical—in contrast to the challenging issues it engages with. smith messes with multiple codes and disciplines, they are at once choreographer, dancer, performer, teacher, comedian. Additionally, the homoshaman is illegible as a figure, it is difficult to keep track of limbs, trunk, neck and head. Such illegibility can be strategic according to Halberstam, it

> points to an argument for antidisciplinarity in the sense that knowledge practices that refuse both the form and content of traditional canons may lead to unbounded forms of speculation, modes of thinking that ally not with rigor and order but with inspiration and unpredictability. (2011: 10)

As part of their queer choreographies, smith utilises instruction and commanding actions in order to expose choreo-policing and the arbitrariness of obedient behaviour within the space of an art gallery. Self-consciously exposing themselves to alternating intersubjective relations of pride and shame, smith performs actions that are lowly as well as celebratory, inviting participation and complicity. An openness, perhaps, even resignation to fakery and failure, is made manifest along with their accompanying positions of queer, deviancy and disorientation. I would argue that smith's performances enact alternative choreo-political actions, offering what Halberstam would call "models of contestation, rupture and continuity for the political present" (2011: 19). Strategically situating themselves in places that spatialise straightness and determine specific gender identities, smith deploys disguise, drag and transformation to interrogate sexual difference, unitary identities and the machinations of power. They delight in counter-intuitive modes of being, knowing and doing and resist the tyranny of received notions of mastery and success.

NOTES

1. smith is spelled with a lower-case 's' and the artist's preferred pronouns are 'they/theirs.'
2. Another aspect missing is the eroticism, a powerful pre-reflective interpretational mode that engages with all of the senses.
3. See Pauline Boudry/Renate Lorenz «Moving Backwards», Pauline Boudry/Renate Lorenz—La Biennale di Venezia 2019, *You Tube* https://www.youtube.com/watch?v=tb7AouZtN7E.
4. See the discussion of vogueing in Chapter 5 as part of Rebecca Hobbs' *Mangere Mall* (2011).
5. *Sprezzatura* is a term coined by Italian courtier Baldassare Castiglione (1478–1529) (Bronstein and Marston 2007).
6. Barry White, *Can't Get Enough of Your Love, Babe* (1974). val smith *Duotones* performed at Artspace, Auckland as part of the exhibition "to and fro" curated by Khye Hitchcock, July–August, 2014.
7. As part of their Caroline Plummer Fellowship smith hosted an evening entitled "This Cloud is Queering" on June 19, 2016, Under Market 177 George Street, Dunedin. One component of the event was a series of gender-inclusive composting toilets illuminated by disco lights.
8. See http://www.newyorker.com/news/news-desk/whos-afraid-of-same-sex-bathrooms.

9. val smith and Kristen Larsen *Meoisis* (2016) performed 13 February, 2016 at Te Uru Waitakere Contemporary Gallery, Titirangi as part of the exhibition "They Come from Far Away: A Performance Series."

10. This concept of *queer failure* is explored in performances by Keith Hennessey and his West Coast Dance Company Circo Zero, see http://circozero.org/ and Halberstam (2011).

11. The use of wigs also evokes another instance of queer performance Alain Buffard's *Dispositifs 3.1* (2001) performed at the Espace Pier Paolo Pasolini in Valenciennes.

12. This ties into Valentina Desideri's practice of "fake therapy." This involves a series of twenty cards, easily available on-line that detail somatic instructions to be performed in twenty minutes sessions in which people take turns trying to "heal" each other. See https://faketherapy.wordpress.com/.

References

Ahmed, Sara. 2006. Toward a Queer Phenomenology. *GLQ: A Journal of Lesbian and Gay Studies* 12: 543–574.

Bennett, Tony. 1995. *The Birth of the Museum: History, Theory, Politics*. London; New York: Routledge.

Boudry, Pauline, Renate Lorenz, and Charlotte Laubard. 2019. *Pauline Boudry/Renate Lorenz: Moving Backwards*. Milan: Skira editore.

Bradford, Mark. 2008. Lisa Tan Mark Bradford at Laxart. YouTube. https://www.youtube.com/watch?v=rI6dIbI6iH0. Accessed 25 November 2016.

Braidotti, Rosi. 2013. *The Posthuman*. Cambridge: Polity.

Brodie, Julie A., and Elin E. Lobel. 2012. *Dance and Somatics: Mind Body Principles of Teaching and Performance*. Jefferson, North Carolina; London: McFarland & Company, Inc.

Bronstein, Pablo, and Rebecca Mar Marston. 2007. Interview between Pablo Bronstein and Rebecca Mar Marston, New York, 4 Nov 2007. Performa. http://07.performa-arts.org/performa_live.php?date=2007-11-15. Accessed 25 November 2016.

Corber, Robert J., and Stephen Valocchi. 2003. *Queer Studies: An Interdisciplinary Reader*. Malden: Blackwell.

Croft, Clare. 2017. *Queer Dance*. New York: Oxford University Press.

Csordas, Thomas J. 1993. Somatic Modes of Attention. *Cultural anthropology* 8.2: 135–156.

Cvejić, Bojana. 2015. *Choreographing Problems: Expressive Concepts in European Contemporary Dance and Performance*. Houndmills; Basingstoke; Hampshire: Palgrave Macmillan.

Deleuze, Gilles, and Félix Guattari. 2008. *A Thousand Plateaus*. Trans. Brian Massumi. London: Continuum, 2008.

Eaton, Jeremy. 2018. Drag Family Values: Lineages of Drag Gesture. Presented at "Minor Activisms 1" convened by Kim Donaldson & Katve-Kaisa Kontturi as part of *Aesthetics, Politics and Histories: The Social Context of Art 2018 AAANZ Conference*, RMIT School of Art, Melbourne Australia.

Ginot, Isabelle. 2010. From Shusterman's Somaesthetics to a Radical Epistemology of Somatics. *Dance Research Journal* 42.1: 12–29.

Goumarre, Laurent. 2014. Disobedience and DIY. In *Danse: An Anthology*, ed. Noémie Solomon, 275–282. Dijon: Les presses du réel.

Halberstam, Judith. 2011. *The Queer Art of Failure*. Durham: Duke University Press.

Jones, Amelia. 1998. *Body Art: Performing the Subject*. Minneapolis: University of Minnesota Press.

Kolb, Alexandra. 2013. Current Trends in Contemporary Choreography: A Political Critique. *Dance Research Journal* 45: 31–52.

Kosofsky Sedgwick, Eve. 1993. *Tendencies*. Durham: Duke University Press.

Kosofsky Sedgwick, Eve. 2008. *Epistemology of the Closet*. Berkeley; Los Angeles; London: University of California Press.

Lepecki, André. 2006. *Exhausting Dance: Performance and the Politics of Movement*. New York: Routledge.

Lord, Catherine, and Richard Meyer. 2013. *Art & Queer Culture*. London, New York: Phaidon Press Limited.

Munt, Sally R. 2000. Shame/Pride Dichotomies in Queer as Folk. *Textual Practice* 14.3: 531–546.

Nathanson, D. L. 1997. Shame and the Affect Theory of Silvan Tomkins. In *The Widening Scope of Shame*, eds., M. R. Lansky and A. P. Morrison, 107–138. Hillsdale: Analytic Press.

O'Sullivan, Simon. 2012. *On the Production of Subjectivity: Five Diagrams of the Finite-Infinite Relation*. London: Palgrave Macmillan Limited.

Rosenthal, Stephanie. 2010. Choreographing You: Choreographies in the Visual Arts. In *Move: Choreographing You*, ed. Stephanie Rosenthal, 8–21. London: Hayward Publishing.

Rothfield, Philipa. 2010. Differentiating Phenomenology and Dance. In *The Routledge Dance Studies Reader 2nd ed.* Eds. Alexandra Carter and Janet O'Shea, 303–318. Abingdon; New York: Routledge.

smith, val. 2015. Gutter Matters Pecha Kucha Styles. Valvalvalsmithsmithsmith. https://valvalvalsmithsmithsmith.blogspot.co.nz/2015/04/gutter-matters-for-dunedin-fringe.html. Accessed 11 October 2016.

smith, val. 2016a. *Personal Interview*. 13 September 2016.

smith, val. 2016b. Mapping a Politics of Queer Pride and Shame. valvalval-smithsmithsmith. https://valvalvalsmithsmithsmith.blogspot.com/2016/07/mapping-politics-of-queer-pride-and.html. Accessed 11 October 2016.

smith, val. 2016c. Mapping Queer Experiences: Caroline Plummer Fellowship—Week 1. valvalvalsmithsmithsmith. https://valvalvalsmithsmithsmith.blogspot.co.nz/2016/02/mapping-queer-experiences.html. Accessed 11 October 2016.

smith, val. 2016d. Meiosis. valvalvalsmithsmithsmith. https://valvalvalsmithsmit hsmith.blogspot.co.nz/2016/10/meiosis.html. Accessed 11 October 2016.

Warburton, Edward C. 2011. Of Meanings and Movements: Re-languaging Embodiment in Dance Phenomenology and Cognition. *Dance Research Journal* 43.2: 65–83.

CHAPTER 7

Walking the Wall and Crossing the Threshold: Angela Tiatia, Kalisolaite 'Uhila and Shigeyuki Kihara's Counter-Hegemonic Choreographies

In her publication *Performing the Margins: An Anthem of Hope* writer and director Louise Tu'u describes performance art as a "processual tool" that can be used to "draw audiences into the dis-ease of social relationships" (Tu'u 2017: 3).[1] The idea is that an emphasis on "dis-ease" or the discomfort that can be created by a performance artwork can re-perpetuate existing dysfunctional or problematic relations and in doing so "develop a system to critique the ethics of [certain] communities." This argument is part of Tu'u's reflections upon a performance she facilitated in the context of the Physics Room, a contemporary art gallery in Christchurch, New Zealand. The artist has described *An Anthem of Hope* (2013) as a process in which her body brought with it a representation of "Pacific Island performance art" however it may have been received (7). Its emphasis on relations means that Tu'u's strategy can also be applied to performances that have taken place in contemporary art contexts and museums and my broader argument about the relationality of choreography. Certain performances can also be considered processual artworks that re-perpetuate the unease of existing relationships so that they might critique such relations as well as the very societies or structures they take place within.

All three artists discussed in this chapter were educated in Tāmaki Makaurau Auckland, New Zealand, the city in which this book was written. As New Zealand's most populous city, Auckland is home to many migrant populations including Pacific peoples, a dynamic and diverse group who either migrated from the Pacific islands or who identify with the Pacific islands because of ancestry or heritage.[2] According to the 2018 Census, 64% of Pacific Peoples in New Zealand live in Auckland and some island nations now have more people living in Auckland and New Zealand than in the island countries themselves. Many migrants from Polynesian islands that have strong historical links with the country such as Samoa, Tonga, Cook Islands and Niue came to New Zealand in the 1960s and 1970s in response to various labour shortages. Currently Auckland's Pacific population is mostly "New Zealand-born, predominantly young, and highly urbanised" (Auckland Council). Pacific peoples, sometimes referred to as Pasifika, are the fourth largest ethnic group, in 2018 they made up 16% of the Auckland population.[3] Tāmaki Makaurau is also home to Polyfest and Pasifika, annual festivals of performing art and cultures from the Pacific Islands.

Before continuing, it is worth noting that this chapter focuses on artworks by Pasifika artists rather than indigenous Māori as *tangata whenua* or "people of the land." One factor that leads to this decision is that recently performances in contemporary art exhibitions by Pasifika artists are more endemic than those by Māori artists in New Zealand art institutions.[4] More research as to why this is the case is needed. Although there is a strong history of Māori western theatrical dance companies, there tends to be more of a focus on *kapa haka* or Māori performing arts in festivals and spaces such as marae where they enjoy more autonomy than within western art museums. There is also the possibility that non-indigenous or *tauiwi* curators who are predominantly white, settler or Pākehā New Zealanders feel less threatened by Pasifika artists. This way they are working *tauiwi to tauiwi* rather than operating within a colonising discipline with artists from indigenous backgrounds.

Just as Tu'u stated that her body brought into the gallery one specific instance of Pacific Islands performance art, I will argue that simple insertions of particular bodies within and around art institutions perform a kind of institutional critique, inflecting the choreo-political so that it can be decolonising or "counter-hegemonic" (Tuhiwai Smith 1999: 189). They do so by drawing on the influence and agency of indigenous Pacific concepts, knowledges and experiences. Through insertions of their own performing bodies, artists Angela Tiatia, Kalisolaite 'Uhila and Shigeuki Kihara activate and interrogate the very thresholds of institutions, disciplines and colonial structures. Each realise relational or intersubjective encounters that undermine authority, they are choreographies performed by Pasifika artists, those previously categorised by the museum and its binary logic as sexualised and racialized others. Exceeding the disciplinary structures so omnipresent in contemporary exhibition spaces, these counter-hegemonic choreographies present their own particular permutations of relations. They evade authority, challenge subjection and enact dissensus, encouraging criticality and enabling novel or more equitable intersubjective relations.

Evoking Tu'u's "dis-ease," these three artists are disobedient, like smith in the previous chapter, their actions promote misbehaviour, other ways of moving and being, ways that deviate. Challenges to verticality take place, together with the performance of pedestrian acts of walking, sheltering and sleeping, they encourage shifts in perspective and orientation. Such bodies can be defiant as well as sexualised, repeating movements from customary Pacific dances with difference and exposing bodily adornment in order to fight against intersubjective relations of shame and stigmatisation. Making such specific bodies visible and exhausted draws attention to their artistic labour, as well as histories of exploitation within the museum. Sites of struggle are occupied so that choreographies might take place within them. Counter-dominant ideologies are performed and presented in acts and dances that are indigenizing and that manifest protest. Prior political events are recounted by presenting dances that are then re-oriented towards a future that might continue to re-negotiate the spaces and disciplines of colonial power.

I will contextualise Tiatia, 'Uhila and Kihara's practices within a specific narrative about Pacific bodies performing and creating interventions in museums and contemporary art gallery spaces in Aotearoa New Zealand and beyond, as part of a response to calls to enliven the museum. These performances will also be discussed in relation to a broader story about an imperialist and colonial order of things that specific bodies were subject to in the nineteenth-century museums and exhibitions described in Chapter 2. This chapter inflects choreo-politics in a specific way, of central importance is how performance art practices can be *decolonising*, particularly when indigenous artists explicitly position themselves in order to disrupt intersubjective structures of power and challenge the categories they have historically been placed within. A theory of decolonizing research methodologies as outlined by Māori academic Linda Tuhiwai

Smith (Ngāti Awa, Ngāti Porou) will be applied to performance art, arguing that such artworks can participate in long-term processes of divestment of colonial power. In the final section of this chapter I will look at an argument from art historian and curator Chloe Weaver that Nicholas Bourriaud's idea of relational space has affinities with the Pacific concept of the *vā*, or the sacred space of interrelations.

7.1   WALKING THE WALL: PACIFIC BODIES IN MUSEUMS AND CONTEMPORARY ART GALLERIES

Angela Tiatia's moving image work *Walking the Wall* (2014, Fig. 7.1) was screened most recently in New Zealand as part of the exhibition *Tatau: Sāmoan Tattooing and Photography* at Te Papa Tongarewa Museum of New Zealand, in Wellington in 2019. In this video the camera is fixed upon the corner of a white-walled space. A pair of black women's high heel shoes has been placed within the frame. A woman walks in from the left, her legs are adorned with Samoan women's tatau known as the *malu,* she wears a black leotard and a gold ring on the ring finger of her left hand. This is Auckland-born, Sydney-based multimedia artist Tiatia. She steps into the tall shoes, adjusting them as they cling to the skin of her

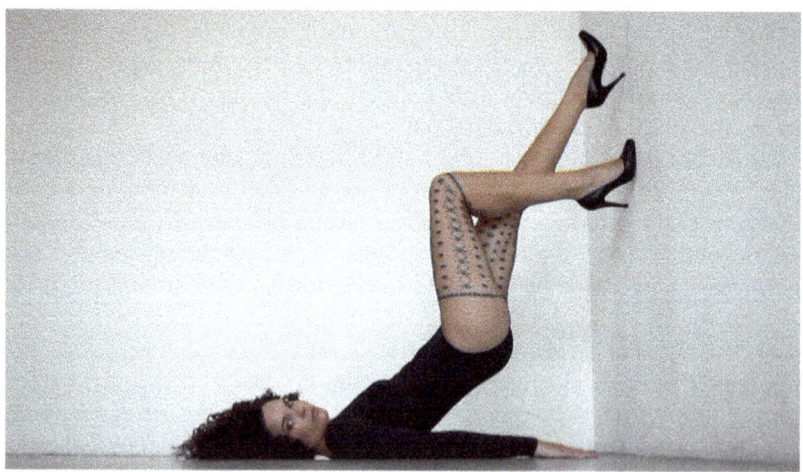

Fig. 7.1   Angela Tiatia, *Walking the Wall*, 2014 (Single-channel HD video, colour, sound, 13 minutes, 4 seconds, looped. Courtesy of the artist)

bare feet. For a moment she stands in profile so that the shoes, her *tatau* and the black costume can be seen. She then slowly turns around, towards the back of the cornered space. She deliberately positions herself, facing the side wall. She slowly approaches it until her hip-bones and pelvis make contact. Keeping her knees touching the wall, she bends and leans backwards, her weight on her hands, placing her body so that the tips of her feet touch the wall, her legs are bent and she lies on her back upon the floor. Tiatia looks straight ahead at the ceiling above her. She then inches forwards with her hands and buttocks until she is close enough to place one foot in its high heel shoe upon the wall. The artist turns her head so that she looks directly into the camera and begins to slowly walk her feet vertically up the wall. When she has walked as far as she can whilst simultaneously lying on her back, Tiatia proceeds to slowly walk her feet back down again, usually taking five steps up and five steps down, before placing her feet on the ground again. This action is relentlessly repeated for around twelve minutes during which time the artist gradually gets fatigued and her movements become more weighted and less precise. Finally failing to trace the careful steps up the wall, Tiatia rolls onto her side and then again onto her back, breaking her gaze with the camera, she looks at the ceiling above her. She kicks off the shoes one by one and lies supine with her legs bent and bare feet on the ground. Breathing heavily, for a moment she is still. She slowly gets up without looking at the camera and exits to the left.

In Tiatia's *Walking the Wall* (2014) a simple everyday action, that of walking, is precisely reperformed with a change in orientation, a switch from a horizontal to a vertical plane.[5] Tiatia enacts a kinaesthetic shift in walking so that it becomes even more prey to gravity and hence more difficult and cumbersome. Harking back to Trisha Brown's 1971 work *Walking on the Gallery Wall* at the Whitney Museum of American Art in New York City, Tiatia's performance is an endurance exercise that consists of a choreo-political repetition and re-orientation of a simple and isolated action, as well as a ludic engagement with the architectural device of the white cube exhibition space. It is a personal, intimate presentation and portrayal of a very specific kind of body in a public space, one that is female, dressed in high-heeled shoes and the modish, intimate-wear of a black leotard. Tiatia presents herself to viewers in a sexualised manner, her legs and upper chest are exposed. Additionally she is slender and youthful, as a former actress and television presenter, her body is one that would generally be considered to be physically attractive. Tiatia's upper thighs with her distinctive adornment or *malu* signify a body that is female as well as Samoan. *Malu* is the name given for women's tatau that is less elaborate than those for men and appears on the legs, starting at the knee and finishing at the top of the thigh (Mallon and Fecteau 2002: 23). The *malu* together with the high-heeled shoes are potent cultural signifiers of femininity, pointing to the way in which intersubjective relations help to produce specific subjectivities. Tiatia's hair and skin-tone also signify a female Pacific body.[6] As Auckland-based artists Lana Lopesi and Louisa Afoa point out, "throughout the Pacific, our hair is big and our skin is dark" (2015, unpaginated). The small steps she makes also evoke the steps a dancer makes in Siva Samoa or Samoan dance though they are more pedestrian, less of a lateral movement of heels and toes. The locked-off camera, with its frame fixed upon a corner, constructs a box-like space or square. This compositional form, together with Tiatia's walking evokes Bruce Nauman's constrained work *Dance or Exercise on the Perimeter of a Square* (1968). Although Nauman occupies the particular private working space of an artist's studio, Tiatia inhabits more of a photographic studio with its neutral white background. The implications of the presentation of such a filmed body within a white cube space, inside a museum, relate specifically to my wider thesis of the ways in which artworks utilise simple choreographies in order to evade or subvert the authoritative relations and hierarchies perpetuated within and by such institutions.

Tiatia alters her orientation as a de-familiarising tactic, it is important to note that she "mis-behaves" and in doing so confronts, as a subject, the intersubjective conventions and stereotypes placed upon the Pacific female body. By openly displaying her sacred *malu*, an act of cultural taboo for Samoans, Tiatia confronts what is usually forbidden and in doing so exposes herself to criticism. It is worth noting that although the origins of the female tatau are sacred, it is becoming more and more common for women to show their malu. According to the artist, "I fix my body in states of conflict between the sacred and the uninhibited" (quoted in Forrest 2016: unpaginated). Part of being a Samoan woman living in the diaspora involves contradictory expectations placed upon her body by minority, indigenous cultures as well as Western, mass global culture. Hence the pressure to "uncover and cover my body at the same time" (Forrest 2016) and the highly feminised cultural signs of black stiletto shoes and the malu. For Tiatia, the action in *Walking the Wall* is absurd, reflecting the ridiculousness of such expectations. On the one hand Tiatia embraces, to the point of exhaustion, symbols of female sexuality and its commodification in mass consumer culture. On the other hand Tiatia protests, openly revealing the sacred malu, highlighting the double standards within Samoan culture when it comes to revealing the male and female tatau, as men are free to openly display theirs with pride in public, whilst women are not. *Walking the Wall* is therefore a protest against patriarchal power, both Samoan and Western. Performing her frustration, Tiatia demonstrates the way in which such expectations are "driving her up the wall."[7]

In contrast to her former employment, Tiatia reflects that presently "I finally have gained control over my own body and image after years of being weighed, measured, dressed and silenced" (Forrest 2016). Instead her body has become a "site for protest," one that exposes "the changing landscape of globalisation and neo-colonial politics on the public and private body." According to Tiatia such politics "sit on the body like a blanket" and create confusion and a lack of clarity. Like val smith in the previous chapter, Tiatia explores the multiple dimensions of the inter-subjective relations of shame, as the shaming of women demonstrates the "sexism and Christian pathology" embedded within diasporic Samoan cultures:

> I wanted to convey the implications of contemporary times and issues on the body, identity and communities... I am empowering young women with the malu (to not shame them and to confront reasons why they think it's so wrong to show it). (Forrest 2016)

By staring defiantly into the camera, Tiatia is resistant, she returns the gaze of those who look upon her, challenging the "dusky maiden" stereotype of "sexually uninhibited and free-loving" Pacific women perpetuated in eighteenth century written accounts from European explorers, nineteenth-century ethnographic and touristic photographs as well as twentieth century Paciflicks (Vercoe 2004: 38).[8] Referring back to Tu'u's provocation, in *Walking the Wall* Tiatia uses her semi-clad body, feminine attire, action and a confrontational gaze to make manifest social relations of shame, discomfort and unease. Tiatia's insertion of herself into the space of the white cube and by extension the museum exists in relation to a specific exhibition history from the 1990s onwards of Pacifika artists performing and intervening in New Zealand museums as, well a broader narrative about the ways certain bodies have historically been displayed within what cultural theorist Tony Bennett has described as the "exhibitionary complex" (1995).

7.2   PASIFIKA STYLES: A SHORT EXHIBITION HISTORY OF PACIFIC BODIES PERFORMING IN MUSEUMS AND CONTEMPORARY ART INSTITUTIONS

Tiatia's *Walking the Wall* (2014) exists within a larger story about Pacific bodies performing and creating interventions in museums and contemporary art gallery spaces in Aotearoa New Zealand. It has been outlined here due to the fact that to date such a comprehensive survey has not yet existed. *Te Moemoea no Iotefa—the Dream of Joseph* curated by Rangi-hiroa Panoho at the Sarjeant Gallery, Whanganui in 1990 is generally recognised as the first major exhibition of Pasifika art in New Zealand (Lythberg 2008: 40). Subsequent exhibitions of contemporary Pacific art included the touring exhibition *Bottled Ocean: Contemporary Polynesian Artists* (1994–1995) and *Paradise Now?: Contemporary Art from the Pacific* at the Asia Society Museum, New York City in 2004. In 2007 Fuli Pereira and Ron Brownson curated *Le Folauga* an exhibition of fourteen Pacific artists at the Auckland Museum, its title courtesy of Samoan artist Johnny Penisula that encapsulates the idea of bringing the learned histories of the past with us into the future, as well as the notion of a flotilla moving together and forward. Since its inception in the 1980s, Tāmaki Makaurau-based, Pacific arts organisation Tautai have consistently facilitated performance events and exhibitions featuring performance art. This must be acknowledged so that the narrative is not dominated by the hegemonic museum and gallery system.

In terms of contemporary Pacific performance art, one important moment was when the Pacific Sisters collective performed at the opening of *Bottled Ocean* at Auckland City Art Gallery in 1994 (Leonard and Vercoe 1997). The membership of the collective shifts over time, however all tend to be born in New Zealand with Pacific Islands and Māori backgrounds. First formed in 1992 by Selina Forsythe, Suzanne Tamaki and Niwhai Tupaea, the collective has been a platform for Māori and Pacific Islands talent that involves fashion shows, multimedia productions and performances (Gordon-Smith 2018). Their signature is various personae clad in elaborate, hybrid and often risqué costumes that combine customary Pacific adornment, high fashion, conservative missionary garments, thrift store finds and costumes crafted from upcycled detritus. At the opening of *Bottled Ocean* curated by Cook Islands artist and curator Jim Vivieaere, the Pacific Sisters wore costumes referencing characters from the Mangaian tale of the maiden Ina and eel-king Tuna. Members mingled with the crowd and this re-telling of the story highlighted the importance of oral history and performance in Pacific art (Leonard and Vercoe). In 2000 Pacific Sisters performed at the 12th Biennale of Sydney in collaboration with Lisa Reihana at the Art Gallery of New South Wales, as well as the Museum of Contemporary Art.[9] In 2013 a performance series *More Than We Know*, curated by Ioana Gordon Smith was staged at the Gus Fisher Gallery in Auckland which included work by 'Uhila as well as Jeremy Leatinu'u, Sesilia Pusiaki, Darcell Apelu, and Nastashia Simeona Apelu. And in 2018, queer Pacific art collective FAFSWAG (also mentioned in Chapter 5) held live events at the Auckland Art Gallery and Auckland Museum.

Tiatia and Kihara both performed within Pacific Sisters as did Rosanna Raymond, an artist with Samoan heritage who would go on to co-curate the exhibition *Pasifika Styles* with Tauiwi Amiria Salmond in 2006 at the Museum of Archaeology and Anthropology (MAA) in Cambridge, UK. *Pasifika Styles* is part of another strand of this exhibition history, that of interventions by Pacific artists in western museums that house anthropological and ethnographic collections. As Tauiwi consultant Billie Lythberg explains, each of these shows acts as a platform for dialogue between living artists, artefacts and the viewing public (Lythberg 2008: 42). According to Lythberg, an earlier template for the Cambridge exhibition was *Redress* which was organised by Samoan artist John Ioane at the Auckland War Memorial Museum in 1997. As a way of mourning and acknowledging the dismantling of the museum's Pacific hall and the lengthy storage of its collections, Ioane and a group of fellow artists dressed the partially emptied space with site-specific works. For Pacific art historian Karen Stevenson *Redress* demonstrated a conflict between the ideologies supporting "captured objects" and "the surging lifeblood of the urban Pacific" (Lythberg 2008: 42). This dynamic was repeated a decade later when the contemporary art exhibition *Le Folauga* was shown at the same time as *Vaka Moana* an historically focussed touring show, though it is worth noting that the contemporary art was displayed separate from the Pacific halls which meant a true dialogue between customary and contemporary did not take place.

In response to a call to "enliven the museum," since the turn of this century there has been an increasing number of collaborative programmes like *Pasifika Styles* that bring together artists, ethnographic museums and originating communities (Raymond and Salmond 2008: 6). As part of an imperative to embrace a more social dynamic, museums such as the MAA twist Bourriaud's edict, acting as an arena for *cultural* rather than just social exchange. Ever since the exhibition *Te Māori* toured the United States in 1984 and 1985 accompanied by Māori kaitiaki or guardians, Pacific bodies have had increasing opportunities to be more physically present at such occasions, intervening in western museum spaces and by doing so exercising sovereignty over their stories and precious treasures. As explained by *Pasifika Styles* Māori artist Wayne Youle:

> Museums are that kind of hush-hush, clean, untouchable, tapu [sacred] kind of space. You wanna touch everything but you can't. It's a thing I'd like to explore... (Youle in Raymond and Salmond 2008: 68)

Recalling the thesis of performing museology mentioned in Chapter 2, according to co-curators Raymond and Salmond, Pasifika Styles was one way of bringing "the people and the song" back into the so-called hush-hush space of the ethnographic collection (Raymond and Salmond 2008: 6). Though it is worth noting that this process of enlivening was far from straightforward. Many of the artists installed their own work in a site-specific way and the exhibition did include various educational work-shops. However, a performing arts festival intended for the museum's courtyard was moved into theatres due to funding criteria (18). And the opening blessing performed by cultural experts Che Wilson and Gerrard Albert were in fact closed to the public so that it was not mistaken for "a performance for the benefit of anthropologists" (7).

This narrative about contemporary Pacific artists intervening in museums in the twenty-first century is part of a longer history discussed in Chapter 2, described by Tony Bennett as the "exhibitionary complex" in which nineteenth-century museums and exhibitions made manifest an imperialist and colonial "order of things" that specific bodies were subject to (Bennett 1995). It is important to note that contemporary art museums and galleries which have specific histories of subjection as these can have an impact on how particular bodies are perceived today. Within such historic structures Samoan bodies were represented as other and belonging to "non-civilised peoples upon whose bodies the effects of

power were unleashed" (1995: 67). There is no doubt about the position of Pacific bodies within the master/slave dialectic of the museum.
In a choreo-policing move, the discipline of anthropology during the
nineteenth century separated races into the civilised and the "primitive" who occupied a "twilight zone between nature and culture" (77).
One example of such framing is the sexualised and derogatory parading
and display of Khoikhoi woman Saartjie Baartman (c. 1770–1815) as a
curiosity in Paris and London.[10] Even after her death intimate parts of
her anatomy were studied then presented to the French Academy which
arranged for their display in the Musée d'Ethnographie de Paris. Her
body was displayed until 1974 and her remains were finally repatriated
to South Africa and buried in 2002. Thus the implied, exhibition-going
public, the white citizenries of the imperialist powers were merged into
an undifferentiated unity as well as the "just beneficiaries, of the processes
of evolution and identified as a unity in opposition to the primitive otherness of conquered peoples" (Bennett 1995: 79). A system of organisation
was created in which the construction of a radically different Other and
the exhibition of so-called other peoples, became a vehicle for imperialist
edification.

This system of ordering or organisation was reflected in the Crystal
Palace as part of the Great Exhibition of London in 1851. The palace
adhered to principles of classification based on nations as well as supra-
national constructs of empires and races, actualised in the form of national
courts and display areas.[11] Pavilions were developed for each participating
country which were then zoned into racial groups. Crucially, within this
system of organisation "black peoples and the aboriginal populations
of conquered territories" were "denied any space of their own, being
represented as subordinate adjuncts to the imperial displays of the major
powers" (Bennett 1995: 82–83). Bennett argues that the exhibition of
non-white peoples themselves and not just their remains or artefacts,
meant they became mere "object lessons of evolutionary theory." One
example is the colonial city within the 1889 Paris Exposition that was
populated by Asian and African peoples in simulated "native villages." The
exhibition of people presented them as "living demonstrations of evolutionary theory." Non-white peoples were thus arranged, as though they
were objects into "a sliding scale of humanity, from the barbaric to the
civilized" and those relations of knowledge and colonial power continued
to be invested in the public display of bodies. It could be argued that
any insertion into art museums of bodies indigenous to the South Pacific

can be read in the context of such a history and the way such imperialist, colonial, intersubjective relations produced certain forms of subjection.

It is in the context of such a history, a history of exhibiting certain bodies as curiosities, monstrosities that were deemed radically other, as well as inferior and primitive, that Tiatia inserts her body. She enters the white cube exhibition space, scantily clad, a sexualised Pacific woman defiantly bearing the adornment that signifies she is Samoan. The actions she performs are simple, entering, slipping into high heel shoes, lying down and walking in a way that hints at Siva Samoa. The simple pedestrian act of walking is disoriented, she walks upon the walls instead of the floor and does so to the point of exhaustion. The way in which her gaze is directed towards the camera and those who view her is unflinching and relentless. *Walking on the Wall* enacts a very particular type of intersubjectivity, highlighting its oppositional, embodied, spatial, affective and emotional dimensions. Tiatia defies those who view her as an eroticised other, challenging those who might prefer for her to feel shame and demonstrates strength for those who identify with her position.

7.3   CROSSING THE THRESHOLD: DECOLONIZING CHOREOGRAPHIES

Another example of a performance that enacts institutional critique via the insertion of a Pacific body in and around the art museum is Kalisolaite 'Uhila's *Mo'ui Tukuhausia* (2014).[12] The title of the artwork can be translated as "to be absolutely stranded; to be left destitute and friendless" (Tonga 2014). In the most recent iteration of this performance 'Uhila lived homeless in and around Auckland Art Gallery for the roughly three-month duration of an exhibition (Fig. 7.2).[13] Prior to the conception of this work 'Uhila conducted a series of experiments in which he slept rough, spending the odd day or night being unkempt and living on the street which contrasted with his employment at the time, working as a security guard in Auckland's central business district (Gardner 2015: 160). One particular day 'Uhila attempted to enter Auckland Art Gallery, only to be denied entry and ushered out. This incident was pertinent due to the fact that 'Uhila himself was often required to move homeless people off the private properties he was guarding (Phillips 2014: 71).

As a former student of dance, 'Uhila's living as though homeless was the execution of a simple plan, score or choreography, yet its actualisation would prove complex, at the outset, there was no way of knowing

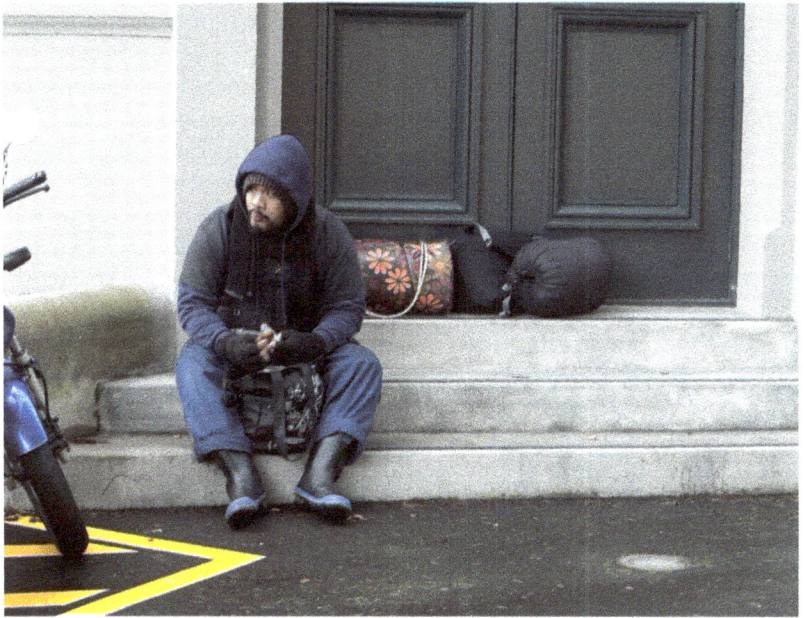

Fig. 7.2 Kalisolaite 'Uhila, *Mo'ui Tukuhausia*, 2014 (Live performance, three months). Performed in and around the Auckland Art Gallery Toi o Tāmaki, as part of the Walter's prize, 12 July–12 October 2014 (Courtesy of the artist and Michael Lett)

what would actually take place when the artist exposed himself to serious vulnerability and risk.[14] The task chosen by the artist was immensely difficult and demanding, both physically as it took place over winter months, but also psychologically as he was separated or exiled from his family and friends.

Complex intersubjective relations were activated, a significant burden was placed upon the infrastructure of the art gallery as the curatorial, security and management staff either worked extra hours or were on-call in order to ensure 'Uhila's safety. *Mo'ui Tukuhausia* bears a resemblance to an earlier work, *One Year Performance 1981–1982* by Taiwanese artist Tehching Hsieh, in which he attempted to stay outdoors for one year without going inside in his adopted city of New York (Heathfield and Hsieh 2009: 160). Hsieh and 'Uhila are both immigrants to the cities and countries they perform within. However, an important difference is that throughout his performance, during business hours 'Uhila used the gallery as a shelter and personal sanctuary, storing possessions and writing reflections upon the walls. But outside of these hours 'Uhila, like Hsieh, slept outside, making alliances and building relationships with a community of rough sleepers in the same area who taught him about survival in the urban environment with its "safe" areas and dangerous "dead zones" (Phillips 2014). The position 'Uhila takes up is that of an artist as immigrant, exile, untouchable, as well as one who is dependent for his very life, security and well-being, upon an art institution. Thus Mo'ui Tukuhausia produced a unique form of intersubjectivity with specific spatial, embodied, kinaesthetic and affective dimensions.

Choreographic authority is inflected in a particular way, 'Uhila's constraints are self-imposed. Spatially, 'Uhila like Tiatia, inserts his body into an art institution in a strategic and subversive way that also questions the location it takes place within. Yet the way he dwells just outside of it is also important. Art historian Nina Tonga discusses 'Uhila's work in reference to the Tongan concept of "*tu'a,* a social and spatial outside," the "back; space or place; time behind or beyond; space outside" or "exterior" (2014). Tonga summarises the term as connoting a "physical, social and temporal periphery." Indeed 'Uhila activated the peripheral spaces of the gallery, its thresholds and environs, its inside and outside, lingering and roaming around its exhibition spaces as well as sleeping beneath the shelter of its external overhanging eaves and resting upon its steps. In terms of embodied dimensions another concept Tonga discusses in relation to this work is that of *haua,* an act of wandering, to be beaten about by wind or rain, "continually wandering about as if more or less insane." Inventive and experimental choreo-politics of wandering and being exposed to the elements is activated. In relation *haua,* 'Uhila's wandering in and around the art museum whilst continuously performing or creating an artwork challenged the physical and conceptual limits of the institution, activating its boundaries and liminal spaces and extending its exhibition space into its social, political and urban context. Such wandering and "being," was part of a simple, yet radical strategy of passivity, a steely, yet gentle endurance. 'Uhila's roaming between exhibition space, the in-between spaces of the gallery as well as its surroundings raised questions about where exactly art, performance and choreography might take place. The affective and kinaesthetic dimensions of 'Uhila's three-month performance are manifold. Having taken place in the coldest and wettest months, basic needs for warmth, food and shelter were crucial, such subsistence living has its own dimensions. Though there was also the emotional and spiritual aspects of being separated from his family and domestic environment.

The intersubjective relations activated or enacted by *Mo'ui Tukuhausia* included the relations between those who sleep rough and those who come to the city and the gallery to live, work or merely visit. Similar to val smith, 'Uhila deliberately assumes a position of lowness, perhaps even shame in order to make visible the plight of those who continue to occupy such a position in the daily order of things and people within the city of Auckland. In terms of Tu'u's thesis, the unfolding, three-month process of *Mo'ui Tukuhausia* activated uneasy relations between artist and audience. Whilst in the social periphery of his performance 'Uhila used cardboard signs and coffee cups to request alms and meals from visitors and passers-by, in doing so he drew witnesses into an uncomfortable relation between artist as beggar and viewer as mark.

This was not the first time that 'Uhila took up an unusual intersubjective relation as part of a performance. Echoing Rosi Braidotti's concerns with post-anthropocentrism, in an earlier endurance-based work *Pigs in the Yard* from 2011 'Uhila cohabitated with a piglet named "Colonist" in a shipping container made into an open straw pen for eight days. The container was located in Aotea Square in the middle of central Auckland and for the duration of the performance 'Uhila mimicked the behaviour of Colonist in full view of the public and exposed to the elements. The appellation of the pig firmly situates 'Uhila's practice in reaction to colonisation of the Pacific by European settlers and missionaries from the eighteenth century onwards. Similar to *Mo'ui Tukuhausia* the work involves performing simple acts of subsistence: sheltering, sleeping and eating.

Taking into consideration 'Uhila's oeuvre as a whole, one can read *Mo'ui Tukuhausia* in relation to the colonisation of the Pacific. He engages with the art museum whilst simultaneously challenging its very boundaries. Such a place is, as previously mentioned, an institution that bears a legacy of imperialist power and a history of desecration of Pacific cultures, bodies and remains. Tiatia refers to her work as a protest, indeed another way of reading her work and that of 'Uhila is that they posit themselves within a specific relation to intersubjective structures of power, performing a function that is *decolonising*, echoing Hannah Arendt's thesis that action can have the ability to produce change. In her discussion of decolonizing research methodologies, Tuhiwai Smith theorises about what decolonising practices might do, with important implications for art making and choreography. Referring back to theorist Edward Said, via Tuhiwai Smith, important questions become "who is making art? For whom is the art being done? And in what circumstances?" (1999: 37). As a woman indigenous to Aotearoa New Zealand, Tuhiwai Smith makes the important definition of decolonising practices for indigenous peoples as being "amongst ourselves, for ourselves and to ourselves" (19). Decolonization is therefore about centring indigenous concerns and world views before "coming to know and understand theory and research from our own perspectives and for our own purposes" (39).

Accordingly, decolonization is a long-term process, one that involves a divestment of colonial power. Tuhiwai Smith writes of spaces that need to be claimed, perhaps such spaces could be that of the white cubes of the contemporary art museum (98, 104). One concept crucial to processes of decolonization is self-determination, though Tuhiwai Smith cautions:

> it is a much more dynamic and complex movement which incorporates many dimensions, some of which are still unfolding. It involves a revitalisation and reformulation of culture and tradition, an increased participation in and articulate rejection of Western institutions, a focus on strategic relations and alliances with non-indigenous groups. (110)

For Tuhiwai Smith, self-determination is a research agenda as well as a political goal of social justice that can be expressed across different terrains including cultural ones, but it must involve "processes of transformation, of decolonization, of healing and of mobilization as peoples" (116). To imagine self-determination involves, for Tuhiwai Smith, "to imagine a world in which indigenous peoples become active participants" (124). A focus upon and situation of a broader indigenous agenda and framework that includes "acts of reclaiming, reformulating and reconstituting indigenous cultures and languages" (140–142). Indeed, if the term *indigenizing* centres around a politics of "indigenous identity and indigenous cultural action," then perhaps this term, or even re-indigenising is more affirming or positive than that of decolonising (146). Importantly for artists, Tuhiwai Smith argues that representation is a project for all those who are attempting "to express an indigenous spirit, experience or world view," one that might counter dominant society's images of them (151). Tuhiwai Smith stresses the importance of the provision of alternatives for each other as well as "the ability to create and be creative" (105, 158). Recalling Tiatia in her white cubic space this can involve *reframing*, in which "indigenous people resist being boxed and labelled according to categories which do not fit" (153). Tuhiwai Smith describes twenty-five indigenous projects as part of her broader thesis of decolonizing methodologies, crucially for art making and choreography these are almost all in the present continuous tense, they are: claiming, testimonies, story-telling, celebrating survival, remembering, indigenizing, intervening, revitalising, connecting, reading, writing, representing, gendering, envisioning, reframing, restoring, returning, democratising, networking, naming, protecting, creating, negotiating, discovering and sharing (142–161). It is in reference to Tuhiwai Smith's thesis that I argue certain choreographed works provide an exploration of processes of intersubjectivity-as-art that perform a *decolonizing* function, though it is important to note that all of the artists discussed in this section are indigenous to one Pacific nation, whilst dwelling in another.

7.4 Dancing as if to Float: Vā and Relational Space

The art museum can be considered what Tuhiwai Smith would call a particular "site of struggle" for indigenous peoples (1999: 191). And it is within this county's most prominent museum, the Museum of New Zealand, Te Papa Tongarewa in the capital city of Wellington, that the next performance took place. *Taualuga: The Last Dance* (2006) was first performed in New Zealand on February 22, 2012 in a gallery within Te Papa.[15] Shigeyuki Kihara, an artist of Samoan and Japanese descent, performed her dance atop a platform raised approximately thirty centimetres from the ground and covered in black cloth. For her costume, she chose Victorian mourning dress, a full-length, high-neck, black gown complete with a corset and hooped petticoats. Such a style of dress communicates a sense of loss, the way in which struggles for power play out, upon and within bodies, how they behave and what they wear. Kihara's "re-dressing" also alludes to earlier colonial encounters and the material effects of missionisation and assimilation (Vercoe 2004: 45). Such dress was introduced to Samoa by the German colonial administration in the 1900s and for Kihara it is a "signifier of colonialism."

> With that dress, I mean it's just so tight and so awkward to move, so it's basically designed to contain your movements rather than be free with it. But I was very interesting in a way that I could use this colonial structure that bondages me and finding a new language, a danced language through this bondaged state. (2015)

Kihara performs elevated, slightly raised above her audience, placed upon a kind of pedestal or stage, again in a position of display. A kind of queering also takes place in this performance due to Kihara's gender identity. Born a man, Kihara is a woman by gender or *fa'a fafine* which translates as "like a woman," that is living as a woman in terms of her dress and mannerisms and occupying a liminal ream between man and woman (Vercoe 2004: 45–46). The choice to perform the graceful Taualuga in such attire was inspired by a studio portrait of a Samoan woman who wears such dress with a sense of elegance, comfort and confidence.[16] For the past decade and a half Kihara has been responding to ethnographic and touristic images of Samoans in museum archives. Upon studying a variety of historical photographs taken by New Zealand photographers in Samoa, Kihara reflected "The more I wanted to know about these people, the more I wanted to be them, by putting myself in the photograph. I wanted to unlock the photograph to free the soul" (Nuku 2015: 10). Part of this process of putting herself within ethnographic photographs involved an exploration of the Biblical character of Salome and her dance as interpreted by Samoans. *Taualuga: The Last Dance* is a syncretic work, one that explores for Kihara "what dance could be when these two distinctive ideologies come together." Additionally Salome, a Samoan woman in nineteenth-century mourning dress, has become a "muse and an alter-ego" for Kihara, which she continues to perform in multiple artworks.[17] Recalling the earlier chapter on post-internet choreographies, the phenomenon of creating choreographies taken from the internet also ties into Kihara's *Taualuga* for which she watched YouTube videos of the Japanese Onnagata specialist Bando Tamasaburo (b. 1950). Tamasaburo was a Kabuki actor who specialised in playing women's roles and known for his willowy physique and haughty demeanour, and Kihara sought to apply the same logic to her characterisation of Salome.[18]

Echoing Tiatia's de-familiarising position and misbehaviour, as well as 'Uhila's occupation of the gallery as a place in which to live, Kihara considered her dance to be a de-colonising and disruptive action that resisted the conformity to a set of behaviours that is generally expected of gallery visitors:

> there is a set of behaviours that the audience is expected to abide by in the gallery space policed by the gallery attendants. We can't spontaneously dance as a response to the artwork or else we get told off or get kicked out of the gallery/museum. So I like the idea of introducing dance in the gallery/museum as a way to disrupt the rules to how we are supposed to engage in art. These situations are no different to missionaries and colonial officers i.e. gallery attendants who ban Pacific Islanders from dancing their culture. (2016)

Kihara's choreography utilises the principles of the classical Samoan dance of Taualuga, a culmination or finishing dance, in order to tell a story and pay tribute to many leaders and people of Samoa in their struggle for independence.[19] It is also a lament that acknowledges the change and loss suffered by Samoan culture through processes of colonisation. Kihara summarises that her intention.

> was to talk about the aftermath of colonialism. After you've gone through all this violence and pain, you need this space of reflection to mourn. For us Samoans, we constantly negotiate the past and the future in the present. (Kihara 2016)

The song Kihara dances to is sung in Samoan by a choir of voices that welcomes a new era of independence after German as well as New Zealand colonial rule. According to art historian Caroline Vercoe, the taualuga is a ceremonial dance traditionally performed at the end of an important occasion or celebration (Vercoe 1994: 137). Performed by the *taupou* or daughter of a Samoan chief who plays an integral and highly respected role in her culture, the dance is meant to demonstrate beauty, skill, grace as well as a myriad of symbolic references to fa'a Samoa or the Samoan way. According to Sydney-based dancer Mary Jane McKibbin-Schwenke the taualuga is meant to be "dream-like" and "mesmerising" (Taualuga 2014). She moves her feet as though she is a spirit floating along the ground, and draws spectators in with her hand movements and eye contact. Other qualities displayed within such a dance include pride, strength, dignity, stateliness as well as an ability to hold oneself well. Central to the dance is an emphasis upon soft and gentle hand movements combined with control and balance. Kihara developed her own choreography based on that of the Taualuga, with each movement alluding to "social, political, economic, spiritual and ancestral matters:"

> the basic movements of the Taualuga still remains with an emphasis on the movements of the arms, hands, stately posture and dancing as if to float between the beats rather than dancing towards the destination of the beat which creates an unnerving feeling for the spectators. (2016)

US-based dance theorist Randy Martin posited a connection between a "decolonized worldview" and a preference for de-centred movement (quoted in Foster 2011: 8) and it is interesting to note how this coincides with Ahmed's thesis of queerness as a kind of wonkiness and disorientation. Indeed both Tiatia and 'Uhila challenge the vertical behaviours of looking and walking within the art museum: Tiatia walks upon the walls and 'Uhila sleeps beside them. A theory of choreography that is decolonizing according to Tuhiwai Smith's thesis is one that involves some of her verbs in the present continuous such as: claiming, indigenizing, intervening, representing, gendering, reframing, creating, and negotiating within the site of struggle that is the contemporary art museum. Kihara ties into this thesis with her elegant colonial attire, elevated position from which she performs a dreamy *taualuga*, simultaneously negotiating the past, celebrating those who protest and resist as well as looking towards the future. Holding herself in a stately manner, her arms and hands alternate between softness and sudden surprising movements, whilst floating between the beats of the music to disquieting effect.

It is important to note that Kihara has been engaging with museums for almost two decades. Her artworks were included in the aforementioned exhibitions *Pasifika Styles* (2006–2008) and *Le Folauga* (2007) and in 2008 she had a solo exhibition *Shigeyuki Kihara: Living Photographs* at the Metropolitan Museum of Art in New York City. Kihara has also explicitly engaged with the idea of the museum as a site for cross-cultural encounters as well as drawing audience members into uneasy relationships. In her work *Culture Court* (2010) at the National Gallery of Victoria in Melbourne, Australia, Kihara hired six cultural performers, including indigenous Australians to either dance or play a musical instrument when audience members gave them money (Weaver 2011: 89). *Culture Court* is similar to 'Uhila's *Mo'ui Tukuhausia* in its inclusion of a request for donations, its transactional nature and the questions this raises about the commodification of indigenous cultures within a museum or art gallery space. It is worth noting that currently Māori cultural performances take place at the Auckland War Memorial Museum Tāmaki Paenga Hira three times a day.

In fact, there exists an even more nuanced story about cross-cultural encounters, or contemporary Pacific artists engaging in museums as well as contemporary art contexts. In 2011 as part of research into works by artists that included Tu'u and Kihara, curator and art historian Chloe Weaver argued that the Pacific "concept of vā shares affinities with the idea of relational space," sociability and the ability for artworks to produce relations as described by Bourriaud (Weaver 2011: 53). According to Weaver, work by artists like Kihara introduces Pacific epistemologies or ways of knowing, doing and being into wider discussions on participatory art. $Vā$ is a fluid term that is present in cultures across the Pacific including Samoan, Tongan, Māori and Japanese ones (Weaver 2011: 49). According to Pacific scholar and educator Melani Anae the $vā$ is made up of "the sacred, spiritual, and social spaces of human relationships" and it is these "that Pacific peoples place at the centre of all human/environment/cosmos/ancestors and animate/inanimate interactions" (Anae 2019). Anae is known for her emphasis upon the Samoan phrase *teu le va* meaning "to value, nurture, and care for (teu) the secular/sacred and social/spiritual spaces (va) of all relationships." Her scholarship in the area of what she calls "Pacific Relational Ethics" plays a crucial role in the area of Pacific research methodologies which has flourished since the publication of Linda Tuhiwai Smith's trailblazing publication in 1999.

Weaver's thesis that relational aesthetics resonates with the concept of $vā$ adds another dimension to my discussion of intersubjectivity and performance art. The importance of such interpersonal space is also highlighted in a point made by Tu'u, that any solo performance, such as those by Tiatia, 'Uhila and Kihara is never truly solo. Questioning her own "singular authority" Tu'u writes:

As a Pacific woman and Samoan daughter... The expectation is for me to acknowledge that the effort was not solely mine, but one that was dutifully shared with others... I am uncomfortable with this concept of being a solo artist, as I feel the pull of collective baggage that comes with acknowledging Pacific people e.g. my parents, God even though I'm an atheist and craving the visibility and applause of bringing people together to make new

work that did not exist before. I name everyone who is present in my work
from audiences to haters as being part of my organization... so we are all
implicit and responsible for the work. (Tu'u 2017: 16)

Kihara concurs with Tu'u adding that such a sentiment would resonate
with "most Pacific artists given our cultural context which places emphasis
on genealogy and kinship" (Kihara 2020).[20] Before moving on it is
important to note that in terms of intersubjective relations between
performer and beholder, in all of the works discussed in this chapter it
is highly likely that each of the artists frequently perform to audience
members from a colonial settler background. This impacts on the thesis
of decolonising choreographies, as Tuhiwai Smith has described these as
by, *with* and *for* indigenous artists. Therefore a more apt descriptor for
these three artworks, ones that are authored by Pacific peoples but that
take place in a settler environment and involve the spectatorship of non-
indigenous audiences, might be the term *counter-hegemonic* or maybe
even *unsettling*. As Tuhiwai Smith has pointed out:

> Personal discomfort and organisation disruption are an inevitable part of a
> change process. Change that destabilises colonial power will be disruptive
> but that needs to be seen alongside the risk of not decolonising which is
> potentially more destructive. (Tuhiwai Smith 2021: 7)

This is also where Tu'u's point about drawing audiences into "dis-ease"
is a useful counter-hegemonic device. In each of the works just described,
Tiatia, 'Uhila and Kihara inflect intersubjectivity and the interpersonal
space of the *vā* in different ways as part of a broader choreo-political
project of *unsettling* the contemporary art museum. From within a white
cube-like, cornered space that also recalls a photographic studio, Tiatia
evokes specific interpersonal relations such as display, particularly sexualised display of a feminine body through her attire and coy, almost
hobbled gait. In *Walking the Wall* her non-functional mincing also recalls
the catwalk or the way in which feminine bodies are often displayed in an
ambulatory mode within fashion industries. This exhibitionist display of a
feminine body encourages a kind of voyeurism on the part of her viewers,
together with the open display of her malu, Tiatia activates broader fields
of feminism that include her particular Samoan inflection. This flavour
of feminism speaks to broader structures and relations of shame derived
from missionisation and Christianity in relation to female and Samoan

bodies. Tiatia's supine pose, silence and confronting gaze combine to directly challenge viewers who may find themselves visually consuming her appearance as well as evaluating or judging her performance in terms of how much exertion it requires and how successful it may be.

In *Mo'ui Tukuhausia* 'Uhila seems to explicitly move in and out of relational fields and in doing so reiterates experiences of migration and displacement. By living as though homeless in and around the Auckland Art Gallery 'Uhila extracts himself from his usual context, his employment as well as his daily life with his family. As Mo'ui Tukuhausia unfolded it became *a process* by which 'Uhila drew his audience into an uneasy relationship, one in which the artist is totally dependent upon those who surround him for his very survival. In following his own script or score his roaming, wandering and very survival become a choreography and instance of performance art. Activating historic artworks that have required extended duration and endurance, 'Uhila inserts himself into a broader narrative in a particular story of twentieth-century performance art. By elevating herself Kihara gives herself a higher status in relation to others, she literally places her body upon a plinth, within a museum, risky business given the aforementioned history of Pacific bodies in museums. Through music and dance Kihara's choreography privileges Samoan performing arts as well as prior histories of counter-colonial resistance and protest. Her embodiment of the character of Salome enables her to take up a position of mourning in relation to prior Pacific histories but also to empower a particular woman whose appearance was captured by processes of ethnographic photography and the accompanying dis-ease it continues to cause Pacific peoples. Finally, and most importantly, in *Taualuga* Kihara's stately, graceful and sometimes surprising movements, upon a plinth positions herself haughtily and highly within the broader phenomenon that is dance in the museum.

NOTES

1. Here the term "dis-ease" can be read as unease, however it also alludes to the spread of European diseases during processes of colonization in the Pacific.
2. See "Pacific Auckland: Who Are Pacific People?" Auckland Council, https://www.aucklandcouncil.govt.nz/plans-projects-policies-reports-bylaws/our-plans-strategies/auckland-plan/about-the-auckland-plan/Pages/pacific-auckland.aspx.

3. For more information on Pacific Peoples see Damon Salesa. *Island Time: New Zealand's Pacific Futures.* Wellington, New Zealand: Bridget Williams Books, 2017.

4. Contemporary Māori artists working in the area of performance include: Hana Pera Aoake, Charles Koroneho, Moana Nepia, Louise Potiki Bryant, Rachael Rakena, Lisa Reihana, Cat Ruka, Shannon Te Ao and Layne Waerea. One exhibition that examined Māori performance, mainly in terms of performing arts, was *Pūkana: Moments in Māori Performance* at the National Library, Wellington, New Zealand in 2019.

5. Angela Tiatia *Walking the Wall* 2014 from the series "An Inventory of Gestures." Single-channel HD video, 16:9, 13:00 minutes (looped), colour, sound, ed.2/8. Purchased 2015. Queensland Art Gallery | Gallery of Modern Art Foundation/Collection: Queensland Art Gallery. Exhibited in New Zealand as part of the exhibition *Tatau: Sāmoan Tattooing and Photography* at Te Papa Tongarewa Museum of New Zealand, Wellington in 2019.

6. Tiatia's mother 'Lusi, was part of a generation from across the Pacific encouraged to migrate to New Zealand in the 1950s and 60s to form a much-needed labour force. These people were considered "overstayers" through the 1970s when the economy began to slow, leaving an enduring negativity toward Pacific communities (Nagesh 2015: 146).

7. This point is deeply indebted to a conversation with art historian Caroline Vercoe. Tiatia's exhausting rituals of performing femininity recalls Janine Antoni's *Loving Care* (1993) in which she painted the gallery floor with her hair and hair-dye.

8. This defiant, de-colonising gaze is utilised in many of Tiatia's works including the early video *Hibiscus Rosa Sinesis* (2010) and *Reflexivity* (2013) another work in which she publicly displays her malu.

9. According to advertisements and ephemera from the Biennale, sourced from the library of the Art Gallery of New South Wales.

10. See Baartman, Saartje C. 1790–1815. 2013. Encyclopaedia of Race and Racism. http://ezproxy.auckland.ac.nz/login?url=http://search.credoreference.com/content/entry/galerace/baartman_saartje_c_1790_1815/0. Accessed 25 November 2016.

11. The remnants of such organisation can still be seen in the national pavilions at the Biennale di Venezia.

12. It is important to note that 'Uhila has performed in a range of contexts, from in and around art galleries, to public squares, city streets, at performance events and at the Wellington waterfront *Ongo mei Moana* (2015).

13. The first iteration of this performance occurred as part of the 2012 exhibition "What do you mean, we?" curated by Bruce E. Phillips at Te Tuhi

Centre for the Arts in Pakuranga, an eastern suburb of Auckland. The duration of this iteration was two weeks.

14. 'Uhila completed a Postgraduate Diploma in Dance from the University of Auckland. "Kalisolaite 'Uhila" *Tautai: Guiding Pacific Arts*, http://www.tautai.org/artist/kalisolaite-uhila/.

15. The performance was presented as part of the opening for the exhibition "Collecting Contemporary" that included a video of the work which was gifted to the museum by the artist in 2011. Previously *Taualuga: The Last Dance* was performed at Haus der Kulteren Der Welt, Berlin, Germany, the Musée du Quai Branly, Paris, France and at the Metropolitan Museum of Art, New York, USA (Tamati-Quennell 2012).

16. Thomas Andrew *Portrait of a Samoan Woman* (1865). Andrew lived in Samoa from 1891 to 1939 and many of his photographs are included within the museum's collection.

17. Works performed as Salome include: *Siva in Motion* (2012), *Where do we come from? Where are we going?* (2013) and *Invocations* (2016). One of the earliest appearances of this persona was in Lisa Taouma's *Pasifika Divas in Performance*, 14 September, 2002 at the Asia Pacific Triennial of Contemporary Art, Queensland Art Gallery.

18. "Bando, Tamasaburo (1950–)". 2000. In *The Cambridge Guide to Theater*, edited by Martin Banham. Cambridge: Cambridge University Press. http://ezproxy.auckland.ac.nz/login?url=http://search.credoreference.com/content/entry/cupthea/bando_tamasaburo_1950/0.

19. It also references the Mau movement, established in 1908, through which Western Samoan's began to assert their claim to independence and also to New Zealand's occupation and to the history of New Zealand's role as colonial power within the Pacific. Tamati-Quennell, ibid.

20. This recalls Bruno Latour's conception of an actor as "the moving target of a vast array of entities swimming toward it... to use the word 'actor' means that it's never clear who and what is acting when we act since an actor on stage is never alone in acting" (Latour 2005: 45–46).

References

Anae, Melanie. 2019. Pacific Research Methodologies and Relational Ethics. https://doi.org/10.1093/acrefore/9780190264093.013.529.

Baartman, Saartje C. 1790–1815. 2013. Encyclopaedia of Race and Racism. http://ezproxy.auckland.ac.nz/login?url=http://search.credoreference.com/content/entry/galerace/baartman_saartje_c_1790_1815/0. Accessed 25 November 2016.

Bennett, Tony. 1995. *The Birth of the Museum: History, Theory, Politics*. London; New York: Routledge.

Forrest, Nicholas. 2016. 8th Asia Pacific Triennial Q&A: Angela Tiatia's Body Battles. Blouin ArtInfo. http://www.blouinartinfo.com/news/story/1348318/8th-asia-pacific-triennial-qa-angela-tiatias-body-battles. Accessed 19 October 2016.

Foster, Susan Leigh. 2011. *Choreographing Empathy: Kinesthesia in Performance*. London; New York: Routledge.

Gallery of Modern Art, Queensland Art Gallery. 2015. *The 8th Asia Pacific Triennial of Contemporary Art*. Brisbane: Queensland Art Gallery | Gallery of Modern Art.

Gardner, Anna. 2015. Project Programme Archive. *Reading Room: A Journal of Art and Culture* 7: 158–169.

Gordon-Smith, Ioana. 2018. From the Margins to the Mainstream: Pacific Sisters at Te Papa. *Pantograph Punch*. https://www.pantograph-punch.com/posts/pacific-sisters. Accessed 14 July 2020.

Heathfield, Adrian, and Hsieh, Teching. 2009. *Out of Now: The Lifeworks of Tehching Hsieh*. London; Cambridge, MA: Live Art Development Agency; The MIT Press.

Henriques, Julian. 2010. The Vibrations of Affect and Their Propagation on a Night Out on Kingston's Dancehall Scene. *Body & Society* 16.1: 57–89. https://doi.org/10.1177/1357034X09354768.

Jones, Amelia. 1998. *Body Art: Performing the Subject*. Minneapolis: University of Minnesota Press.

Kihara, Shigeyuki. 2015. Shigeyuki Kihara—Taualuga: The Last Dance. Museum of New Zealand, Te Papa Tongarewa. https://www.youtube.com/watch?v=ev-vIeSDb4I. Accessed 18 November 2015.

Kihara, Shigeyuki. 2016. Personal Interview. 19 October 2016.

Kihara, Shigeyuki. 2020. Personal Interview. 31 May 2020.

Latour, Bruno. 2005. *Reassembling the Social: An Introduction to Actor Network Theory*. Oxford; New York: Oxford University Press.

Leahy, Helen Rees. 2012. *Museum Bodies: The Politics and Practices of Visiting and Viewing*. Farnham, Surrey; Burlington, VT: Ashgate.

Leonard, Robert, and Vercoe, Caroline. 1997. Pacific Sisters: Doing It for Themselves. *Art Asia Pacific* 14: 1997.

Lopesi, Lana, and Louisa Afoa. 2015. Body Language. In *Love Feminisms, The Occasional Journal*, eds. Alice Tappenden and Ann Shelton. http://enjoy.org.nz/publishing/the-occasional-journal/love-feminisms/. Accessed 18 November 2015.

Lythberg, Billie. 2008. Pasifika Styles: Where the Bellbird Sings. In *Pasifika Styles: Artists Inside the Museum*, eds. Rosanna Raymond and Amiria Salmond, 37–47. Cambridge, United Kingdom; Dunedin, New Zealand: University of Cambridge Museum of Archaeology; Anthropology and Otago University Press.

Mallon, Sean, and Fecteau, Uili. 2002. Tatau-ed: Polynesian Tatau in Aotearoa. In *Pacific Art Niu Sila: The Pacific Dimension of Contemporary New Zealand Arts*, eds. Sean Mallon and Pandora Fulimalo Pereira, 20–37. Wellington: Te Papa Press.

Nagesh, Tarun. 2015. The Social Medium. In *The 8th Asia Pacific Triennial of Contemporary Art*, 118–161. Brisbane: Queensland Art Gallery | Gallery of Modern Art.

Nuku, Maia. 2015. Standing on the Edge of the Abyss: Shigeyuki Kihara, Catalyst for Change. *Broadsheet* Summer: 10–14.

Phillips, Bruce E. 2014. A Voice for the Voiceless. In *The Walters Prize 2014*, ed. Clare McIntosh, 71–74. Auckland: Auckland Art Gallery Toi o Tamaki.

Raymond, Rosanna, and Salmond, Amiria. 2008. *Pasifika Styles: Artists Inside the Museum*. Cambridge, United Kingdom; Dunedin, New Zealand: University of Cambridge Museum of Archaeology and Anthropology; Otago University Press.

Salesa, Damon. 2017. *Island Time: New Zealand's Pacific Futures*. Bridget Williams Books.

Tuhiwai Smith, Linda. 1999. *Decolonizing Methodologies: Research and Indigenous Peoples*. London; New York; Dunedin: Zed Books Ltd.; University of Otago Press.

Tuhiwai Smith, Linda. 2021. Decolonising Cultural Institutions—An Urgent, Necessary, Challenging Yet Hopeful Journey Beyond Colonialism. In *Uneven Bodies (Reader)*, eds. Ruth Buchanan, Aileen Burns, and Johan Lundh, Hanahiva Rose, 6–7. New Plymouth: Govett Brewster Art Gallery.

Tamati-Quennell, Megan. 2012. Taualuga: The Last Dance. Museum of New Zealand, Te Papa Tongarewa. http://blog.tepapa.govt.nz/2012/03/09/tau aluga-the-last-dance/. Accessed 18 November 2015.

Taualuga. 2014. Tangata Pasifika. Television Documentary. Directed by Lisa Taouma. New Zealand: TV One, Television New Zealand.

Tiatia, Angela. 2016. Tautai: Guiding Pacific Arts. http://www.tautai.org/art ist/angela-tiatia/. Accessed 25 November 2016.

Tu'u, Louise. 2017. *Performing the Margins: An Anthem of Hope*. Christchurch: The Physics Room, We Should Practice.

Tonga, Nina. 2014. Roaming All Levels. *Off the Wall* 6. http://www.arts.tepapa. govt.nz/off-the-wall/7959/roaming-all-levels. Accessed 18 November 2015.

Vercoe, Caroline. 1994. Samoan Dance—A Visual Art, Master of Arts in Art History, University of Auckland.

Vercoe, Caroline. 2004. The Many Faces of Paradise. In *Paradise Now? Contemporary Art from the Pacific*, ed. Melissa Chiu, 34–47. Auckland: David Bateman.

Weaver, Chloe. 2011. *Art as Experience: Collaborative and Participatory Practice in Contemporary Pacific Art*. Thesis MA Art History, The University of Auckland, New Zealand.

CHAPTER 8

Conclusion: Unsettling the Museum

During the second decade of the twenty-first century, there was an emergence and flourishing of dance exhibitions in contemporary art biennales, galleries and museums and it was this "new performance" or *choreographic turn* that provided the impetus for writing this book. From the late 1960s onwards, critical exhibition-making practices have built in intensity, leading to a shift from an informing to a *performing* museology, as outlined by performance studies scholar Barbara Kirshenblatt-Gimblett and museum studies scholar Barbara Rees Leahy (2012: 203). Leahy describes a shift in attention from the museum as a collection of objects to the museum as a site of social and corporeal practices. The idea is that a *performing museology* enables institutions to adopt more reflexive positions in relation to their own operations, functions and processes.

In this book, I have tracked some of the shifts in performing museology that have been created by experimentation with installations, performance events and curated actions in the museum, beginning with the Eurocentric disruption of male subjectivity by leading male performance artists, through to the decolonising of borders and bodies provided by queer and indigenous artists in the Pacific.

Leahy's thesis of *museum bodies* is crucial not only for thinking about performance art as exhibition practice, it is also important for understanding the roles visitors to such institutions are expected to play and

© The Author(s), under exclusive license to Springer Nature Switzerland AG 2021
V. Wynne-Jones, *Choreographing Intersubjectivity in Performance Art*, New World Choreographies,
https://doi.org/10.1007/978-3-030-40585-4_8

the ways they are expected to perform. Processes of habit acquisition and familiarity with the operation of the museum provide visitors with a repertoire of potentially appropriate actions and activities (100). Hallmarks of a *performing museology*, such as the Turbine Hall Commissions at the Tate Modern since 2000, have involved the art museum deliberately changing the script, disrupting the repertoire and altering the familiar choreography of viewing. Part of the self-reflexivity of *performing museologies* is a deliberate *unsettling of spectatorship*, in which artists like Tino Sehgal may disrupt visitors' habits and their expectations of museum comportment by distorting or interrupting their experience of gallery spaces. As I have argued, commissions like Sehgal's *These Associations* (2012) act as machines that provoke and manage individual and group encounters, often licensing a more relaxed and playful occupation so that, with the blessing of the institution, visitors might temporarily abandon the decorum of the contemporary art museum.

Attending to the topology of such performance artworks requires giving attention to their constituent parts and much is at stake, given that these include the very subjectivities of those who participate. As I have outlined in my discussion of radical and sociological accounts of intersubjectivity, there is no self without the other, the group and interaction come first, and distinct individuation can only emerge from an interactional context (Crossley 2005). Subjectivity develops in and through intersubjectivity, it is a social or dialogic relationship with another person, in a shared, between world, one that connects individual human subjectivities. The contemporary art museum is a very specific interactional context, one that has its own scripts to follow.

Within this book's extension of these complex shifts in the organisation of museum subjects—performance artist or spectator—the concept of choreography comes into significance as an analytic lens. In Chapter 2, I examined how dance theorist André Lepecki described the tension between conformity and freedom in terms of two oppositional forces: choreo-policing and choreo-politics (2013). Choreo-policing involves systems of obedience, commands, imperatives and the controlling of movement, whereas choreo-politics involves the redistribution and reinvention of bodies, moving politically and experimental exercises of freedom (20).

Throughout this book I have explored this tension as a way of reading works of performance art. Each of the artists discussed, negotiates the oppositional forces of choreo-policing and choreo-politics in their own particular ways. Given the imperialist and discriminatory foundations of what theorist Tony Bennett has called the 'exhibitionary complex,' (1995) there is a pressing need for artists to re-invent the museum as what Lepecki calls "a site of choreographic imagination" (Lepecki 2013: 20). The hope is that in such a space, highly mobile and political subjects can evade pre-assigned modes of circulation and perhaps even temporarily enact forms of intersubjectivity that make manifest experimental exercises of freedom.

As I argued in Chapter 3, from the 1960s onwards performance artists like Bruce Nauman and Vito Acconci began to test the parameters of the white cube, making various attempts to evade pre-assigned modes by isolating themselves within chamber-like spaces and labouring towards acts of transformation, or at the very least appearing to transform themselves before an audience. Such endeavours were continued by figures like Stelarc and Mike Parr, through to the examples of Xavier Le Roy and Oleg Kulik during the 1990s, each has demonstrated a real dedication to challenging the limits of subjectivity, as defined by the male artist. Such limits include the fragility of masculinity as well as the always-already legitimising function of the male performing body. Becoming-minoritarian, or at least performing or choreographing oneself in attempting to become-minoritarian, is one strategy available to the singular, authoritative, unitary subjectivity of the male performance artist, who wishes to temporarily try-out a subordinate relation to the standard of white man and adult male. Though it is worth noting that such endeavours are still *theatrical* and intersubjective, as they are contingent upon the presence of beholders and audience members.

Just as Le Roy pushed the boundaries of recognition in order to temporarily suspend acts of identification, in his 2012 works *These Associations* and *This Variation* Tino Sehgal orchestrated swarming bodies as well as darkness, as a way of challenging individuation. In Chapter 4 I looked at how intersubjectivity as a shared, between-world connecting individual human subjectivities has been deftly explored in smaller scale works like Sehgal's *Instead of allowing some thing to rise up to your face dancing bruce and dan and other things* (2000), Sean Curham's *Gentle Resting on the Bonnet of a Popular Car* (2016) and Kalisolaite 'Uhila's *First will be last and last, first* (2018). Each of these three artists uses pared-back performances to consider the ethics of interpersonal encounters, as well as to attune to the ramifications of proximity and touch.

Post-humanism has proven a fruitful strategy for artists enacting instances of choreo-politics in performance artworks, particularly in terms of the redistribution of bodies, affects, and senses. Works such as Alicia Frankovich's *Defending Plural Experiences* (2014) and *World is Home Planet* (2016) manifest Rudi Laermans' idea of *choreography in general* as a making and modulation of assemblages or people and things brought together (2008: 11). Laermans' concept of choreography can account for performances that involve the "explorative associating" of a whole range of materials, including the human and non-human. Such performance artworks can be considered part of a broader project of challenging the humanist prejudices of the museum, as well as promoting the kinds of planetary perspectives currently required by the climate emergency. The various assemblages, groupings and multitudes that temporarily come together in such artworks allow for connective reverberations to take place, commingling materials, creatures, performers and participants. Further extended through the use of darkness as a de-familiarisation technique, one that challenges visual recognition and judgement as normative attributes of museum aesthetics, collective works such as these activate intersubjective encounters that are not merely visual but multi-sensorial.

Whereas Sehgal and Frankovich organise significant amounts of performers who swarm, swell and shrink in order to modify and reinvent groupings and different ways of relating, Rebecca Hobbs' video works capture networked choreographies by highly-connected individuals whose subjectivities are cyborg-like and shaped by the connective tissue of the internet and digital technologies. The performers in *Otara at Night* (2011) and *Mangere Mall* (2011) use various devices as well as online movement archives as choreographic prostheses to implicate themselves in broader, global networks of dancers and popular dance styles, taking intersubjectivity to the next level. The post-internet choreographies captured in Hobbs' dance videos as well as in performance artworks by artists like Joshua Rutter, offer another kind of challenge to the museum and present a different sort of choreo-politics. These contemporary art practices engage with collections that are more accessible and inclusive than the contemporary art museum, using video repositories like YouTube and TikTok that have been dubbed 'movement archives' by theorist Harmony Bench (2017). Choreographies performed to camera, that were self-taught subsequent to viewing dance content uploaded to the internet, further collapse the distances between dancing bodies and audiences. Just like images found through on-line search engines, such performances can circulate and be permuted through scores of bodies to be tried and tested, de-virtualised and re-virtualised ad infinitum.

It is worth re-iterating that throughout their histories, museums have perpetuated a dominant cultural model of universal humanism, one driven by a cultural logic that has been formed by the binary of identity and otherness. As theorist Rosi Braidotti explains, according to such a model, difference is positioned as pejoration (2013: 15). Braidotti argues, those branded as so-called others "are the sexualised, racialized and naturalized others, women, indigenous peoples and animals who are reduced to the less than human status of disposable bodies (2013: 26)."

In Chapter 6 I examined performance artworks involving queer chore-ographies created by those who have been categorised by the museum and the exhibitionary complex as sexualised and other. There are two propositions that arose from my exploration of performances by val smith that are particularly pertinent. The first is the way in which they demonstrated queer choreographic authority in *duotones* (2014) by manipulating their audience around the gallery with energetic, arbi-trary, deliberate and confusing hand gestures, together with repetitive commands. Through such playful manipulations smith manifested an instance of choreo-policing that was in fact choreo-political in a clas-sically *queer* act of blurring the binary. The second proposition worth noting is that instances of intersubjectivity, or shared in-between worlds, are not necessarily positive. As psychologist Sally R. Munt has explained, shame is a deeply relational, choreo-policing force that demands confor-mity. There is a tendency for queer identities to be shaped and formed by the binary opposition of pride and shame (Munt 2000: 533). In the performance *Gutter Matters* (2014) smith maps a politics of queer pride and shame, manifesting a "Gay Shame Parade" in the gutter and executing a slow-motion pom-pom routine while lying on the ground (smith 2015). In *Gutter Matters* smith demonstrates that although shame might be something familiar to those persecuted within an intersubjective environment of compulsory heterosexuality, it can also be claimed and used as a methodology for creating choreographies.

As Leahy has pointed out, much of the impetus for re-orienting museum theory and practice from an informing to a performing muse-ology was a response to the fraught and contested formation of collections as well as a re-examination of underlying assumptions about the trans-mission of knowledge and cultural value (2012: 2–3). As I have argued through this book, the exhibitionary complex has a history of perpetuating an imperialist and colonial "order of things," a regime of space and vision that bodies were subject-to. In such a context, where stolen artefacts and human remains are displayed and live bodies exhibited, the term *choreo-policing* is something of an understatement. According to this system indigenous peoples have been and often still are framed as racialized others, yet it is these "hush-hush" sites of struggle and those derived from them that contemporary Pasifika artists are choosing to perform in and around, activating *choreo-politics* on their own terms. Artists like Angela Tiatia, Kalisloaite 'Uhila and Shigeyuki Kihara are vastly different from the singular, authoritative, unitary subjectivity of white male artists like Xavier Le Roy, Vito Acconci and Paul McCarthy, not only that, the relations activated by their performance artworks function in a very different way.

As Louise Tu'u has explained, sometimes performance art can be a processual tool used to draw audiences into the dis-ease of pre-existing social relationships (2017: 3). In addition to a performing museology, when indigenous artists are self-determining, they can choreograph the exhibitionary complex on their own terms and for their own families and communities, and such artworks can be indigenising and decolonising. When choreographies take place before beholders from colonial settler backgrounds they can be considered *counter-hegemonic* and there may be an *un-settling* of spectatorship. As Linda Tuhiwai Smith has stated "Personal discomfort and organisation disruption are an inevitable part of a change process. Change that destabilises colonial power will be disruptive" (2021: 7). Participating in a broader, emancipatory project, Tiatia, 'Uhila and Kihara are just three examples from a rapidly growing number of artists experimenting with ways of moving politically. In this book I have offered some theoretical challenges to the constituent parts and underlying ideologies of art history and the contemporary art museum. I have also provided innumerable examples of intersubjective performances that shift the hierarchies of museum reception. It is for future artists to widen these initial cracks, spill through and crowd, walk, perform or dance in and out of the gallery.

References

Bench, Harmony. 2017. Dancing in Digital Archives: Circulation, Pedagogy, Performance. In *Transmission in Motion: The Technologizing of Dance*, ed. Maaike Bleeker, 155–167. New York: Routledge.

Bennett, Tony. 1995. *The Birth of the Museum: History, Theory, Politics*. London; New York: Routledge.

Braidotti, Rosi. 2013. *The Posthuman*. Cambridge: Polity.

Crossley, Nick. 2005. Intersubjectivity. In ed. Nick Crossley, *Key concepts in critical social theory*. Sage UK. Credo Reference: http://ezproxy.auckland.ac.nz/login?url=https://search.credoreference.com/content/entry/sageukcst/intersubjectivity/0?institutionId=181.

Laermans, Rudi. 2008. 'Dance in General' or Choreographing the Public, Making Assemblages. *Performance Research* 13.1: 7–14.

Leahy, Helen Rees. 2012. *Museum Bodies: The Politics and Practices of Visiting and Viewing*. Farnham, Surrey; Burlington, VT: Ashgate.

Lepecki, André. 2013. Choreopolice and Choreopolitics: or, the task of the dancer. *TDR: The Dance Review* 57.4: 13–27.

Munt, Sally R. 2000. Shame/pride dichotomies in Queer as Folk. In *Textual practice* 14.3: 531–546.

smith, val. 2015. Gutter Matters Pecha Kucha Styles. Valvalvalsmithsmithsmith. https://valvalvalsmithsmithsmith.blogspot.co.nz/2015/04/gutter-matters-for-dunedin-fringe.html. Accessed 11 October 2016.

Tu'u, Louise. 2017. *Performing the Margins: An Anthem of Hope*. Christchurch: The Physics Room, We Should Practice.

Tuhiwai Smith, Linda. 2021. Decolonising Cultural Institutions—An Urgent, Necessary, Challenging Yet Hopeful Journey Beyond Colonialism. In *Uneven Bodies (Reader)*, eds. Ruth Buchanan, Aileen Burns, and Johan Lundh, Hanahiva Rose, 6–7. New Plymouth: Govett Brewster Art Gallery.

INDEX